D0909130

THE FUTURE OF LAND WARFARE

The Future of LAND WARFARE

CHRIS BELLAMY

ST. MARTIN'S PRESS
New York

First published in the United States of America in 1987

Printed in Great Britain

Library of Congress Cataloging-in-Publication Data
Bellamy, Chris.
The future of land warfare.

Includes index.
1. Military art and science — History — 20th
century. I. Title.
U42.B45 1987 ' 355'.009'04   86-31364
ISBN 0-312-00725-6

For my parents

'Give me a child to the age of seven,
and I will show you the man'
                                    Jesuit saying

'War is a matter of vital importance to the
State; the province of life or death; the
road to survival or ruin. It is mandatory
that it be thoroughly studied.'
                    Sun Tzu, The Art of War
                    4th Century BC

Important. Several national agencies helped in research for this book. However, a wide variety of published sources were also used, which may conflict with the views of those agencies and may not meet with their approval. Therefore, statements in this book referring to the armed forces, equipment or doctrine of a particular nation do *not* necessarily reflect the official views of that nation's government or armed forces.

Contents

Figures and Tables

FIGURES

TABLES

Acknowledgements

I would first of all like to thank my friend and colleague over several years, Dr Philip Towle, Defence Lecturer at Cambridge University, for introducing me to Croom Helm and for suggesting that I might be a suitable author to write this volume in the family of books on the future of conflict, an honour which I accepted without hesitation. It brought me pleasure and excitement as well as work. I must thank the National Westminster Bank, Oxford High Street (again), for lending me the money to go to Israel; the Israeli military attaché in London and the public relations staff of the Israel defence forces for all their help; Lieutenant Colonel (res.) 'Shaike' Dranitzky for an adrenalin-pumping tour of the Golan Heights, dropping in at Armageddon on the way back; Martin van Creveld of the Hebrew University of Jerusalem for his time and assistance; General Katz and General Tal and their staffs; and Mr Doron Arazi, a pupil of Martin's who continued the Israeli connexion in London. From the new world I am indebted to Mr D.A. Grant, Director General of the Operational Research Department, Department of National Defence, Canada, for his personal interest which extended to physically carrying the 1985 revision of the Compendium of Major Armed Conflict across the Atlantic the moment it was available so as to help ensure that this book was as up to date as humanly possible; at The US Army Command and General Staff College, Fort Leavenworth, Kansas, my friend and colleague Dr Bruce Menning, for giving me the opportunity to discuss the subject with those in the US Army working on future operational art and tactics; Major Roger Cirillo for information on various armies; Gary Bjorge for allowing me to benefit from his research on the Chinese

Army's conduct of war at the operational level and the Huai-Hai operation, including translating place and formation names and statistics from the Chinese; and the US Army TRADOC liaison officer in London, Lieutenant-Colonel Bob Aylor, for all his help. From the old world, Gilbert Kutscher of the Industrieanlagen Betriebsgesellschaft allowed me to benefit from their research on demographic and military manpower trends. Not to neglect my own country, I would like to thank Major-General Edward Fursdon, formerly Defence Correspondent of the *Daily Telegraph*, for sharing with me his experiences of the Gulf War and for general advice on military affairs; Richard Holmes and John Keegan of the Department of War Studies, the Royal Military Academy, Sandhurst, for initial advice; the International Loans Section of the University of London Library (again) and the British Lending Library (again), the British Library and Public Records Office and especially the military, scientific and technical and general sections of the Ministry of Defence Whitehall Library. Michael Chapman, head of the General Section, Sheena and Carolyn get special mentions, but all deserve them for their unfailing enthusiasm and competence. The Director and Staff of the Royal United Services Institute for Defence Studies played an indispensable role with the provision of topical lectures which updated and honed my own ideas and perceptions. My friends Captains John Hyden and Charles Dick helped, again, by noticing press reports and lines of enquiry that I missed. So did my friend John Romano, applying a professionally trained translator's skills to a number of German texts, German not being my best foreign language. I must thank The Soviet Studies Research Centre, RMA Sandhurst, for making sure I received the latest and best information on the top land power and Eric Grove, formerly of Dartmouth and the Council for Arms Control, for reading the manuscript, making a number of helpful suggestions including the elimination of some polemic, and for detailed assistance with nuclear weapons. Finally, I must once again thank my friends at the Polytechnic of Central London School of Languages, not only for teaching me the language of the superpower which does not speak English, but also for going easy on the coursework requirements. With a little help from my friends, the impossible became possible. Thank you.

Note on Military Organisation and Terminology

In this book, the term military art is usually used to describe the conduct of war. In the west, the term doctrine is often used, and that is explained further in Chapter 4. Military art is divided into three levels, as understood by the American, British, German, Israeli and all Warsaw Pact armies. These are strategy (the higher conduct of war, incorporating economic and political considerations), operational art (the manipulation of higher formations) and tactics (operations by smaller formations and units). The dividing line varies from country to country. A higher formation is generally a Corps, Army or Army Group (Warsaw Pact front); a formation is a division or brigade (but not a Warsaw Pact regiment), and a unit is a regiment and/or battalion. A sub-unit (Warsaw Pact) or minor unit (western) refers to a battalion and below in the former case, a company or below in the latter. The term regiment is confusing: in some armies it comprises three or four battalions, very nearly equivalent to a brigade: in the British Army it is often used to describe a battalion-sized organisation. The British Parachute Regiment (three battalions) is the nearest the British have to a 'regiment' in the continental sense. A battalion normally comprises in the order of 500 troops, and is subdivided into companies, each comprising in the order of 100. The next division down is the platoon. This comprises in the order of 30 troops or three tanks. Infantry platoons are subdivided into sections (British) or squads (American).

An idea of the size of major land powers' formations can be gained from the accompanying table.

Land formations and units — comparative strengths

| | Division | | | | | Brigade or Regiment | | | |
| | Armoured | | Mechanised | | Airborne | Armoured | | Mechanised | |
	Men	Tanks	Men	Tanks	Men	Men	Tanks	Men	Tanks
United States	18,300	324	18,500	216	16,800	4,500	108	4,800	54
Soviet Union	10,500	322	12,500	271	7,000	1,300*	95*	2,300*	40
China	9,200	300	12,700	30	9,000	1,200*	90*	2,000*	—
UK	8,500	122	—	—	—	—	—	—	—
FRG	17,000	300	17,500	250	8-9000	4,500	110	5,000	54
India	15,000	200	17,500	—	—	6,000	150	4,500	—
Israel	—	—	—	—	—	3,500	80-100	3,500	36-40
Egypt	11,000	300	12,000	190	—	3,500	96	3,500	36

*Indicates a regiment, the equivalent to a brigade in normal communist structures. However, the Soviets may introduce brigades consisting of reinforced regiments for special tasks. UK strengths will rise on mobilisation: FRG's is under constant review. Other NATO countries tend to follow German organisation; Iran, Pakistan and South Korea have followed American organsiation.

Source: *The Military Balance, 1985-1986* (IISS, London, 1985, p. vii).

Introduction

Armed conflict will be as prevalent on this planet in the next quarter century as it has been since the dawn of history. There were 654 identified instances of major organised armed conflict in the 265 years 1720-1985, of which 162 started in the years 1951-85. It is highly unlikely that the incidence of conflict will diminish, although the balance between different types of conflict has shifted and will continue to do so.

Historians and analysts tend to define wars according to their causes and political objectives, rather than their military nature, which is both understandable and easier. The study of major armed conflict carried out under the auspices of the Canadian Defence Department's Operational Research and Analysis Establishment, divides wars into seven categories: conventional interstate, unconventional interstate, internal with external involvement, primarily internal, colonial, imperial and crisis.[1] Unconventional interstate wars tend to be of a guerrilla type, for example the PLO campaign against Israel or North Vietnamese incursions into Laos.[2] It might be tempting to assume that conventional interstate war is the main forum for large-scale mechanised air-land operations, but this is not necessarily so. Some of the most important wars for the developments of military art, which presaged future wars, were internal: notably the American (1861-5), Russian (1917-22) and Spanish (1936-9) civil wars. The latter two were also characterised by external intervention. In the 265-year period examined by the Canadian team, 230 of the 654 conflicts were primarily internal and 164 conventional interstate.

Another method of categorising wars is by scale, but this is subjective unless pinned to a specific index, like the number of

1

deaths attributable to the conflict. Although conventional interstate conflict is a leading cause of death in warfare, the two internal modes of conflict have been the leading cause since the end of World War II. On the evidence of the last 35 years, the three major modes of conflict in the next quarter century are likely to be internal, conventional interstate and internal with external involvement.[3] The latter is relatively the most costly in human life.

Table Introduction 1 categorises conflicts by numbers of known deaths. Straightaway, we can see that there are problems: the one conflict with the 'Doomsday' designation, World War II, includes 13.8 million military casualties and over 18 million civilian, including the six million European Jews of the Holocaust. Whilst it might be legitimate to include accidental civilian victims of armed conflict in an assessment of the relative size of major wars, deaths in concentration camps are in a different category, attributable to the internal policies of certain states involved, and not to operations of war as such.

World War I was a class I war. By the same token the Spanish Civil War was a class II and the Russo-Finnish Winter War of 1939-40 a class III. If internal purges and atrocities are counted as conflict, a single small German concentration camp deals the same number of deaths as a class III war. The Vietnam War is a category II, but many of those deaths are attributable to massacres or privation which are peripheral to the military operations themselves. The Russo-Polish War of 1920, so crucial in the development of military art, which exercised two of the most talented commanders of this century Pilsudski and

Table Introduction 1: Classes of conflict according to fatalities

Number killed	Class of conflict
More than 32 million	Doomsday
3,162,278 to 31,622,777	I
316,228 to 3,162,277	II
31,623 to 316,227	III
3,163 to 31,622	IV
317 to 3,162	V
32 to 316	VI
less than 32	VII

Source: Hoover Institution on War, Revolution and Peace, *Wars and Revolutions: a Comprehensive List of Conflicts Including Fatalities, Part 2 1900-1972* (Stanford, California, February 1973), p. v.

Tukhachevsky, was a class V in terms of known lives lost. So was the Anglo-Argentinian conflict of 1982. The latter is admittedly a prime example of air and sea warfare, which tend to be much less expensive in terms of blood than war on land, if more so in treasure.[4] Numbers of deaths alone are clearly not enough to assess the relative importance of major land conflicts.

Information available from Soviet and Warsaw Pact sources suggests that they define conflicts according to political criteria, the number of states involved and a rather subjective concept of scale. Broadly speaking, major wars occupy an entire Theatre of War (TV), while minor ones are confined to a single TVD, usually translated either as a Theatre of Military Operations or, perhaps more accurately, Theatre of Strategic Military Action (TSMA) (see also Chapter 4). Major recent local wars, according to Soviet writers, include Korea, Vietnam, the Arab-Israeli Wars of 1967 and 1973, and the Anglo-Argentinian conflict of 1982.[5] Warfare is conducted at both the tactical and operational levels (see also Chapter 4), and what the Soviets call local wars are clearly examples of major land-air warfare. Indeed, the criterion adopted for deciding what is or is not a local war is more related to politics than to scale, reflecting a peculiarly eurocentric view of the world. Any war outside Europe and not involving the USSR would seem to be a local war, in the Soviet view. Future conflicts of this type could involve the use of chemical and nuclear weapons — indeed, the Iran-Iraq War has already seen use of chemicals (see Chapters 1 and 3).[6]

A number of trends can be observed affecting the location, nature, frequency and duration of major conflict. The first is that the number of conflicts and the number of deaths in major conflict have increased more or less in proportion to world population. Conventional interstate and primarily internal wars account for about 60 per cent of conflicts, and these have increased in numbers in the same way as the overall trend, while the balance between the others has shifted. Colonial wars, very prominent in the eighteenth and nineteenth centuries, have shown a sharp decline. World Wars I and II together account for 55 per cent of the total deaths over the last quarter millennium, more than in the other 502 conflicts since 1721 for which deaths are recorded put together. This suggests that the superpowers and Europeans are right to attach top priority to avoiding World War III, whether or not it has a nuclear component, even if this means doing less to prevent conflict elsewhere. Conflicts are getting more numerous, but also more ill-defined. Even with the difficulty in defining what is and is not a major armed conflict, it is clear that the number of conflicts starting has increased since 1951. They are also getting longer. The average duration of wars remained roughly constant up to about 1850, followed by a decline to 1950. After 1950, there was a sharp rise, a surprising statistic which calls into question the belief that 'the next war will be a short war' (see especially Chapter 8). Many of these are low intensity or guerrilla conflicts which smoulder for years, but the average length of conflicts now is about five years. The Iran-Iraq War is therefore about average up to the end of 1985. If we take the increase in the number of conflicts starting and the increase in duration, the net result is an increase in the number in progress at any one time: about 40 at the time of writing, or twice what it was in 1950.

Until the end of the nineteenth century, the starter of a war ('committer') was more likely to win than to lose, making war as an act of deliberate policy seem a fairly rational phenomenon. Since 1900, the chance has declined and the probability of a committer 'winning' in a discernible way had fallen to 21 per cent in the period 1951-85, as against a 34 per cent probability of losing and 45 per cent of a draw. This may have some effect on nations' willingness to initiate conflict.[7]

* * *

This book is part of a family covering various aspects of future conflict. It is axiomatic that conflict on land interacts with that in the other main elements, at sea or in the air. As The Soviet Fleet Admiral Sergei Gorshkov pointed out in *The Sea Power of the State*, technological developments have enabled navies not only to bring force to bear on a narrow coastal strip but, with the advent of long-range ballistic and cruise missiles and carrier-borne aircraft, far into the hinterland.[8] Air power has been critical to the land battle since at least the 1930s. Air forces began life primarily as support for armies and navies, and it is significant that in most countries (Britain and Commonwealth nations being the exception) air force officers have army ranks. Although air power was used to strike directly at centres of power and population, its most effective use in World War II was arguably for close support of ground troops. As the fixed-wing aircraft has become more expensive and vulnerable, the helicopter has simultaneously emerged as an outstanding army vehicle and weapons platform. The use of the helicopter to move ground forces and as an attack weapon in its own right has led to the emergence of the integrated 'AirLand Battle' (American designation) or 'land-air battle' (British). It is quite impossible to disentangle what happens on the battlefield from the air above it and wherever the word 'land' appears in this book, read 'air-land'. Future 'land' warfare will also be totally dependent on systems carried in the air and in space for surveillance, target acquisition and communications.

Land warfare is profoundly different from fighting in the other elements. Generally speaking, the more complex the environment, the simpler the technology needed. Thus ground is infinitely complex and ground forces' weapons tend to lag behind those of navies and air forces in technological sophistication, although this trend may be changing (see Chapter 5). Conversely, the simplest environment — space — requires the most costly equipment. In some senses, however, the trend is reversed. It is easier to blast a laser or charged particle beam through space than to make it travel any distance through the soup-like atmosphere of a wet west-European dawn, and a relatively small explosion near an aircraft in flight will bring it down. Not so with a tank.

This book does not specifically address terrorism, low-intensity or guerrilla war. The dividing line between guerrilla war and large-scale, more conventional land operations is often blurred. General Giap began as a guerrilla leader in Indo-China, but his later operations, and those of the North Vietnamese Army in the closing stages of the Vietnam War, were clearly conventional operations involving large amounts of artillery and armour, in the tradition of the world wars and employing in an exemplary fashion many of the classic principles of 'open' warfare. Mao is thought of primarily as a guerrilla leader, and the doctrine of people's war still dominates the concept of operations of the world's largest land army, that of the People's Republic of China (PRC), although this may be changing (see Chapter 4). Conversely, 'guerrilla' type wars are often associated with conventional interstate wars. The Spanish *guerrillas* in the Peninsular War, whose operations led Wellington to introduce the word to English, the *francs-tireurs* in the Franco-Prussian War of 1870-71, and the Resistance in World War II, all acted to some extent in concert with regular forces of friendly powers.[9] At the top end of the scale are the

Russian partisans in World War II, organised in whole brigades and divisions.[10] As far as the author is concerned, these formations roaming in the enemy depth and operating in close cooperation with conventional forces are part of 'conventional' land warfare. The distinction is not confined to those writing about war with the comfort of hindsight. The officers of the French Foreign Legion, one of the toughest professional military outfits in the world, were well aware of it in their mess at Dien Bien Phu in 1954, the night before the final Vietminh assault began:

'Giap's boys are already giving us their best cards. 81 millimetre mortars, 120 millimetre mortars, 105 millimetre howitzers — the whole works.'
'It's going to be like Na San only ten times bigger.'
'Or almost Verdun! This time they'll put all their big artillery here and will show us what they have learned about big war fighting.'[11]

This book is about big war fighting over the next quarter century. That period has been selected because major weapons sytems being introduced or envisaged at the time of writing are likely to be in service during that period, and few demographic or other projections are reliable much beyond 2010. We can therefore make some sensible projections for that period based on reliable information about technology, tactics and military thinking, demography and the lessons of recent wars.

NOTES

1. G.D. Kaye, D.A. Grant and E.J. Edmond, *Major Armed Conflict: a Compendium of Interstate and Intrastate Conflict, 1720 to 1985* (Operational Research and Analysis Establishment, Department of National Defence, Ottawa, 1985), ORAE Report R95, p. 22. This is a revision of A.D. Mitchell, D.A. Grant and E.J. Edmond, *Major Armed Conflict: A Compendium of Interstate and Intrastate Conflict 1730 to 1980* (ORAE, Directorate of Strategic Analysis, Ottawa, May 1981), ORAE Report PR 161.
2. Mitchell, Grant and Edmond, *Major Armed Conflict,* 1980 report, pp. 227-8.
3. Ibid., p. 21, and Kaye, Grant, Edmond, *Major Armed Conflict,* p. 30.
4. Hoover Institution on War, Revolution and Peace, *Wars and*

Revolutions: A Comprehensive List of Conflicts Including Fatalities, preliminary edition, part 2 (Stanford, California, February, 1973), pp. 76, 89, 145.

5. N.K. Glazunov and I.S. Nikitin, *Operatsiya i boy: inostrannye armii (The Operation and [tactical] Battle: Foreign Armies)* (Voyenizdat, Moscow, 1983), pp. 13, 279-309. Although the book is about foreign armies, it is an example of 'mirror-imaging' which gives an insight into the Soviets' own perceptions; Lieutenant Commander Zygmunt Binieda, '*Geografia wojenna: ogólne pojecie teatru dzialan wojennych*' ('Military Geography: the General Concept of a Theatre of Military Operations'), *Przeglad morski (Naval Review)*, 12/1981, pp. 3-4; Major General V. Larionov, '*Nekotorye voprosy voyennago iskusstva po opytu lokal'nykh voyn*' ('Certain questions of Military Art According to the Experience of Local Wars'), *Voyenno-Istoricheskiy Zhurnal, (Military Historical Journal*, henceforward *VIZh*), 4/1984, pp. 46-52.

6. Glazunov and Nikitin, *Operatsiya i boy*, p. 279.

7. Kaye, Grant and Edmond, *Major Armed Conflict*, pp. 2, 3, 22, 27, 51-3. The Canadian compendium is the most complete analysis available. The statistical approach was begun by Quincy Wright, *A Study of War* (University of Chicago, 1942), and Lewis F. Richardson *Statistics of Deadly Quarrels* (Quadrangle, Chicago, 1960).

8. Admiral of the Fleet of the Soviet Union Sergei M. Gorshkov, *The Sea Power of the State* (Pergamon, Oxford, 1979), pp. 221-2, a translation of the Russian *Morskaya moshch'gosudarstva*.

9. The first authoritative use of the term *guerrilla* seems to have been by Wellington in 1809 (*Oxford English Dictionary*).

10. *Sovetskaya Voyennaya Entsiklopediya (Soviet Military Encyclopedia*, henceforward *SVE*), Vol. 6 (Voyenizdat, Moscow, 1978), pp. 229-34, '*Partizanskoye dvizheniye*'.

11. Bernard B. Fall, *Hell in a Very Small Place*: *the Story of Dien Bien Phu* (Pall Mall Press, London, 1967), p. 136.

12. On the career of Giap see Robert O'Neill, *General Giap, Politician and Strategist* (Cassell, Victoria, 1969), esp. pp. 195, 203, and for a revised opinion, *The Strategy of General Giap Since 1964* (Canberra Papers on Strategy and Defence, Australian National University Press, Canberra, 1969), p. 19.

1

Hell on Earth

The impossible had happened. The two opposed camps had been watching each other for years, aided by the latest and best in electronic and airborne surveillance. Yet one side had managed to concentrate large land forces secretly and launch them across a major obstacle achieving complete tactical, operational and strategic surprise. The other, in spite of holding strong and carefully prepared positions, was forced back and reeled from the blow. Some said that elaborate mechanical devices had been installed on the border to engulf and delay the attackers, but even if they had been the specially trained engineer teams which operated in the latter's van would have found them and rendered them inoperable. And there was another shock. The attacking troops, who had always been regarded as a mass of brave but badly led and motivated peasantry, fought with aggression, coolness and skill which did full justice to the brilliant and original plan for the surprise attack.

Fiction? An imaginary scenario for a future war in Europe? Warsaw Pact troops attacking across one of the wide European rivers and overcoming a barrier of electronic sensors and preplaced mines? No. This actually happened on Saturday 6 October 1973 when operation Badr, named after a battle which Muhammad won against great odds was launched by the Egyptians against Israeli forces in Sinai. General Ahmed Ismail's troops were not concentrated for the attack in an orthodox way but crossed the Suez canal at points all along the hundred miles from Port Said to Suez. The 'mechanical devices' were a system which the Israelis allegedly had for pouring oil on to the surface of the canal and setting fire to it: in fact, such a system had been tried on a small scale in 1970 but found to be

8

unworkable. However, the Egyptians believed in it and sent special squads across the canal on the night of 5-6 October to sabotage these fictitious installations.[1]

The Israeli plan to defend Sinai was based on the Bar-Lev line of fortifications which, like so many other defensive lines, has been much maligned, although the concept behind it was sound. The Bar-Lev line was designed to buy time for the defenders and conserve precious manpower behind concrete and sand while an Egyptian thrust lost its momentum and its main axes became clear. A strong armoured reserve would then counterattack. Besides the value to the Egyptians of total surprise and their novel use of man-portable anti-tank guided weapons to hold the ground they had seized against armoured counterattack, the main element in the Israeli plan — adequate artillery and a strong armoured reserve — was missing: only one brigade of 200 Patton tanks under Colonel Resheff was actually in place, and there was not enough artillery to beat down the anti-tank weapons.

The first wave of Egyptian troops carried the canal bank with aggression and *élan*, and when the Israelis roared down upon the Egyptian bridgeheads they were halted by the barrage of unimposing but deadly Sagger anti-tank missiles with a maximum range of about 3,000 metres. This is a classic example of how new technology *used as part of a coherent tactical or operational plan* and *deployed in significant numbers* can have a dramatic and surprising effect. The Israelis knew the Egyptians had Sagger missiles, and they knew what that missile's capabilities were. It was the way they were used and the scale which shocked them. Two other factors upset the Israeli defensive plan. The first was that the Israelis reasonably expected the Egyptians to exploit their initial success and drive for the Ismailia, Gidi and Mitla passes, the rocky portals opening the way to Sinai. The majority of Resheff's armour was therefore held back in reserve against this contingency. In fact, the Egyptians did not go for the passes as expected, but sat tight consolidating their bridgehead. This shows how a lack of aggression, drive and confidence at the operational level can negate spectacular tactical success: some of the Egyptian armoured commanders wanted to press on and exploit tactical progress that seemed almost too good to be true. However, the political objectives of the Egyptian plan called only for the seizure of a narrow canal side strip, showing how the actions of commanders in the field are limited by political direction, which seems to be implemented more and more closely and rigidly in modern war. The Egyptians were also anxious to remain within the umbrella of surface to air missiles (SAMs) which would shield them against Israeli air power. The Israelis were also confident that they could bring up reserves in 48 hours, which was, they thought, as long as it would take the Egyptians to consolidate their bridgehead and construct bridges to get heavy armour and ordnance across the canal. In fact, the Egyptians had devised an ingenious method which cut the time taken by half. Slots had to be cut in the steep canal banks before bridges could be laid, involving the movement of thousands of cubic yards of sand. High-pressure water jets were found to break down the walls more effectively than any explosives, and within five hours the necessary slots had been hosed out. The use of Soviet mobile bridging equipment further reduced the time needed before heavy armour could roll from Africa into Asia. In fact, this operation was more successful in the north than the south, where the sand granules were bigger and more cohesive, and the carefully calculated schedule was upset when it took longer to hose gaps than had been anticipated. This is a startlingly clear and obvious example of the way terrain — and the very soil — can critically affect military operations. Even so, by dusk on 6 October the Egyptians had ten bridges across the canal and in the night which followed 500 tanks rolled across, one of the greatest military, engineering and logistical achievements of modern major land war.

* * *

The Golan Heights occupy a surprisingly small area, about the same size as the Salisbury Plain training area in southern England. The surface of the plateau is not dissimilar, either: very open, dotted with bushes, and criss-crossed by tracks and what were once asphalt roads, cut into deep furrows by the tracks of tanks and armoured personnel carriers. The Heights are not only of enormous military importance because they lie on the Israeli-Syrian border and were therefore inevitably the place where their forces clashed in October 1973. They are also vital to Israel's survival. Water cannot be taken for granted here, and 85 per cent of Israel's water comes from the Jordan valley. This water comes in from the north through the Sea of Galilee and the Golan Heights shield its source. Without Golan, Israel

Figure 1.1: Opening moves, Sinai, 6 October 1973

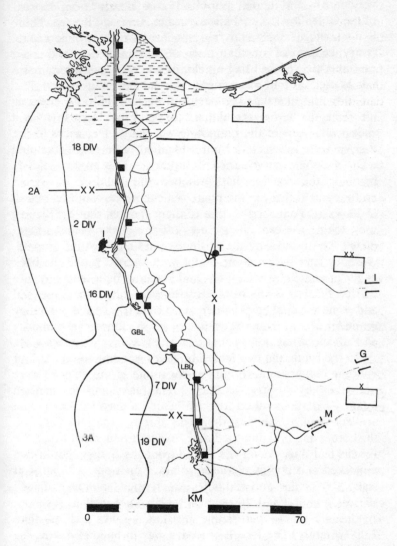

A – Army (Egyptian); G – Gidi Pass; GBL – Great Bitter Lake; I – Ismailia and Ismailia Pass; LBL – Little Bitter Lake; M – Mitla Pass; T – Tasa; Black squares – Bar-Lev line strongpoints; Israeli formations are shown with standard symbols: x – brigade, xx – division (these symbols will be employed throughout this book).

can, quite simply, be parched into submission. Also, Israel is a very narrow and densely populated coastal strip: from the rear of the Golan it is only 50 kilometres to Acre and the sea. There is no strategic depth, no free space in which to manoeuvre. Every centimetre of that slab of terrain which had been captured in 1967 had to be held, at all costs: every centimetre was in itself crucial: war on land, war for land.

To the north stands the beautiful Mount Hermon, shielding the flank of the heights like a bastion. From here there is a spectacular view of the plain below as far as Damascus to the east, and the Israelis had built a fortified eagle's nest crammed with electronic surveillance equipment. The young soldiers manning the position had watched the build-up of Syrian armour and artillery in the plain, but carried on as normal until, at 13.45 on Yom Kippur, one of them shouted that the Syrians were taking the camouflage nets off the guns. Almost immediately Syrian shells hit the position, and fierce fighting erupted. An hour later Syrian commandos were carried round the back of the mountain by helicopter, and began to fight their way into the fortification. Some of the Israelis were killed, some escaped and some were taken prisoner to be butchered alive, a chilling reminder of the incongruous juxtaposition of medieval barbarity and advanced technology that characterises many modern wars.

To the south, the two Israeli brigades standing to on the four volcanic mountains forming the backbone of the defence were not taken by surprise as the Syrian tanks and mechanised infantry battalions rolled forward behind a massive Soviet-style artillery barrage, clearing their way through the minefields on the border and bridging the impressive anti-tank ditch which the Israelis had dug. Along the whole front the Syrians put in two armoured and two mechanised infantry divisions, a total of at least 900 tanks and 30,000 infantrymen, although Israeli sources give 1,200-1,400 tanks, which may include reserves. Against this, there were some 180 Israeli tanks and less than 1,000 infantry. The Israeli objective was to blunt and slow the initial attack to buy time for the reserves which were being mobilised to come up. It was an exemplary 'covering force battle' and has many analogies with the likely course of a future European conflict. In fact the first Israeli reserves were appearing within 24 hours, a miracle of organisation and speed, although 7 Brigade had to go on fighting for four days and three nights before being relieved. In this narrow area unfolded a tank

Figure 1.2: Initial dispositions, Golan Heights, 6 October 1973, 14.00 hours

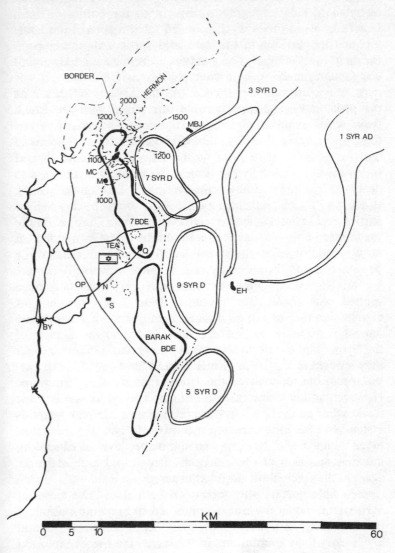

BY — Bnot Yaakov (Jacob's Daughters') Bridge; EH — El Hara; M — Masaade; MBJ — Mazraat Beit Jinn; MC — Majdel Chams; N — Naffakh Camp (Kafer Naffakh); OP — Oil Pipeline Road; Q — Qnaitra; S — Sinndiane; TEA — Tel el Aaram; Dotted lines are terrain contours, heights in metres; AD — Armoured Division; D — Division battle of a scale and intensity unparalleled in the history of war. Although the Soviet-German battle of Kursk in 1943 involved many more tanks, roughly equivalent to the battles on both Israel's fronts in this war, the concentrated nature of the fighting, and the attrition in this area and particularly the engagements in the Valley of Tears between the hill called Hermonit and Qnaitra, make it the archetypal tank battle to date. It was massive, violent and continuous. As the Syrians rolled across the plain they sometimes became intermixed with the Israeli tanks which swung their turrets round as the Syrians passed them and continued to fire. Some of the Israeli strongpoints in the plain continued to hold as the advancing armour lapped round them, delaying Syrian forces which had to be diverted to deal with them, providing valuable intelligence and adjusting Israeli fire, a clear indicator of the value of such 'stay behind parties' and strongpoints in a similar situation in Europe. As the battle raged crews ate, swilled a mouthful of water, nodded off for a second or so on their vehicles. As the Syrian tanks came on they engaged them one by one: target — traverse! — range! — fire! The average time taken to destroy a Syrian tank once spotted was about five seconds. When they ran out of ammunition they had to go back and get more — it was virtually impossible to bring resupply forward. At the beginning most of the Syrian tanks were Soviet-made T-54s and T-55s, but later they brought in the T-62s, which should have been able to out-shoot and out-manoeuvre the Israeli Pattons and Centurions. However, another timeless truth of war worked for the Israelis; it takes time and practice to learn to operate a complex weapons system, and the long experience the Israelis had of theirs combined with superior training and the higher level of education, initiative and skill of the individual Israeli told time and time again as they picked off target after target.

Incredible bravery was shown on both sides. The crews of Syrian tanks hit in the tracks continued to fire from stationary positions until they were shot apart. Because the T-54s and T-55s carry their ammunition in the turret, the risk of explosion was great, and even if they did not blow up immediately they caught fire, those inside screaming as they could find no escape, clawing and scratching vainly at the inside of the tank until they were consumed by the flames. Tank casualties tend to be of two types: burns, or major amputation as High Explosive Squash Head (HESH) shells strike, knocking jagged scabs of metal off the inside which rip through everything in their path. For the Israelis, there was the thought of what would happen to their families not very far behind if the Syrians got through, and they held on like grim death.

As night fell the Syrians gained an advantage, as they had better night vision equipment. However, the Israelis managed to avoid disaster by using illuminating shell fired from artillery. Artillery was also brought down right on top of the beleaguered strongpoints to sweep off Syrian infantry while from direct fire positions the Israeli tanks engaged their Syrian counterparts, a clear example of the need to use each weapon for what it is best at in a mutually supportive scheme.

The Syrians continued to advance head on, wave after wave. They did not change the direction of their attacks, more out of pride, one suspects, than inability to conceive other courses of action. Although the tactics were clumsy, their major objectives had been selected with skill and showed detailed knowledge of the Israeli dispositions. One division's objective was the Jacob's Daughters' (Bnot Yaakov) Bridge, the main line of communication for all the Israeli forces in the central Golan Heights. Other Syrian tanks swung south, down the oil pipeline road, connecting north Golan with the south. This had to be held, and one Israeli tank did so all night, stopping an entire Syrian division until dawn revealed the fact to the Syrians. Sheer weight of numbers had to tell, and by midday on Sunday 7 October Syrian forces were within 8 kilometres of the Jacob's Daughters Bridge, the maximum Syrian penetration, but at this stage the first trickle of Israeli reserves was beginning to arrive.

The stand by the Israeli 7 Brigade was the most spectacular of all. A major element in its success was its commanders' intimate knowledge of the ground. They knew the advantages and disadvantages of every piece of high ground instinctively, and the area had been prepared for a defensive holding battle, with hull-down positions and ramps, while range tables had been prepared to various landmarks to give an outnumbered force the maximum advantage against an oncoming enemy. Even so, the Syrians located the various positions one by one and shelled the Israelis off them. Most Israeli casualties were from artillery fire, the tank commanders faced with the unenviable choice of fighting closed down and blind or opening their tank hatches to face death in the swirl of fragments and blast. The Israelis were pushed back and by Tuesday were holding the

15

Figure 1.3: Maximum Syrian penetration, Golan Heights, midnight, Sunday 7 October

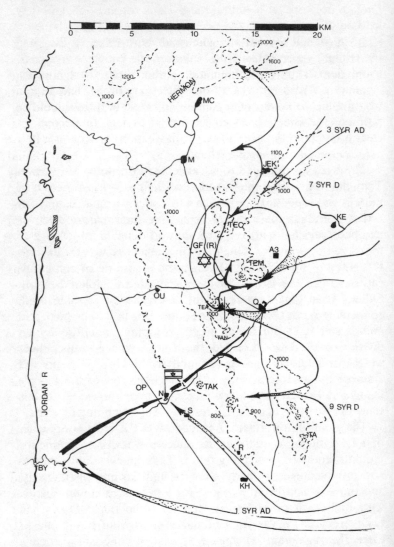

BY — Bnot Yaakov Bridge; C — Customhouse; GF(R) — Northern Group of Forces (Raful); JEK — Joubbata el Kachab; KE — Khane Erenbe; KH — Khoehniye; M — Masaade; MC — Majdal Chams; N — Nafakh; OP — Oil Pipeline Road; OU — Ouasset; Q — Qnaitra; R — Ramsaniye; S — Sinndiane; TA — Tell Aakacha; TAK — Tell abou Hannzir; TAN — Tell abou Nida; TEA — Tel el Aaram; TEC — Tell ech Cheikha; TEM — Tell el Makhfi; TY — Tell Youssef; X — maximum Syrian penetration, Valley of Tears, from which panorama is drawn; Dotted lines are contours, heights in metres edge of the high ground, their position still giving them a good field of fire across the valley of Tears towards Qnaitra, as Figure 1.4 shows.

By Tuesday 7 Brigade had been fighting without let up for four days and was utterly exhausted. The situation was critical as reinforcements from the southern sector at last appeared imminent. The front commander, Raful, begged Avigdor, commanding 7 Brigade, to hold on, 'Give me another half an hour. You will soon be receiving reinforcements. Try, please, hold on!' By now 7 Brigade had seven tanks left out of an original total of about 100. One battalion was down to two shells per tank. At this point the beleaguered troops in strongpoint A3, far behind the foremost Syrian forces, radioed that the Syrian supply columns were turning round and withdrawing. The Israelis had stood the pounding for longer. The scene before them in the Valley of Tears was one of utter devastation, with about 500 armoured vehicles broken and burning:

> None of the Syrian tanks managed to pass the crest ... it was one huge graveyard of hundreds of pieces of steel still burning ... ashes ... explosions ... armoured brigades completely wiped out, our bodies, their bodies ...[2]

This graphic description of part of a recent war is included to remind the reader that war is messy, exhausting, horrible. The Yom Kippur war is worthy of exhaustive study: its main lessons can be summarised as follows:

— The continued critical nature of terrain, both in terms of vital routes (the Golan and routes across Sinai) and the nature of the soil itself.
— Any defensive system, no matter how strong, whether based on natural or artificial barriers may be penetrated with surprise, ingenuity and determination.
— That said, defensive systems properly used can channel, delay and perhaps critically affect an offensive.
— The importance of knowledge and preparation of the terrain in the tactical defensive battle (Golan).
— The ability of new technology used as part of a coherent doctrine and plan and *en masse* to create major surprise (Saggers).
— The value of fortified strongpoints in conjunction with

17

18

Figure 1.4: The Valley of Tears. Scene of the greatest tank battle of modern times

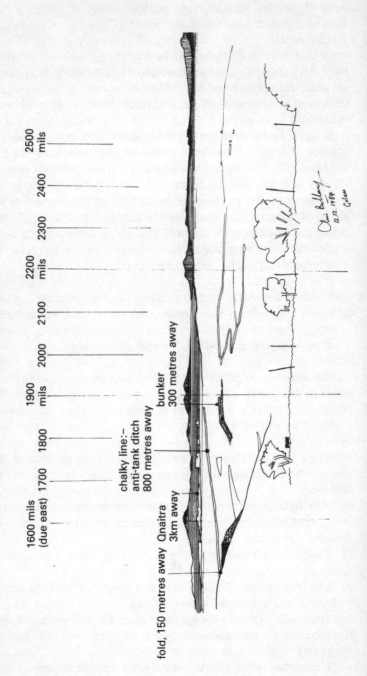

mobile reserves for diverting and delaying an attacker and reporting from behind attacking forces.

— The potential of a well organised air defence system comprising a mix of guided missiles and guns.

— Connected with this, the concept of absolute 'air superiority' has perhaps lost some of its validity as a result of dispersal and hardening of air forces on the ground and potent ground based air defence.

— In the Israeli counterattack across the Suez Canal (14 October) the plan hinged on overrunning Egyptian Surface to Air Missile (SAM) sites, thus creating a corridor which opened the way to the Israeli Air Force.

— Because of the capabilities of anti-armour weapons, it has become impossible to ensure the success of any attack, whether of tanks or mechanised infantry, without destroying or neutralising these weapons in advance.

— Connected with this, the re-emphasised role of artillery.

— Also, the role of tactical surface to surface missiles in destroying large targets in the enemy depth, especially where there is a good air defence system which prevents the air forces from operating.

— The need for improved reconnaissance to target artillery and longer range surface to surface missiles.

— The vital role of electronic warfare, and the way in which its effectiveness can be minimised through good security and training.

— The importance of continuous operations (especially Golan), operations at night (Israeli counterattack in Sinai), especially under enemy air superiority and in desert terrain.

— Surprise remains a decisive factor in attaining success, and with meticulous planning and execution can be attained even in spite of modern electronic and other surveillance.[3]

SPACE-AGE VERDUN

'A sand grey coloured billiard table extending in every direction as far as the eye can see' is how one observer described the setting for Iraq's operations on its southern front in March 1984. In such terrain, camouflage is impossible. The only alternative method of survival is to disperse vehicles and stores widely, and protect them with deep scrapes cut in the sand and a network of sand walls. Everything is expanded, and everything is dug in. Because of this, engineer plant has acquired greatly increased significance: the commander of the Iraqi 3 Corps, Major-General Maher Abed al-Rashid, ordered special patrols to capture or destroy Iranian earthmoving equipment, and captured specimens are displayed as trophies as prestigious as tanks or guns, thus fulfilling Tizard's prophecy that the humble bulldozer would play an increased role in future war (see Chapter 5). The fine alluvial sand disintegrates when driven over, and in the rain during winter and spring it immediately becomes very boggy, severely hampering mechanised operations. Unlike North Africa, which is mostly hard, rocky terrain, this desert is far from ideal for mobile war. To overcome the hard going, the Iraqis hit on the device of spraying the sand with liquid tar, which immediately binds and strengthens the sand. A large network of these instant roads now criss-crosses the desert, and there is a well organised system of traffic control with recovery vehicles stationed at key points. There has probably never been as much construction plant on a battlefield, and such investment made in manipulating the terrain and making it suitable for military operations. Not far away, around the island of Majnoon, electrodes have been immersed in the water which transmit a powerful current between them. Anyone trying to infiltrate through the marsh water is electrocuted, and because no mark is left on the bodies it was suspected that chemical weapons had been used. Even more ingenious a barrier is a giant man-made lake about 24 kilometres long and 1 kilometre wide, running from west to east and straddling the border just to the south of Majnoon. It was made by pumping billions of gallons of water from the Tigris river and the Hawizah marshes through a 20-metre-wide canal. Some analysts believe that the Iraqis began the project before the war, and that it is part of a geo-strategic plan to drain the Iranian rivers flowing through Khuzestan. Whereas the original trench was more than sufficient to block the passage of infantry across the flat desert northeast of Basra, by 1983 it had expanded at its southern end into a 10-kilometre-wide lake. Either way, in this part of the world native ingenuity and Soviet equipment have combined to create an elaborate network of fortifications all along Iraq's southeast border. Nature and art have been combined to turn land and water into a single fortified complex.[4]

The dominance of ground and position and the elaborate

Figure 1.5: The Southern Front, Iran-Iraq War, 1980 onwards

1 — Iranian offensive, February 1984; 2 — Iranian offensive, March 1985; Palm trees indicate cultivated area

way the environment has been sculpted are not the only similarities with those great positional struggles, the Russo-Japanese and Great wars. When the war began in late September 1980, it was confidently expected to be over in seven or 14 days. Yet after a fortnight it was reported that the Iraqi army was 'inexorably bogged down in the Iranian desert'. As in Europe in World War I, the Iraqis resorted to artillery bombardment to break the Iranians, both in Khorramshahr and Ahwaz. The Iraqi heavy artillery, the classic weapon of positional warfare, hardly moved for five days. The fighting became concentrated around fortified cities, Khorramshahr and Abadan, whose resemblance to other sprawling conurbations like Stalingrad became more than geographical. In October, *The Times'* defence correspondent noted that 'these artillery barrages are beginning to resemble those on the Somme in that they are doing a grotesque amount of damage without achieving very much'. Khorramshahr eventually fell but Abadan continued to hold. After nine weeks it became obvious that this war, like another, was not going to be over by Christmas, and that it would 'settle down to a conflict characterised by artillery duelling'.[5] By January 1981, the war had developed a familiar pattern of long-range artillery duels punctuated by infrequent border skirmishes. In the northern and central sectors the Iraqis quickly secured the strategic road controlling the border towns of Qsar-o-Shirin and Mehran and dug in in front of an Iranian mountain range which had withstood previous Arab penetration for 500 years. The main theatre remained the southern during 1981 and 1982, the Iranians resorting to 'human wave' attacks with hundreds of thousands of young and poorly trained troops against strong and growing Iraqi defences. As with the World War I, stalemate on the main battlefront led both sides to pursue the struggle on the economic plane, especially with Iraq attacking Iran's oil trade. Meanwhile Iran sought to bring its population advantage to bear in the most direct manner, with more frontal attacks on the Iraqi line throughout 1983. By 1984, the conflict had assumed 'Passchendaele proportions' in both its futility and the scale of the slaughter, both sides just too exhausted to achieve the decisive breakthrough which they sought. The same comments and parallels with the Great War continued to appear. In March 1984, newspaper captions described scenes of Iranian dead littering the desert as 'reminiscent of the First World War', and the casualty figures and tactics employed by the Iranians bore this out. At least 20,000 Iranians and 7,000 Iraqis were killed in a month between February and March 1984, many fewer than both sides claimed but still carnage on a colossal scale. In June, General Rashid spoke of scything the Iranians down like ripened wheat, destroying two million Iranians with any means at their disposal, a veiled reference to chemical weapons (see also Chapter 3). In October, nearly 2,500 Iranians were killed in a five-day period in the border area east of Baghdad. 50,000 in all are reported to have died in the Iranian offensive in early 1984, and perhaps half a million in the first four years of war. The ubiquity and density of death led commentators on World War I battlefields to remark how the bodies seemed to merge with the clay, and in the Gulf War they said exactly the same, corpses 'starched with grey, merely matching the alluvial sand on which they had fallen'.[6] The numbers engaged, certainly on the Iranian side, also attained World War I dimensions. Reports that Iran had mobilised half a million men and boys near the Iraqi frontier from January to July in 1984 can be discounted, but there were probably 140,000 deployed against Iraq in July. Even these numbers were not adequate to force a passage through the dense Iraqi defensive line, perhaps 20 kilometres or more deep all along the front with ingenious obstacles, underground headquarters and interlocking fire positions.[7] Those who have to defend Europe against a possible Warsaw Pact thrust might care to take note.

Some would argue that this return to World War I techniques and casualties is a function of the relative technological backwardness of the participants compared with the industrialised and superpowers, and the low level of training of most of the troops. However, this is hard to sustain as some aspects of the conflict are undeniably very modern. For example, at the end of February 1984 the Iranians launched a carefully planned and bold attack from their side of the Hawizah marshes. Travelling at night in large powered rubber boats a small force surprised and captured the undefended village of Al-Bayhda. They immediately dug in while thousands of reinforcements, weapons and ammunition were poured in using the Iranians' large American-built helicopters and more boats. This was in spite of the fact that the force comprised many more revolutionary guards than the Iranian army regulars who would be expected to have greater expertise in this sort of operation. Another force landed at the adjacent village of Sakhra. The two forces linked up and established a strong base which threatened the main Basra-Baghdad road a mere 10 kilometres away. The essence of operational art in the defence is to identify a breakthrough and destroy it before the trickle becomes a flood. For the Iraqis who are greatly outnumbered this is a particular problem: no one can be strong all along a defended front, but the Iraqis have fought the problem skilfully using, in particular, the helicopter gunship. The Iraqis immediately hit the Iranian positions with artillery whose range enables it to cover wide threatened sectors, and then brought in helicopter gunships and air strikes. Within a day of the Iranians establishing their position the Iraqis had launched a difficult three-pronged infantry counterattack, and destroyed the penetration after an exceptionally hard and bitter battle. The gunship helicopter is the weapon *par excellence* for plugging breaches quickly, with its high speed of reaction, mobility and firepower and the Iraqis' use of them in this way mirrors American and Soviet views of their employment. The Iraqis' use of gunships increased considerably as the war went on, and general al-Rashid was a major pioneer in this. By June 1984, the Iraqis were mounting raids with up to 50 Soviet-built gunships in a single day.[8] Iraqi armour is held back in reserve to counterattack really major penetrations and massed artillery employed to interdict (isolate and channel) breakthroughs.

On 11 March 1985 the Iranians launched a six-day offensive in the area around Majnoon island with seven divisions totalling 100,000 men moving by boat and helicopter and assisted by Korean pontoon bridges. The most successful penetration was the southern one, which drove through to a point northeast of Qurna where the Tigris, otherwise running roughly parallel to the Baghdad-Basra road, makes a distinctive bend towards the border (see Figure 1.5). Here they quickly put across three bridges made of styrofoam blocks — an exceptionally light, water-resistant plastic — and then poured across to cut the Baghdad-Basra road. To ward off the expected Iraqi armoured counterattack they were stiffened by a lavish scale of RPG anti-tank rockets and jeep-mounted 106 mm recoilless guns. The Iraqis fell back with the attack and then launched counterattacks from north and south to cut off the Iranian penetration. Having boxed the bridgehead in armour, artillery and helicopter gunships went to work to destroy them. About 25,000 Iranian and 10,000 Iraqi troops were killed. The Iraqis deployed 25 brigades (eight divisions) to defeat the offensive, and proved adept at moving large formations about the country rapidly. As an example of a very large scale, mobile defensive battle, with both sides using modern technology in congruence with doctrine, this grand battle must be one of the most important of modern times.[9]

Another thoroughly modern aspect of the war is the employment of large operational-tactical surface to surface missiles, probably on a larger scale than at any time since World War II. These are mainly Soviet-built Scuds but in 1984 it was reported that the Iraqis might also be getting the extremely accurate SS-21s, as well as the latest T-72 tanks and fighter aircraft. The employment of the surface to surface missiles is particularly instructive: to date they have been used mainly against large civilian targets although there is no reason why SS-21s with conventional or chemical warheads could not be used with devastating effect against headquarters and reserves. The Iraqis have also apparently been able to pinpoint the sites from which Iranian missiles have been launched against them, a sign that this is far from an old-fashioned war in the spheres of target acquisition and intelligence also. On the Iraqi side, at least, this new equipment has been handled competently and in some cases with considerable skill and imagination.

General al-Rashid has emerged as an aggressive and capable military leader: a brigade commander at the start of the war, he rose swiftly through divisional command to direct 3 Corps to defeat the Iranian offensives of early 1984. At this time, 3 Corps comprised ten divisions of 10,000 men each and held a 200 kilometre sector.[10] This is somewhat more extended than would be the case in a European conflict, but not totally unrepresentative. As with the American Civil and Russo-Japanese wars, we should be wary of saying that the particular circumstances of this war lessen its relevance for future wars elsewhere.

The greater long-term strength of Iran may have begun to show in a new and surprisingly successful offensive in February 1986. Iran launched a major offensive across the Shatt-al-Arab waterway on the night of 9 February, called 'Dawn-8'. A week after the fighting began total casualties were reported to be about 30,000 and the Iranians claimed to have pushed west along the coast so as to cut Iraq off from the Persian Gulf. On 11 February they claimed they had captured the coastal town of Al-Faw although reports that they had advanced the full 40 kilometres as far as Kuwait cutting the Iraqis off from the sea proved to have been premature. The Iraqis fought back resolutely, claiming to have mounted 1,200 air sorties in the four days from 11 to 15 February, and loosening the Iranians' hold on the area around Faw in vicious and costly fighting. By the time the Iranians were into their third week on the strategic peninsula the signs were that the Iraqi three-pronged counterattack was making slow but steady progress. However, in the last week of February the Iranians still controlled large areas of the Faw peninsula. This was still the situation in late May, although the Iranians had not advanced so far west as to reach the Kuwaiti border. Gunfire could still be heard in Kuwait at this time.

The main lesson of this continued energetic and bitter fighting is that there are not necessarily any quick results in land warfare: progress over ground is slow, requires enormous effort, and is costly in life. A report in February 1986 assessed that Iran was apparently prepared to contemplate a war of attrition for 10 or 20 years. Her losses would be greater than Iraq's, but the population difference (Iran's 45 million to Iraq's 15) would ultimately guarantee victory for Iran, the more so since individual Iranians were displaying greater commitment which would ultimately combine to outweigh Iraq's great advantage in equipment.[11]

At the time of writing the war's main lessons appear to be: the extreme difficulty of breaking through a defended front, even with greatly superior numbers, the value of air-mobile forces in plugging any gaps before the trickle turns into a flood, the continued importance of massed artillery fire, the ability of surface to surface missiles to substitute for expensive manned aircraft, the continued cardinal importance of fortifications and terrain, and the interrelationship between the two, the ability of a conflict to drag on and on, assuming a positional form, and the effect this has on the populations of the countries engaged. The fact that strong positions, weaponry and training has enabled a nation of 15 million to defeat or contain fanatical, concentrated attacks by one of 40 to 45 million, albeit unsupported by fighter ground attack aircraft, for six years up to the time of writing should also lead us to be more optimistic about the potential of NATO to hold any assault by a Warsaw Pact numerically inferior to itself.

PEACE FOR GALILEE?

Although the Israeli involvement in Lebanon from 1982 to 1985 is remembered primarily as a guerrilla conflict, the initial Israeli invasion by eight divisions known as operation Peace for Galilee and the 48 hours' fighting between Israel and Syria from 9 to 11 June 1982, constitute a brief but full scale conventional war which had enormous, perhaps unparalleled, implications for the future of major war. The high quality of the Israeli armed forces, their effective and sophisticated use of advanced weaponry and use of innovative tactics have put Israel at the 'cutting edge of modern warfare'.[12] Israel's use of Western style equipment and tactics against an enemy relying on Soviet systems makes specific aspects of the conflict highly relevant to those concerned with the defence of Western Europe.

The operation opened with a brilliant exercise of administration and logistics, eight divisions concentrating in an area deep inside the country, and driving right across Israel. At the same time beginning at 1400 hours on 9 June the Israelis attacked Syrian air defences in Lebanon. Unmanned drones were launched over the Syrian air defences, forcing the Syrians to open up with SAMs against fake targets and protecting the Israeli Phantom aircraft following behind. The Israelis also used ground-based weapons against the Syrian missile sites: probably, 175 mm guns, basic range 32 kilometres, Israeli MAR-290 rocket launchers (range reported in western sources as anything between 25 and 40 km) and LAR-160s (reported range varying between 13 and 30 km). Published reports say the latter had cluster bomb warheads. The Israelis used remotely piloted vehicles to direct this fire, achieving great accuracy.

It is also reported that the Israelis used ground-launched anti-radiation missiles, but it is impossible to confirm this. One report says they were called *Zeev* ('wolf') fitted with radar homing warheads and a range of 40 kilometres. This means they could have been based on the 290 mm rocket launcher MAR-290. Others indicate they could have been a surface-launched version of the American *Standard* anti-radiation missile. It is also claimed that ground-launched rockets carrying chaff were fired at Syrian radar sites to mask Israeli air activity and supplement active electronic jamming techniques. Chaff — a sort of metallic confetti — is a very simple but effective way of confusing radar, which was called 'window' in World War II. Finally, a small drone may have been used to upset fire control radars like the Gun Dish radar on the ZSU-23-4 *shilka* radar controlled anti-aircraft system. This would have flown over areas packed with anti-aircraft installations until a radar of the right sort was detected. At this point the drone would do a kamikaze dive into the radar emitter.

In co-ordination with air and artillery – rocket – missile attacks the Israelis, according to reports derived from open sources, mounted a commando operation against the main command post for Syrian air defence in Lebanon. It apparently succeeded, dislocating the air defence network and forcing each anti-aircraft unit to operate in isolation.[13]

It is clear from this that one cannot talk about 'land warfare' and 'air warfare' as two separate things. Air was critical to the ability of ground forces to move and fight and ground systems and forces made a passage for aircraft, as in 1973 but in a far more complex and multi-faceted way. The degree of ground-air co-operation achieved was greater than even most NATO countries could have achieved, partly because the Israelis have more practice in hot war conditions and partly because the unified structure of the Israeli Defence Forces (IDF) precludes much of the inter-service rivalry and competition for resources which characterises the different services in NATO and perhaps even Warsaw Pact countries. Also, the Israelis obviously had a very sophisticated range of electronic warfare equipment for this sort of operation.

As always, terrain exercised an all-pervading influence on considerations of air defence as well as ground fighting. The Bekaa valley where most of the fighting took place is surrounded on three sides by mountains, and these reduced the coverage of the Syrian early warning radars. The Syrians also made certain mistakes, leaving radars switched on when they were not needed, making it easier for the Israelis to locate them, and did not take advantage of the mobility of the Soviet SA-6 anti-aircraft missiles, and left them in one place for long periods. Finally, their anti-aircraft sites were not fortified, which made them much more vulnerable to attack, especially ground attack.

The manoeuvre war on the ground did not go so well for Israel. Most combat took place in a 32-hour period from dawn on 10 June. The operation went like clockwork until they entered Lebanon, when the narrow roads channelled them between high ground broken by terraces with groves, vineyards and scrubby woods. Any attempt to move off the roads took a terrible toll of equipment, the sharp dry rocks ripping into equipment in a way totally unfamiliar to those used to operating in European terrain. Forced to stick to the roads, the Israelis could only drive straight ahead, and a single position could hold them up for hours. There was no place for initiative, tactical skill or manoeuvre — all considered to be the IDF's forte. The Israelis did not move flexibly on foot. Instead, they used American M-113 armoured personnel carriers as infantry fighting vehicles. Prior to 1982, most Israelis considered that these vehicles, designed to carry infantry to the battlefield rather than for fighting from, would survive. In fact, they sustained terrible casualties and in disgust Israeli paratroops rode to Beirut sitting on top of tanks, which they thought was safer. The Israelis have taken these lessons to heart, as will be seen in Chapter 4.

A great deal can be learned about tank design and employment, from this most recent example of intensive armoured combat, and this will be explored when considering the future of tank design in Chapter 5. The Israeli *Merkava* acquitted itself well, its computer fire control system and armour-piercing fin stabilised ammunition providing the 'main technological advantage' enjoyed by the Israelis on the ground.[14] The *Merkava*'s design and various systems for preserving human life also worked well. According to some published sources, this was the first time ICMs were fired from artillery and multiple rocket launchers in war. If so, this presages major increases in artillery's effectiveness generally. There is no evidence that 'smart' (terminally homing) munitions like the American Copperhead were used. Finally, both the Israelis and Syrians used helicopter gunships to attack each other, the Israelis equipped with American Cobras and 500 MDs and the Syrians with French Gazelles. Some sources say that Soviet Hinds were used but this is uncertain. The Israelis used helicopters with great effect against the Syrian tanks. Although the Israelis enjoyed air superiority high above the battlefield, they were unable to prevent Syrian attack helicopters skimming along below, in spite of the fact that the Syrian pilots were mediocre. They avoided detection by Israeli air defence radars and in one case surprised Israeli columns moving through the Chouf mountains, causing mayhem. Tank crews were very concerned about attack by these. On the other hand, helicopters cannot occupy ground and vertical envelopments were not attempted, possibly because such aerial *desants* might be considered too lightly equipped to survive for very long.

The most fundamental and disturbing lesson of this brief, savage war does not hinge on terrain, tactics or technology but on the ability of men to cope. The widespread introduction of advanced technology, especially command control and communications (C^3), had led to many of the most intelligent and best educated men being employed in communications and support units. This had two effects. One was that the cream of the cream was not necessarily employed commanding in the front line, as has traditionally happened (in Britain, for example, the brilliant generation of whom so many died in the Great War or aircrew in World War II). However tragic and wasteful this may seem, combat is the most demanding activity known to man and requires the very best. This undoubtedly hampered Israeli effectiveness in battle. Secondly, for some strange reason those in the rear, perhaps because they faced a potential threat which never actually materialised, suffered far more psychological casualties than those right up front. In the 1973 war, the Israelis suffered what they regarded as excessive battle shock casualties: taken overall, 30 psychological casualties to every 100 physically wounded. As a result, the Israelis took active steps to deal with the problem, the first nation to do so. A team of six staff psychologists forms the central IDF agency responsible for prevention and treatment of psychiatric casualties. The Invasion of Lebanon provided the first opportunity for the IDF to test the effectiveness of this, divisional and brigade psychologists going into battle with briefcases full of questionnaires designed to measure morale, stress and a host of other factors and to help relieve stress among soldiers who had come away from the fighting. The results were not encouraging. The head of the Israeli Defence Psychological Research Unit noted that 10 per cent of casualties were psychological, ranging from fatigue to paralysis. Other estimates put the rate higher: 23 psychiatric casualties for every 100 physically wounded or 20 for every 100 physical casualties (killed and wounded) overall. The percentage successfully treated and returned to their units also varies between reports: 40 to 80 per cent, with 60 per cent returned within 72 hours seeming about right. The Israelis' 20 psychiatric casualties to every 100 physical (17 per cent) is higher than the 2.6 per cent reportedly suffered by the Germans in World War II, but better than the 26 per cent suffered by the Americans. In Vietnam, 12 per cent suffered some type of battle reaction. The Germans returned 80 per cent of their psychiatric casualties to the front, the Americans in the same war returned 65 per cent. One suspects that the widely varying statistics reflect varying attitudes to the problem and different methods of diagnosis. Nevertheless, given the Israelis' strenuous efforts to deal with the problem, it is clear that the greater power of modern weapons, the mental demands of operating complex equipment and the pace and incessant nature of modern operations make it more likely that soldiers will crack up.[15] Given that a future European conflict might involve very intensive operations for many days, not just two, the implications are very worrying indeed.

An equally important lesson of operation Peace for Galilee is clearly the increased importance of Electronic Warfare (EW). It was not the first war in which EW featured prominently (see Chapter 6), but it demonstrated how electronic weaponry has become pivotal on the modern battlefield. The lessons of Lebanon will dominate military thinking for the next ten years, and if there are no more high intensity, high technology wars in that time, it will be for longer. Electronic warfare works both ways: as the Israelis demonstrated, electronic counter measures (ECM) can make sophisticated weapons like SAMs ineffective. Clearly, it is unsatisfactory to see a trade-off between electronics and the weaponry which actually strikes the target: they are mutually supportive — without support from electronic countermeasures, weapon systems may not reach the target. The Israeli experience of using EW in the 1982 war has been exhaustively studied, especially in the United States. According to the Deputy Under-Secretary of State for Research and Advanced Technology, 'Experience clearly demonstrated the advantages of combining tactics with various EW techniques, for example drones, decoys, stand-off jammers and defense suppression in order to achieve a decisive victory with minimum losses.'[16]

Two things should be noted. Firstly, that the side equipped with Soviet systems, the Syrians, was actually weaker in artillery than the Israelis. In a conflict with Soviet or their allied armies, this would not be the case. Secondly, the Syrians had only two early warning air defence radars deployed in the Bekaa to supplement those of the individual missile batteries. If provided with these on a scale comparable with the Soviets (two to every four or five missile batteries) that would have given them eight to ten to forewarn their 19 battery force. The inability of combat air patrols to prevent low-level penetrations by helicopters hugging the terrain also highlights the importance of organic, point air defence systems, an area where the Warsaw pact forces are far better provided than the West. The armed helicopter threat to ground forces needs to be taken every bit as seriously as that from tanks. However, all this new technology apart, what sticks in the mind most about Peace for Galilee are two things as old as war. First was the influence of ground and its tendency to channel, constrict and wear out. The second was the demands placed on men. The Israelis were definitely short on leg infantry. According to the published reports, their attempts to reduce psychological casualties were not as successful as they had hoped. Above all, war is the province of danger and uncertainty, as Clausewitz knew: terrifying, exhausting, confused, messy, requiring brave, fit men and women who are complete masters of the equipment they have to operate.[17]

Other recent wars worthy of particular attention because of their relevance to the future are the closing stages of the Vietnam War, especially operation Lam Son 719 in 1971 as an example of air-mobility; The Ogaden campaign, especially the Jijiga operation in 1977, because of air mobility again and the fact that it was devised by Russian generals; and the Indo-Pakistan War of 1971, especially the Bangladesh operation as a *Blitzkrieg* offensive using technology chosen for its suitability in the terrain.[18] Before analysing the nature of future war in detail, there are a number of critical factors which have a bearing on it and which need to be evaluated.

NOTES

1. Colonel A. Barker, *Yom Kippur War* (Ballantine, Random House, New York, 1974), esp. pp. 33-42; Chaim Herzog, *The War of Atonement* (Weidenfeld and Nicolson, London, 1975), esp. ch. 4, 'Eyes they have but see not'; 'Kar', 'A Personal View of the Yom Kippur War', *British Army Review* (August 1975), pp. 12-18.
2. Eye witness account. The account of the Golan is based on the author's visit and conversations with Israeli officers. Also Barker, *Yom Kippur War*, pp. 69-89, 7 Brigade: Herzog, *War of Atonement*, pp. 106-15.

3. Brigadier Mohammed Ibrahim Nagaty, 'Some Lessons of the Ramadan War', *Pakistan Defence Journal (PAJ)* 1975, pp. 8-9, 45; Arnon Soffer, 'The Wars of Israel in Sinai: Topography conquered', *Military Review*, April 1982, pp. 61-72; Martin Van Creveld, *Military Lessons of the Yom Kippur War: Historical Perspectives* (The Washington Papers 3, Sage, Beverly Hills, 1975).

4. Sand grey billiard table, terrain and dispersion: Major-General Edward Fursdon, 'Iraqi army masters techniques of desert dispersal', *Daily Telegraph*, 8 March 1984, p. 4, and interview; electrocution: Fursdon, 'Rival Gulf armies face tough obstacles', *Daily Telegraph*, 20 June 1984, p. 4; giant moat: David Ottaway, 'Confident Iraqis wait behind giant moat', *Guardian*, 31 July 1984, p. 7; and David Fairhall, 'Mystery of Iraqi ditch', *Guardian*, 17 January 1985, p. 7. The ditch is illustrated on maps compiled in 1983.

5. Over in 7-14 days, *Daily Telegraph*, 27 October 1980, p. 5; 'Inexorably bogged ...', *Times*, 10 October 1980, p. 1; great amount of damage without achieving very much, *The Times*, 15 October 1980; artillery duelling, *Daily Telegraph*, 14 November 1980.

6. General course of war 1981-3 and Passchendaele proportions: James MacManus, 'No winners as bloody gulf war drags on', *Daily Telegraph*, 29 January 1985, p. 5; captions, 'The Holocaust', *Daily Express*, 2 March 1984, p. 6; Casualties February and March: Jon Swain, '27,000 die in month', *Sunday Times*, 11 March 1984, p. 13; scything down: 'We are ready to scythe down 2m Iranians', *Observer*, 17 June 1984; 2,500: 'Thousands die in Gulf battle', *Financial Times*, 23 October 1984, p. 3; 50,000: Ross Benson, 'General Blood's Harvest of Death', *Daily Express*, 22 June 1984, p. 17, and 'Iraqi Secret Weapon Threat ...', *Daily Express*, 6 June, p. 6; corpses merging with sand: Fursdon, 'Iran bloodbath in land of the Marsh Arabs', *Daily Telegraph*, 2 March 1984, p. 1.

7. Edward Mortimer and Henry Stanhope, 'Exiles ridicule Tehran troop strength', *Times*, 4 July 1984, p. 6. Previous reports had varied from 300,000 to 500,000: depth of defences: 'We are ready ...', *Observer*, 17 June 1984.

8. Iranian attack and Iraqi response: Fursdon, 'Iran bloodbath ...', *Daily Telegraph*, 2 March 1984, and interview: use of gunships, also David Fairhall, 'Iraq's last trump', *Guardian*, 20 April 1984, p. 19; 50 sorties: Shaun Usher, 'Gulf fears Iran epic day', *Daily Mail*, 5 June 1984, p. 44.

9. March 1985, Fursdon, 'Iraqis continue their pressure on Iranians', *Daily Telegraph*, 23 March, 1985, p. 6, and Derek Wood, 'Iran uses Scud Missiles against Iraq' (includes offensive and number of divisions), *Jane's Defence Weekly*, Vol. 3, No. 13, 30 March 1985, p. 532.

10. Surface to Surface Missiles: Wood in *JDW*, 30 March 1985; Scuds (range 300 kilometres) were reported to have been used by Iraq against Navahand in June 1984, and have been used against other targets. The Iraqis also received SS-12 'Scale board' missiles (range 900 kilometres), Ian Glover-James, 'Iraq threat of mass destruction', *Daily Telegraph*, 8 June 1984, p. 4; SS-21s, *ibid.*, 'Russian arms to help Iraq

long range war', *Daily Telegraph*, 4 June 1984; Iranian use: 'Iran rocket Baghdad', *Daily Telegraph*, 27 March 1985, p. 1, and other dailies; 'Iraq has detected Iran missile sites', *Guardian*, 30 March 1985, p. 8, and 'Iraq traces Iranian missile base', *Daily Telegraph*, 30 March, p. 6. The former claims that the Iranian missiles were 'REF 17s with a range of 125 to 150 miles' (Scuds, presumably); Rashid: interview with Maj.-Gen. Fursdon, who knows him well; strength of 3 Corps, 'Iran says Gulf War offensive crushed', *Guardian*, 29 January 1985, p. 7.

11. Nick Childs, 'Anniversary Offensive: Gulf flare-up', *JDF*, 1 March 1986, p. 365; David Hirst, 'Iran claims new ground in advance on Basra', *Guardian*, 13 February 1986; Ian Black, 'Iran looses hold on peninsula in vicious fighting', *Guardian*, 24 February 1986, and 'Iran pushes further into Northern Iraq', *Guardian*, 27 February 1986: advice on situation in May 1986, International Institute of Strategic Studies, London.

12. Professor W. Seth Carus, *Military lessons of the Israeli-Syrian Conflict, 1982*, unpublished typescript, pp. 1-2.

13. Ibid., pp. 8-10.

14. Ibid., p. 23, citing the head of the Israeli Armoured Corps in 1984, General Amos Katz.

15. Helicopters: conversations with Israeli officers and Martin van Creveld; psychological casualties: Major Richard A. Gabriel, 'Lessons of War: the IDF in Lebanon', *Military Review*, August, 1984, pp. 63-4 and ibid., 'An Israeli Lesson Learned: Stress in Battle: Coping on the Spot', *Army*, December 1982, pp. 36-42. Gabriel revised his statistics to become much less favourable to the Israeli psychologists between the two articles. The most consistent account is Lt.-Col. Gregory Belenky, (USA), Lt.-Col. Shabtai Noy (IDF) and Major Zahava Solomon (IDF), 'Battle Stress: the Israeli Experience', *Military Review*, July 1985, pp. 28-37, which gives the 30 to 100, 23 to 100 and 20 to 100 figures, plus the 60 per cent return in 72 hours. The percentage of psychological casualties was far from uniform: out of four battalions selected, the ratio of psychological to physical casualties (killed and wounded together) varied from zero in the unit under least stress to nearly 1:1 under conditions of maximum stress.

16. Carus, p. 45, citing Leslie Wayne, *New York Times*, 20 June, 1982, p. III-4.

17. Carl von Clausewitz, *On War*, Michael Howard and Peter Paret (eds.) (Princeton University Press, 1976), Book 1, chapters 4 and 5, pp. 113-16.

18. On Lam Son 719 see Major-General Dave Richard Palmer, *Summons of the Trumpet: A History of the Vietnam War from the Military Man's Viewpoint* (Ballantine, New York, 1978), pp. 302-9, and Captain Jonathan M. House, *Towards Combined Arms Warfare: a Survey of Tactics, Doctrine and Organization in the 20th Century*, Research Survey No. 2, Combat Studies Institute, Fort Leavenworth, Kansas, 1984, pp. 164-8; On Ogaden, Lieutenant-Colonel I.E. Mirghani, 'Lessons from the Ogaden War', *British Army Review*, August 1981, pp. 28-33; on the India-Pakistan War of 1971, see Chapter 4.

2

Factors Affecting Land Warfare: Geography, Demography and the Major Land Powers

RIVER DEEP, MOUNTAIN HIGH

On land, the ground itself is of critical military importance. If well used it can conceal and protect, multiply and project one's forces and strength. Men live on land, not in the sea or air. Aircraft and naval vessels must return to land at some point, and require special facilities on land to keep them operational. Of the countless millions of dead whose agony is recorded in the cold statistics in the Introduction, the vast majority died on land and in land operations. Land warfare is generally more expensive in human life than any other form, unless nuclear weapons are employed against civil populations. Virtually all conflicts are finally resolved on land. The British naval victory at Trafalgar in 1805, the blockade of Germany in World War I and the air bombardment of the same country in World War II were all immensely important contributions to victory but in all three cases it was not until the enemy's ground forces were defeated and his territory occupied that he could be relied upon to 'do our will'.

Unlike water or air, terrain is infinitely variable. Its clever use is the most important and difficult aspect of military art. The slightest bump provides cover from direct fire. Gently rolling ground provides an infinite number of concealed fire positions for powerful artillery and missiles. The unprecedented potential for electronic warfare assets to multiply force many times is highly dependent on the way they are sited (see Chapter 6). A small slot cut in the softly swelling ground is a haven for rest and sleep, and can be a fire position of enormous strength.

There is something almost supernatural about it, defying analysis.

From the earth, from the air, sustaining forces pour into us, mostly from the earth. To no man does the earth mean so much as to the soldier when he presses himself down upon her long and powerfully, when he buries his face and his limbs deep in her from the fear of death by shell-fire, then she is his only friend, his brother, his mother; she stifles his terror and his cries in her silence and her security, she shelters him and gives him a new lease of ten seconds of life, receives him again and often for ever.

Earth! — Earth! — Earth!

Earth with thy folds and hollows and holes into which a man may fling himself and crouch down! In the spasm of terror, under the hailing of annihilation, in the bellowing depth of explosions. O Earth, thou grantest us the great resisting surge of new-won life. Our being, almost utterly carried away by the fury of the storm, streams back through our hands from thee ...[1]

Psychological and sexual significance apart, ground has an undeniable, almost animal-like effect on tactics and operations. Take the Argentinian position at Goose Green in the Falklands conflict of 1982. These death-concealing crevices, invisible from ground level, stretched away into the oppressive distance. It took the utmost physical and moral exertion to reach and take each small objective, and as soon as one position was painfully prized from the ground there was another to be laboriously fought and chewed through, and another: trench, after trench, after trench. The rocky terrain on the approach to Port Stanley afforded the opportunity to build far stronger individual positions, and was cleverly exploited. These examples concern terrain which is relatively flat, firm and open. How much more influence is exerted by high mountain ranges, forbidding and treacherous marshes, wide and fast flowing rivers, scorching desert or freezing tundra. Some examples will already be apparent from Chapter 1. National boundaries often coincide with natural barriers. Much land warfare, at least in the initial phases of a conflict, therefore takes place in an environment which is decidedly hostile even before the shooting starts. Recent examples of this are the Sinai desert, the Hawizah marshes between Iran and Iraq, or the high Himalayan glaciers which have been the scene of protracted disputes between India and Pakistan.[2] These frontier areas are all parts of the world which the first great strategist known to us, Sun Tzu, would have called 'difficult ground'.[3] Major obstacles to the conduct of land operations are shown in Figure 2.1.

Closely related to terrain are climate and weather. The effect of the Russian winter on Napoleon's and Hitler's forces is well known, although in the author's view this is often used to derogate the capabilities of the Russian and Soviet armies. The Russians had to fight in it too. Clever combatants can turn weather to their advantage.[4] Less spectacular but often equally significant is straightforward rain; it was not just the weight of artillery fire on the Western Front in World War I, but the heavy soil and temperate climate of northern France, bringing frequent rain, which made no-man's land so difficult to negotiate. The element of mud has reasserted itself very recently, in the Iran-Iraq War (see Chapter 1).

Once again, Warsaw Pact views are useful. Warfare in 'special conditions' takes place in five different environments: mountains; major forests (for example, the northern coniferous forest or *taiga* which stretches uninterruptedly across much of Siberia); deserts; 'northern regions' (the Arctic); and, finally, winter. It is notable that warfare in the Arctic and in the very severe conditions of the east European and Russian winter are considered as two separate problems, whereas for NATO conditions are either arctic or normal. Operations in high mountains (over 2,000 metres) usually require specially trained troops with mountaineering equipment. At over 3,000 metres altitude, breathing becomes difficult and the efficiency of petrol engines is reduced by nearly 50 per cent. For these reasons, heights over 2,000 metres above sea level are treated as 'high mountain ranges' on Figure 2.1. In addition to the obvious problems caused by steep slopes, hard and slippery rocks, absence of roads and rarefied atmosphere, mountain rivers, with their fast flowing current and steep, rocky banks are a particular problem for attacking troops. This is partly because they are not amenable to bridging with standard equipment, which is designed for slower, wider rivers with gently sloping banks.

In forests, movement off the roads by heavy military vehicles is virtually impossible. The effect of forests on military operations in other respects varies with the soil conditions, the

37

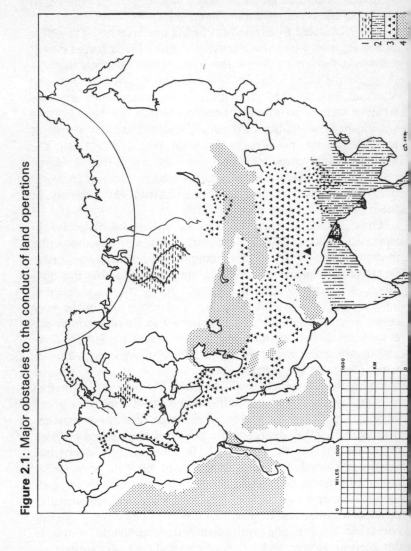

Figure 2.1: Major obstacles to the conduct of land operations

A — Arctic Circle (Ice); 1 — Major swamps; 2 — Tropical rain forest and monsoon forest; 3 — Very high mountain ranges (mostly over 2,000 metres, except Carpathians and Yugoslavia, which are shown because of military significance); 4 — Desert and semi-desert

Note: this map is only intended to give a quick impression of the major features of relief and areas where warfare would have to be conducted in special conditions. It is important to distinguish between *relief* (height above sea level) and *terrain*. Much of the land shown white is in fact hilly or mountainous and this can be exploited tactically and operationally. Conversely, an area like the Gobi desert south of lake Baikal although high above sea level (1,000 metres), is nevertheless relatively flat. The major features shown here would, however, place very severe constraints on operations by large land armies. For more precise details of elevation and type of country at any point, consult any large atlas. Terrain can only be deduced from a large scale map or an air chart.

The scale is shown in the form of a grid to show that this is an equal area projection. Distances measured from one point to another will not be true.

presence of marshes, rivers and lakes, and the type of vege-tation. Mature pine forests, for example, impair vision and fields of fire in comparison with open country, but not as much as other types of forest. In forest areas the value of fortifications is substantially increased, and the effect of fire reduced. Young coniferous forests mitigate the effect of fire least, and decidu-ous forests the most. In deserts, concealment, cover and the construction of strongpoints are all made enormously difficult (see Chapter 1), and the maintenance of troops and vehicles demands much more attention and effort than in temperate climes. The same is of course true in arctic regions. Frozen ground tends to swell and crack, causing landslides and gen-erally impairing the construction and maintenance of field works and roads. Natural obstacles such as lakes and rivers, which in other conditions would secure a flank, cannot be relied on. High winds and bitter cold, besides being fatal to human beings if experienced for too long or without special equipment, will freeze hydraulic fluid and oil. Blizzards and the long nights of the arctic winter reduce the availability of air support very significantly. Radio equipment, radar and magnetic compasses are all affected by the proximity of the magnetic pole, and the latter, combined with the paucity of natural and man-made features, makes navigation extremely difficult. Finally, special conditions have a major influence on the effects of nuclear weapons (see Chapter 3). In mountainous areas, the effects of nuclear explosions are channelled and concentrated by valleys, and correspondingly reduced on reverse slopes. In forests, con-tamination by nuclear and chemical weapons is more prolonged. In arctic conditions, overpressures near the epicentre of a nuclear explosion are increased, but the speed at which the shock wave travels outwards is reduced. This means that the effect on dug-in positions is relatively greater than in normal conditions, while that on men and vehicles in the open is relatively less. In deserts, the effect of nuclear weapons is generally increased by the openness of the terrain and the nature of the soil, which will remain contaminated for longer. Conversely, however, the rarefied desert air permits the shock wave to travel outwards faster, so that the effect on dug-in positions and heavy vehicles is diminished.[5]

It is not for nothing that the world over, armies' orders begin with the heading *ground.*

THE STAGE AND THE PLAYERS

Armed conflict will continue to take place over the entire land surface of the globe. The places where wars happen have changed significantly in the last 250 years. Africa and America were particularly prominent for colonial wars, but otherwise with the exception of Europe other major areas are not showing any marked decrease in conflict. The disappearance of conflict from Europe is the most remarkable and unprecedented change and is so out of character that one must seek a specific explanation. The nuclear balance of terror might be it. However, there have been long periods of peace in Europe before. The period 1871-1914 was peaceful for western and central Europe at least, if not for eastern Europe, and this was followed by the second most destructive war in history and the most politically traumatic of modern times. Europe has led the world for conventional interstate wars for the last 265 years, followed by Asia and then the Middle East.[6] If the two superpowers ever fight each other on land it will probably be in the Middle East or Europe, and in Europe the most technologically advanced nations face each other with land forces which are still numerically greater than anywhere else except for the Russian and Chinese forces facing each other in the Far East. Within a month of mobilisation the opposed pacts could put four million men, ten thousand fixed-wing aircraft, 25,000 artillery pieces and 40,000 main battle tanks into the field in Germany alone.[7] So, although major war has disappeared from Europe since 1945,

Figure 2.2: Where wars have happened, 1730-1980

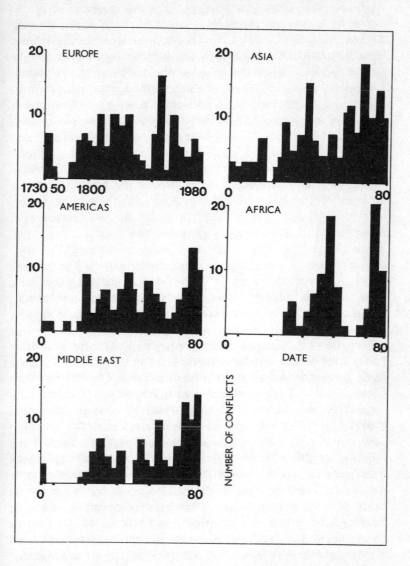

Note: This analysis indicates number of conflicts, some of them low intensity. This is why some are still shown for Europe even though there has not been a major war there since 1945. There may well have been other conflicts in Africa, the Americas and the Middle East before the nineteenth century, of which no record survives.

41

it remains potentially the most important theatre of land warfare. The other areas where large-scale conventional land operations have occurred recently and are likely to recur are the Middle East, the USSR-China border, South and South-East Asia. Coincidentally, perhaps, these three areas of Europe, Asia and the Middle East are also those which are top of the league for conventional interstate conflict. United States forces are unlikely to be involved in major conventional operations other than in these areas. The author believes that conflict in the Americas and Africa, though bitter and protracted, will incline to smaller scale and guerrilla operations. Egypt and North Africa, abutting as they do on to the Middle East and Mediterranean Sea, are considered to be part of the Middle Eastern area and distinct from sub-Saharan Africa. The one thing that is certain when talking about warfare is that the unexpected will happen, and there may be exceptions to this generalisation. The Falklands conflict might be one example, although in the author's view its main lessons concern sea and air operations and it hardly qualifies as an example of major land conflict. New trends in military technology, operational art and tactics will almost certainly be worked out in Eurasia, even if subsequently employed elsewhere.

This trend is reflected in the incidence of conflict within the boundaries of individual countries. Over the last 265 years the leading countries have mostly been in Eurasia. The first five are China, India, Turkey, Russia and Argentina. Conflict in Argentina has, however, mainly been of a small scale or guerrilla type and this does not affect the overwhelming dominance of Eurasia in major air-land warfare. The other notable exception is South Africa which has seen important wars from the point of view of developments in military art, notably the Boer War of 1899-1902, and is today in the forefront of certain major land warfare developments, notably artillery. The South African Army is likely to be employed mainly in guerrilla type operations in the next few years, but full scale mechanised land warfare against other states is possible. On balance, the author has decided to omit South Africa from specific examination in this book, but it is arguably a potential major land warfare state.

Another way of assessing the most important potential participants in major land warfare is simply to look at the strength of their armed forces and the level at which they are organised.

This can be seen from Table 2.1, which aims to give an initial impression of the premier powers on land. Peacetime strengths do not reflect war potential exactly, although they usually determine a nation's strength in the opening phases of a war. The more highly organised and developed NATO and Warsaw Pact countries can increase their armed forces very quickly in the event of hostilities: West Germany's total armed forces would be more than doubled in the first three days of a major war, from 478,000, and the army has 645,000 reserves. Switzerland has regular armed forces of only 1,500 but could mobilise them to 1,100,000 in 24 hours.[8] Numbers of troops and quantities of equipment are always changing, and there are problems with interpretation. Should the US Marine Corps be included in ground forces? To what extent do the Soviet Air Defence Service, KGB and Border Guards fulfil functions which in other countries would fall to the ground forces? How strong would Iran and Iraq's armies be if they were not fighting each other? Raw numbers of men and women do not reflect military competence and the amount and quality of equipment available to various armies varies enormously. Nevertheless, raw numbers of troops do provide a surprisingly good rule-of-thumb indication of what constitutes a premier land power, when matched against other criteria. Number one in terms of peacetime ground forces' strength, China, also has the world's largest population, and is a nuclear weapon state with a formidable intellectual and scientific tradition. Number two, the Soviet Union, has been a major land power throughout recent history, has invested 'more intellectual capital in the study of war' than any other nation and is a superpower militarily and technologically.[9] It also occupies the centre of the Eurasian land mass, and we will return to the significance of that point at the end of this section. The third in size is India. India's army, furthermore, is all-professional. India is a sub-continent, capable of making its own nuclear weapons and ballistic missiles. India should receive more attention in analysis of the development of armed forces and military thinking than she does. China and India have also been the scene for most conflict within their own borders in the 265-year period examined by the Canadian Department of Defence. In general, the leading countries for conflict within their own borders are large agricultural areas with restless minorities.[10] Most of these conflicts have been internal but there is a surprising — or perhaps not so

Table 2.1: Top nineteen nations for ground forces, 1986 (over 200,000 strong)

Nation	Ground forces' strength (1985-6)	Number of conscripts (if known)	Number of women (if known)	Highest operational/ tactical formation	National population (million)	Ground forces as percentage of population
1. People's Republic of China	2,973,000 (25% reduction underway)	2,040,000		Army Group	1,055	0.28
2. Soviet Union	1,995,000[a]	1,400,000		Front (Army[b] Group)	267.5	0.73
3. India	1,100,000	none		Corps	759	0.15
4. Vietnam	1,000,000	high %		Corps	60	1.6
5. United States	978,900[c]	none	84,700	Army Group[d]	239	0.4
6. North Korea	750,000			Corps	20	3.75
7. South Korea	520,000		1,600 in 1978	Army	42	1.2
8. Turkey	520,000	475,000		Army	49	1.06
9. Iran (war)	500,000[e]	100,000		Army	43	1.16
10. Iraq (war)	475,000			Corps	15	3.1
11. Pakistan	450,000	none	55,000 in 1978	Corps	95	0.47
12. Federal Republic of Germany	335,600	180,300		Army Group[d]	61.2	0.54
13. Egypt	320,000	180,000		Army	48.5	0.65
14. France	300,000	189,000	6250	Army	55.17	0.54
15. Taiwan	290,000			Army	19.89	1.45
16. Syria	270,000[f]	135,000		Corps	11	2.45
17. Italy	270,000	205,000		Corps	57.15	0.47
18. Spain	230,000 (to reduce to 195,000 in 1985-8)[g]	170,000		Corps	39.5	0.58
19. Poland	210,000	153,000		Army	37.5	0.56
Iran (peace, estimate)	220,000[h]					
Iraq (peace, estimate)	220,000[h]					

44

Source: Compiled from *The Military Balance, 1985-86* (International Institute of Strategic Studies, London, 1985). The balance aims to record the situation in July of the first year it represents. This edition was just published before the manuscript was completed and should still be current at the time of publication. The notes draw, in addition, on the balances for 1979-80, 1980-1, 1981-2, 1983-4. 1978 women's figures from Kütscher, *Übersicht Frauen in Streitkräften*.

a. Excludes 600,000 paramilitary forces (KGB troops, border guards) and Air Defence Troops (*voyska* PVO), 635,000 strong, some of whom perform functions which in other states would be performed by ground forces. Take, say 300,000 *voyska* PVO and all paramilitaries and the Soviet Union vies with China for first place.
b. See Chapter 4. The Theatre of Military Operations (TVD) has no manoeuvre elements of its own and is therefore not counted as a formation.
c. Army 648,000, US Marine Corps, 189,241. Women 75,500 and 9,200, respectively. For these purposes, USMC including substantial air elements is counted as ground forces.
d. NATO's highest operational level formation is the Army Group, and major nations (US, Germany, Britain) are assumed to think in such terms.
e. Iran's regular army is estimated at 250,000, of which the conscripts are a part. The Revolutionary guard corps (also 250,000) is obviously playing a major part in land conflict and is included.
f. This has probably been inflated by the continuing uncertainty over Lebanon.
g. The reduction is clearly due to Spain's accession to NATO, which has subsumed some of the responsibilities which Spain formerly had to undertake herself.
h. Before the Islamic revolution in 1979, Iran's army was 285,000 strong. After the revolution, 60 per cent was reported to have deserted. In 1980 it was reported as 150,000 strong. In 1981 it was the same strength plus 40,000 revolutionary guards and 30,000 Mujaheddin. The author believes that if peace returned, Iran would probably retain a number of Revolutionary guards, estimated at the 1981 level, 70,000, plus regular forces (1981 level) of 150,000, giving 220,000. Iraq's army was 190,000 strong in 1979, before the conflict, so it is feasible that it would keep pace with Iran, putting both powers in the over 200,000 bracket.

surprising — correlation between this and readiness for major interstate war.

The scale of land operations is a theme which will recur throughout this book. For this reason the 'highest operational-tactical formation' given in the table is of significance. The Soviet Union, for example, thinks big. Given the intellectual effort the Russians have invested in the study of war and their experience of conducting land operations of enormous scale and scope not only in the Great Patriotic War but going back at least to the eighteenth century, this is not surprising. Having been invaded by the Mongols, Napoleon and Hitler, to name a few, probably helps. The United States, Britain and West Germany now work on the same level, but probably as a reaction to Soviet concepts of scale (see Chapter 4). On the whole, the highest level of operational-tactical formations mirrors the dimensions of a nation's army to a surprising degree.

Other countries in Table 2.1 because of numbers deserve to be there for other reasons, too. Spain has a fine tradition on land (the *tercios* in the sixteenth century) and the high degree of political involvement by the army is probably reflected in its numerical strength. The same is true of Poland, which has also produced some of the most original and perspicacious writing on the development of Warsaw Pact military thinking, notably the OMG whose resurgence was first identified from Polish open sources. Turkey also has a long history as a formidable land power.

A common-sense look at the major land powers today would produce a list surprisingly similar to Table 2.1. In addition, we must include Israel since, as noted in Chapter 1, she is at the spearpoint of modern warfare, especially mechanised warfare, is more advanced in the crucial electronic warfare area than anyone else except the United States (see Chapter 6), and has nuclear weapons (see Chapter 3). Although her peacetime army is only 104,000, that is a lot for a country of only 4.3 million (2.4 per cent), and it can be mobilised to 400,000 in 24 hours.

Two nations are conspicuous by their absence so far: the United Kingdom and Japan. Both are island nations, oddly symmetrical, mirror reflections at opposite ends of Eurasia. Although geography has suited them both for a role as maritime and air powers, they have been major continental powers in their time. Japan showed an aptitude for continental operations in the Russo-Japanese War of 1904-5, and continued as a continental power for 40 years, until defeated on land by the Soviet Union. Her army today is 155,000 strong (oddly enough, almost exactly the same size as the British). However, it is unlikely that Japan would play a major role in conflict on the mainland of Asia, unless there is a very significant political change in the east of that continent. Japan would seem most suited to concentrate naval and air strength. Having lost her toe-hold on the Asian mainland, land operations against the Soviet Union, China or Korea would have to be preceded by major amphibious landings, unless Japan was acting in concert with a mainland Asian ally.

Because of her commitment to NATO, and the continued presence of a substantial army on the European peninsula, the

United Kingdom is in a different position. The British army is not much smaller than the armies at the bottom of Table 2.1, 163,000 strong at the time of writing, and being a force of professionals it may be as militarily effective as much larger armies. It has been involved in more fights than any other NATO country since World War II.[11] Although for much of its history it had been an army of 'limited liability', it played a major continental role from 1916. The situation since World War II has forced the continental commitment on the British, whether they like it or not. The British Corps in Northern Army Group has considerable mobilisation potential and the Russians consider that corps to be the 'main striking force' of the Group.[12] The Army Group commander is a Briton, and either he or his West German counterpart commanding Central Army Group would face the main thrust of a Soviet attack on Western Europe. That makes the British Army, and British understanding of continental land warfare, a very important thing. The British should therefore be considered as a major continental land army with associated air power.

Another relevant factor is that the world's major arms developers, manufacturers and exporters are all in the USA/ Eurasia area. The United States and USSR are approximately equal as exporters, each representing about 35 per cent, with the USSR pulling ahead at the time of writing. Then come France (9.7 per cent) and West Germany (2.6 per cent). Of the Third World arms importing regions, two of the top three are in Eurasia: the Middle East (44.7 per cent) and the Far East (13.2 per cent). The USSR exports most arms to the Third World (36.9 per cent in 1978-82).[13]

There is one other possible theatre of continental land warfare. Soviet and United States territory face each other across the Bering Strait and part of the Pole (see Figure 2.3). In the event of conflict between NATO and the Warsaw Pact the arctic north could become a theatre of military operations, which could spill over on to the North American mainland. The Soviets might see a land invasion of Alaska as providing a useful diversion from operations in Europe (as the United States might see an invasion of Siberia). Furthermore, in addition to their enormous mineral resources, which would only be a very long-term objective, Alaska and Canada are of immense strategic signficance. This is because any early warning system designed to protect the United States from missile attack must be based

Figure 2.3: Superpowers across the pole

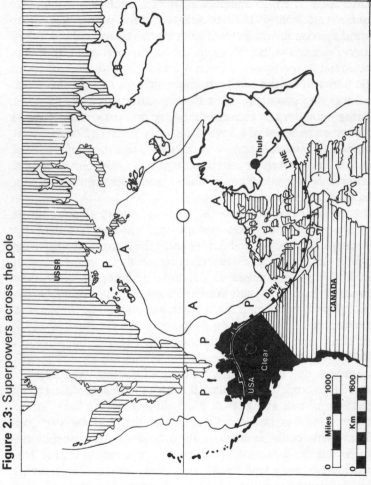

Azimuthal equal-area projection; A = Arctic ice; P = Pack ice; B = Gulf of Bothnia (Russian ice march, 1809)

there. The DEW line, which is obsolescent but might be revived, stretches across the north of the continent, and one of the three key Ballistic Missile Early Warning System (BMEWS) stations is at Clear in Alaska.[14] Although these might be targets for missile attack or special forces detachments, a conventional land invasion could conceivably pose a dilemma for the Americans. It could immobilise an early warning or part of a future Anti Ballistic Missile (ABM) system, without itself justifying a strategic response. It could therefore put the Soviet Union in a good bargaining position. The Russians have projected land forces over ice before. In February 1809 three Russian armies were pushed across the frozen Gulf of Bothnia to force the Swedes to capitulate before the ice melted and the British and Swedish fleets could be brought into play.[15] It was a very daring operation since, besides being utterly exhausting for the men, there was always a possibility that the ice might break up and swallow all or part of the army. The Russian gamble succeeded, however, and the Swedes capitulated immediately. Recently, the Soviets have been placing stress on arctic operations in the open military press. The historical examples used are usually from Soviet operations against German forces in north Norway in 1944. The relevance of these operations to the mid-1980s and further ahead is stressed in the most unsubtle fashion: 'even today, in spite of the appearance of qualitatively new weapons systems, all these [climatic and geographical] factors must be studied when planning for military operations in the arctic'.[16] This may reflect increased Soviet interest in outflanking NATO via the same route — northern Norway — or it may have other connotations. In the event of superpower conflict in the future, the possibility of land operations in the Arctic north of America or even on the arctic ice cannot therefore be ruled out.

The size of armed forces, the nature and frequency of conflict, the sources of technological, tactical and operational innovation and the face of the land itself all highlight Eurasia as the hub and almost exclusive theatre of major air-land warfare. Halford MacKinder (1861-1947), the great geographer and founder of the school of geopolitics, graphically evoked the historical and strategic significance of this colossal slab of land, which he called 'the geographical pivot of history'.[17] For this operation, ground is, therefore, the pivot of history, the Eurasian land mass.

THE EFFECT OF DEMOGRAPHIC CHANGE ON THE MAJOR LAND POWERS

Demographic factors have received much attention when discussing the future of armed forces, particularly land forces, and rightly so. Besides the total population, crucial factors are the number of people, particularly men, in the young adult age group, typically 18 to 30. The age of 18 is the baseline used for most recruitment, whether in countries with all volunteer armed forces or those with conscription. Basic military training and professional soldiering is a young man's or woman's business, although older citizens may be recalled in the event of real national emergency. Total population has a bearing, where there is a major disparity between potential or actual belligerants (Iraq's 15 million versus Iran's 43: Pakistan's 95 million against India's 759). The difference can be made up to some extent by different policies, different states mobilising widely varying percentages of their populations. In total war on land, overall population strength will, however, tell eventually. The overall populations of the major land powers up to the year 2000 are shown in Table 2.2.

Put simplistically, if India continued to retain ground forces at the present percentage of the total population, she might be fielding a regular army of over 1.4 million by 2000. In fact, such a force would be very expensive and possibly unnecessary. The present army of 1.1 million is gigantic for a relatively poor country, and there would be problems assimilating new weaponry and training soldiers in a larger force. China's army has reduced from 3.25 million in 1983 to 2.97 million at the time of writing and a further 25 per cent reduction was underway. As this book was going to press a 'further reduction' of one million was announced: this would appear to be below the 2.97 million, bringing China's forces below the two million mark, although it remains to be seen whether it will be achieved. There seems to be an optimum size for armies in peacetime, a maximum beyond which increases in size are counter-productive. Even in total war, there are limits to how much of the population can be mobilised. Between 9.6 and 12.9 per cent of the world's population is disabled in some way, and although certain disabilities need not prevent someone doing certain military jobs, it provides a useful rule of thumb.[18] Armies still have to be fed and resupplied, and industry has to function —

Table 2.2: Historical and projected population of selected
countries

Country	1965	1975	1985	1990	1995	2000
European Community	243.5	258.4	263.3	266.8	270.4	273.6
Belgium	9.5	9.8	9.9	10.0	10.1	10.2
Denmark	4.8	5.1	5.2	5.3	5.3	5.3
FRG	58.6	61.8	61.0	60.9	61.0	61.0
France	48.8	52.7	54.6	55.6	56.8	57.9
Italy	52.0	55.8	58.0	59.0	60.0	61.0
Netherlands	12.3	13.7	14.6	15.0	15.4	15.6
UK	54.4	56.0	56.2	56.9	57.6	58.0
Other developed countries						
Australia	11.4	13.8	15.4	16.3	17.2	18.0
Canada	19.7	22.7	25.3	26.6	27.7	28.5
Japan	98.9	111.6	121.5	125.5	129.2	132.8
Spain[a]	32.1	35.5	39.1	40.7	42.1	43.5
USA	194.3	213.6	232.9	243.5	252.8	260.4
Warsaw Pact and Allies						
USSR	230.9	254.5	276.8	286.6	294.9	302.5
Czechoslovakia	14.1	14.8	15.7	16.1	16.5	16.9
GDR	17.0	16.9	16.9	17.1	17.3	17.5
Poland	31.3	34.0	37.3	38.7	39.9	41.0
Cuba	7.8	9.3	10.3	11.0	11.7	12.4
Vietnam	38.2	47.7	60.4	66.5	72.3	77.9
Other communist countries People's Republic of China	736.1	949.7	1,026.9[b]	1,057.3	1,095.2	1,138.5
North Korea	12.2	16.5	22.6	26.5	30.8	35.8
Selected developing countries						
Egypt	29.4	36.9	47.8	53.7	59.5	65.4
India	494.9	616.6	744.0	811.7	883.6	958.9
South Korea	29.1	36.7	43.3	47.1	51.0	54.7
Turkey	32.0	40.5	51.2	57.1	63.0	69.0

Source: Chief of Foreign Demographic Analysis Division, US Department of
Commerce, 1980. Figures for 1985 will vary from those given by *The Military
Balance* (see Table 2.1) but the original 1980 figures have been retained here so as
to be consistent with the future projections.

a. Spain was not a member of the Common Market when this analysis
was compiled.
b. China's population in 1985-6 is estimated at 1,055,million (*The Military
Balance*). The 1985 and subsequent figures here are from the low series of
estimates, which the author believes is reasonable given the stringent
measures the Chinese are applying to keep population down.

defence industry more so than in peace. In peacetime, it is usually reckoned that 65 per cent of the young men reaching the age for conscription (usually 18) are available for military service.[19] In war, this might go up to 85 per cent, all those without some disability or criminals leaving all the other essential jobs to older men and women.

If we consider the developed countries first, they almost all show a decline in births from the mid-1960s, which is therefore having a marked effect on military manpower. Britain, France, the Federal Republic of Germany and the USA are showing a distinct decline in the number of births while the German Democratic Republic, although enjoying an upward trend from the late 1970s, will see a decline from the late 1980s. The Federal Republic shows the sharpest decline of all. Although the USSR is showing an upward trend overall, the western industrialised regions are showing a decline as against the less industrialised Islamic regions of Central Asia. The available military manpower supply is compared with requirements in Figures 2.4 and 2.5.

The Federal Republic, the principal land power in European NATO, faces the greatest demographic problems. This will become acute at the end of the 1980s. The first possible remedy is to reduce the required size of the ground forces by changing their role. This could result from a major revolution in conventional disarmament talks or the accession of a left-wing government which would withdraw West Germany from NATO. If something resembling the present political situation continues, however, this is out of the question. The favoured approach is to encourage voluntary enlistment by offering incentives in the form of trade training. As the number of conscripts declines with the declining total manpower, it is hoped that the proportion of volunteers will increase, which will also have a beneficial effect on Bundeswehr morale and professionalism, not that there is anything wrong with it at present. Other major possibilities are the recruitment of women for non-combatant posts, or extending the time which conscripts serve. The latter would be unpopular politically and would probably have an adverse effect on the economy. Another solution, which the Germans do not seem to be considering seriously at the moment, would be to make greater use of non-ethnic groups — immigrant workers, and so on, or the creation of a voluntary foreign legion like that so successfully employed by the French

Figure 2.4: Available versus required military manpower, NATO countries

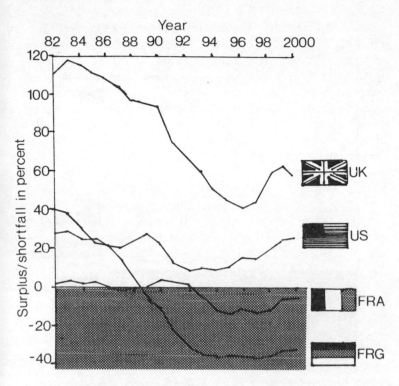

Source: Kütscher, *The Impact of Population Development on Military Manpower Problems: an International Comparison*, Industricanlagen Betriebsgesellschaft mbH).

for many years.

France is permanently confronted by manpower shortfalls, but the French remain convinced that conscript forces of half a million are preferable to smaller professional forces. A recent cost benefit analysis came down in favour of France's present national army as against a 350,000-strong professional one.[20] The fear of Bonapartism and of political intervention by a highly motivated professional military force probably has a considerable affect on French attitudes.

Britain and the USA have all-volunteer forces, and that is unlikely to change in the foreseeable future. Volunteer forces are clearly not directly affected by population development. The

Figure 2.5: Available versus required military manpower, Warsaw Pact countries

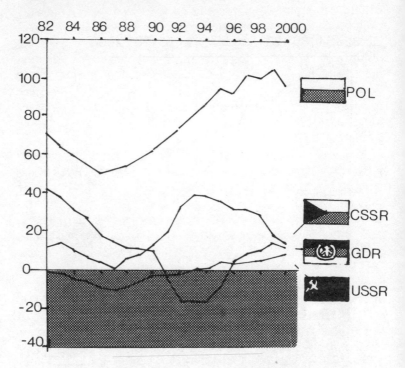

Source: Kütscher, *The Impact of Population Development on Military Manpower Problems: an International Comparison*, Industrieanlagen Betriebsgesellschaft mbH).

British Army suffered from the drain of personnel to civilian life in the 1970s (known as the 'black hole'), and in 1979 granted massive pay increases which remedied the situation. The drive to create a highly professional and motivated reserve force, the TA, which is an integral part of the British potential for continental war, has also been successful. The British should have no problem maintaining their army at the present level, especially if unemployment continues at current rates, but the quality of personnel might be a problem.

The United States has returned to voluntary enlistment — the all volunteer force (AVF), and seems pleased with the results. The British experience in the Falklands is considered to have overwhelmingly demonstrated the effectiveness of an all-professional force, and the Americans' own operation in Grenada has further reinforced that. The United States, like Britain, can probably maintain its present ground forces into the twenty-first century with judicious use of financial and other incentives, plus the selective employment of women. Given the distance between the continental United States and potential theatres of land conflict, there is little point in having armed forces much bigger than they are now. If the Warsaw Pact were to punch through to the Rhine by day five of a war (see Chapter 4), it would not be because the American Army was not big enough. It would be because they were not there in time.

The geography of Europe and the wide expanses of east Europe in particular place more stress on numbers on the ground. In Czechoslovakia and Poland there are few problems with military manpower. Poland employed a fairly lax method of military call-up until 1979 but tightening up on conscription laws has resulted in as comprehensive an induction of the able-bodied as possible. The GDR's population will decline from the late 1980s but they have taken determined steps to maximise the potential of the population by instructing school children in military subjects at an early age.[21]

The USSR mobilises surprisingly few of its young men into the ground forces *per se*: 0.73 per cent, as against 0.54 for France and Germany (interestingly, identical proportions), or 0.58 for Spain, arguably comparable developed countries. However, if we add 300,000 PVO troops employed on tasks which in other nations would be the preserve of the ground forces and 600,000 paramilitaries, we get nearly 1.1 per cent of the population, which is nearer Third World levels. There is a perceptible decline in the number of young males in the western USSR as against the east, in the 15 to 19 and 20 to 24 year old age groups. Whereas in 1975 there were 18.8 million western Soviet males between 15 and 24 years, by 2000 there will be 16.8 million. In comparison, the number of males of that age will have increased from 23 to 24.4 million in the USSR overall during the same period. Given, say, the standard 65 per cent availability for military service, this gives 12.2 million western Russians in this age group either in service or ready for recall in 1975, as against 10.9 in 2000. This compares with 14.95 and 15.9 million overall, respectively.[22] So, the western Russians will have reduced from 81.6 to 68.5 per cent of the total available Soviet manpower. Many analysts have said that this is a problem for the Russians. Is it? In parallel with this, equipment is getting more sophisticated and the demands on initiative from lower level commanders greater. The more educated and urbanised western Russians could probably cope better. Given the Soviet Union's economic problems generally, but its high standard of military technological achievement, it would make sense for the Russians to move towards a high technology, volunteer (or semi-volunteer) army. If we take the French analysis and equate a professional force of 70 per cent with a conscript one of 100, the Russians could make do with ground forces of 1.4 million, or what India can field on a professional basis on present trends by 2000. The Russians have made strenuous efforts to create a professional NCO cadre, as in the introduction of the *praporshchik* (warrant officer) class in 1972, and all the officers are professionals. Given the USSR's position as the second major technological power in the world, a nation with a tradition of intellectual achievement, and one faced with demographic problems, 'going professional' would make a lot of sense. Maybe this is what Marshal Ogarkov had in mind, alongside developing high technology arms (because high technology arms are no use unless you have someone qualified to operate them) when he was shifted sideways. The main Russian objection towards the creation of a professional army would seem to be political. Fear of the military asserting themselves, of Bonapartism, must be endemic in the Soviet system. But can the Soviet Union afford to go on fielding a nineteenth-century style mass army into the twenty-first century?

Developing countries do not face the same problems. From Table 2.2 we can see that between 1990 and 2000 alone China's population is likely to increase by 5 per cent, India's and Vietnam's by 8, North Korea's by 16 per cent and Egypt's by 10. Furthermore the birth rate in all these countries is much higher than in developed countries and the chances of the old and infirm surviving correspondingly slimmer, giving a much higher proportion of younger people. Between 1965 and 1975 India's population increased by 25 per cent, from 495 million to 617 million. Although that rate has slowed now, it means that there will be a bulge of a couple of hundred million Indians aged about 20 between 1985 and 1995. That is of great military significance. Developing countries' conditions can also work against the military use of those population resources. In Bangladesh, the most densely populated state in the world after

Singapore and Hong Kong, one in four children die before the age of five and 15 out of every 100 surviving children suffer from tuberculosis.[23] The number fit for military service is unlikely to exceed 50 per cent of the ideal age group (the same as British volunteers for the Boer War of 1899-1902).

One way which a number of Third World countries have managed to increase the pool of available manpower is the widespread employment of youths and children. Preconceptions about 'coming of age' vary from culture to culture. In the next quarter century, children and youths will play a major part in terrorism and guerrilla warfare, but less so in major conventional operations. The exceptions so far have been the *Hitlerjugend* units employed very effectively in World War II and the recent employment of youngsters by Iran in the Gulf War. They have tended to be employed in straightforward infantry roles, but there is no reason why an intelligent child should not, for example, man a radio set. In major air-land warfare over the next quarter century the availability of medically fit manpower of an appropriate age is, however, unlikely to be a problem for developing countries. Training, quality and the ability to use new technology will be.

THE FEMALE OF THE SPECIES

From Boadicea to Elizabeth I of England to Maria Theresa of Austria, military history has a number of outstanding examples of female military leaders. They tend to excel at the political and strategic level rather than in any subordinate capacity, although Maria Theresa reportedly knew as much about the mechanics of military operations as many of her generals.[24] The employment of women as a numerically significant element of the combat power of armed forces is, however, a relatively new phenomenon. Women have always formed a component of armies, and in an army as well organised and professional as the French in the Crimea the *cantinières* fulfilled a valuable logistic function. Women were employed on a large scale and a more formal basis in the Great War, for non-combatant duties, and the Russians in particular took the trend further, with women's battalions of combat troops. Accounts of the latter's effectiveness vary but in 1941-5 the Russians employed large numbers of women near the front line, often in very active capacities such as military police, political officers and interrogators. Others, like Tanya Chernova, a lady sniper at Stalingrad, accounted for 80 'sticks' — dead Germans.[25] Generally speaking, it has required dire necessity to force armies to overcome a traditional reluctance to use women in or very near combat, and the Russians in 1941-5 were one case. The Israelis today are another, but impressions of glamorous girls brandishing Uzi sub-machine guns in commando-style raids are exaggerated. They carry Uzi sub-machine guns, yes, but within Israeli Defence Forces units the responsibilities break down into more traditional roles for men and women. Israeli front line combat units are almost exclusively male. However, in 1978, women comprised 20 per cent of the Israeli ground forces' total strength, and 25 per cent of naval and air force personnel.[26]

In recent years the United States and Britain have made extensive efforts to assimilate women into the combat structure of ground forces. In Britain this has been particularly noticeable with commissioned personnel, a phenomenon which seems to have begun with the University Officers' Training Corps (OTCs) in the early to mid-1970s. Some of the keenest young women 'went regular', and now female personnel may be found doing jobs which are really crucial to front line effectiveness. The integration of female regular commissioned personnel has been further emphasised by the decision to train them at the formerly all-male military academy, Sandhurst. The regular army started giving women officers combat training in 1980, long after it had begun in OTCs. The tendency to employ women in more active capacities is more pronounced among officer personnel, but this could change. The Americans have endeavoured to incorporate female personnel with all the enthusiasm to be expected from that nation, and have perhaps gone too far in attempting to make them perform exactly like men, notably at West Point.[27] After the initial experiments, it is likely that the role of women in front line formations and units will settle down in accordance with a natural division of responsibilities as it has in the Israeli Defence Forces.

The Soviet Union has recently adjusted its military laws and may now call women up for 'voluntary' two-year national service periods. This is in response to the shortage of young men, particularly, one assumes, educated young men from the western USSR. Young women with 'specialised training' are particularly sought after. The Soviet Army has employed women extensively since the Great Patriotic War, but often as civilians and for administration or teaching. Women conscripts, on the other hand, would receive the minimal pay of conscript men.[28]

In spite of its chronic shortage of manpower, the Federal Republic of Germany seems reluctant to make more extensive use of women soldiers. The Chief of Staff of the Bundeswehr, General Meinhard Glanz, has proposed conscripting women, extending male conscription from 15 months to two years, calling up the medically unfit in support roles, as well as pay inducements to attract volunteers. On the other hand, if your problem is, in the long term, one of a low birth rate (the FRG is the only country considered here where the population is actually remaining about static), the last thing you want is to make rearing families more difficult, which conscripting young women might do. Furthermore, there seems to be a surprisingly old-fashioned attitude to the employment of women in more active roles in the armed forces among West Germans. One analysis opined that 'the problem dealt with here [the reducing birth rate] cannot be solved by the admission of women to the military service. In accordance with the social function of armed forces, women should be represented in them, but it would be wrong to assign an exclusive stopgap function to women because of the shortage in male military personnel.'[29]

Women have not been assimilated into the ground forces' structure of developing countries to the same extent, and generally speaking have no combat role within them. Surprisingly, however, they do play an important role in the Egyptian armed forces, where they are employed on general staff and support duties, in the medical services, and in signals and communications work. Another major Muslim land power, Pakistan, had women comprising 1.1 per cent of its army strength in 1978, and employs them in the same capacities as Egypt. Jordan has women general staff and medical personnel, which, considering the role of women in Islamic society generally, is perhaps noteworthy. Iran employed women on general staff, medical and signals-communications duties in 1978, but the Islamic revolution (or reaction) of 1979 has probably led to a reassertion of more traditional Islamic attitudes. India employs women of commissioned status as army doctors and nurses, and as army teachers.[30] It is perhaps a paradox that most armies are willing to employ women as officers more readily than as enlisted personnel, and in more active capacities. This trend will probably continue in the next quarter century.

Within the structure of the armed forces as a whole, even within a higher formation, there are many jobs which women would do as well or better than men. The modern air-land formation, indeed, has so many technical, administrative, communications, logistic or intellectual tasks that it really is quite unnecessary to assign women to highly active combat roles to which they are, in the main, physiologically less suited than men. It is not just a question of immediate muscular strength. Women's personal hygiene requirements, for example, are far more demanding than men's, making them less suited to continuous combat operations over a considerable time. Women in military formations and headquarters must be trained to use weapons and in minor tactics to fight off enemy troops who may appear hundreds of kilometres behind the FLOT, in accordance with the deep strike doctrines being pursued by NATO and the Warsaw Pact (see Chapter 4). In the author's view, a headquarters or communications node (see Chapter 7) far behind the NATO FLOT might well contain a high proportion of women and should be able to defend itself. Generally speaking, young men are still more suited to continuous combat operations in close proximity to the enemy.

CONCLUSION

Nations possessing contiguous land frontiers with potentially hostile states (France, the two Germanies, the USSR) have retained conscript armies. Those which do not, like Britain and the USA, have only had them in times of national emergency and have eschewed them for the present. Certain nations, such as India and Pakistan, have all-volunteer armies, which is perhaps a function of their economic circumstances and also of the high prestige which the military profession enjoys in those countries. This makes conscription unnecessary and the emphasis on volunteer forces probably owes a good deal to British precedent. The trend in developed countries would seem to be the decline of the mass army. In the next quarter century the Federal Republic of Germany may move from a predominantly conscript army to a predominantly or wholly volunteer one. In view of its demographic problems, the USSR could well move in the same direction. A smaller high technology force could be a more appropriate way of meeting its defence needs, and the army as a school of the nation may have outlived its historical relevance. The problems with a small, professional army for Russia are political and ideological. The same goes for China. As technology becomes more complicated and it becomes more difficult to train people to use it, the traditional need for numbers of bodies and male muscle will become less important. However, on land, unlike the other elements, numbers of people are still a very important facet of military power, and the great powers are still measured by the size of their armies as well as by their technological sophistication and operational and tactical expertise.

NOTES

1. Erich Maria Remarque, *All Quiet on the Western Front*, trans. A.W. Wheen (London, G.P. Putnam's Sons, 1921), p. 64.
2. 'India and Pakistan fight for control of Himalayan glacier' *Guardian*, 25 July 1984.
3. Sun Tzu, *The Art of War*, translated and with an Introduction by Samuel B. Griffith (Oxford University Press, New York, 1982), pp. 124-40. Two chapters are relevant: 10 ('Terrain') and 11 ('The Nine Varieties of Ground').
4. See the author's 'Heirs of Genghis Khan: the Influence of the Tartar Mongols on the Imperial Russian and Soviet Armies', *Journal of the Royal United Services Institute for Defence Studies* (henceforward *RUSI*), March 1978, pp. 52-3.
5. V.K. Shamshurov, *Inzhenernoye obespecheniye boyevykh deystviy voysk noch'yu i v osobykh usloviyakh* (*Engineer support of Military Operations at Night and in Special Conditions*), (Voyenizdat, Moscow, 1969), pp. 58, 101-3, 128-30, 160-2, 187; *Voyenno entsiklopedicheskiy slovar'* (*Military-encyclopaedic dictionary*) (Voyenizdat, Moscow, 1984), p. 204; Lieutenant General V. Lobov, '*Boyevye deystviya v zapolyar'e*' ('Military Operations in the Arctic'), *Voyenny Vestnik* (*Military Herald*, henceforward *VV*), 7/1984, pp. 18-22.
6. A.D. Mitchell, D.A. Grant and E.J. Edmond, *Major Armed Conflict: A Compendium of Interstate and Intrastate Conflict 1730 to 1980* (ORAE, Directorate of Strategic Analysis, Ottawa, May 1981), ORAE Report PR 161, p. 33; and G.D. Kaye, D.A. Grant and E.J. Edmond, *Major Armed Conflict*, a revision of Mitchell, Grant and Edmond, 1985, p. 47.
7. International Institute of Strategic Studies, *The Military Balance 1985-1986* (London, 1985), pp. 22-3, 29. The USSR has some 30 divisions in central and eastern Europe, and 53 in the Far Eastern TV/ TVD (see Chapter 4). If the divisions in the western USSR are added to

the 30, this places the emphasis on Europe as far as the USSR is concerned but then China has 66 regular infantry and armoured divisions in the northeast, north and west Military Regions, that is, facing the USSR; men and tanks in Europe in the event of a war: Elmar Dinter and Paddy Griffith, *Not Over by Christmas: NATO's Central Front in World War III* (Antony Bird, Chichester, 1983), p. 6.

8. *The Military Balance 1985-1986*, pp. 49, 67.

9. 'intellectual capital,' from Harriet Fast Scott (ed.), *The Soviet Art of War: Doctrine, Strategy, Tactics* (Westview Press, Boulder, Colorado, 1982), p. 287. The difficulties of assessing the military balance are well summarised in the essay in the United Kingdom's 1986 Defence White Paper, *Statement on the Defence Estimates 1986*, Vol. 1, Cmnd 9763-1 (HMSO, London, 1986), pp. 58-9.

10. See Kaye, Grant and Edmond, *Major Armed Conflict*, 1985, p. 45.

11. Michael Kidron and Dan Smith, *The War Atlas: Armed Conflict — Armed Peace* (Pan, London and Sydney, 1986), map 1, 'A world at war'.

12. '*Predstavlyayet soboy glavnuyu udarnuyu silu severnoy gruppy armii*', Glazunov and Nikitin, p. 258.

13. Thomas Ohlson and Evamaria Loose-Weintraub, 'The Trade in Major Conventional Weapons', *SIPRI Yearbook*, 1983 (Stockholm Peace Research Institute, 1983), pp. 269, 271, 273. Military strengths and populations from *The Military Balance 1985-86*.

14. DEW line entry 2567.181 and BMEWS 2525.181, *Jane's Weapon Systems, 1977* (Jane's, London, 1977), pp. 221-2.

15. Michael Jenkins, *Arakcheev, Grand Vizier of the Russian Empire* (Faber & Faber, London, 1969), pp. 117, 119.

16. Lobov, 'Military Operations', p. 18. See also Major Yu Zavizion, '*Nastupleniye v zapolyar'e*' ('The offensive in arctic regions'), *VV*, 2/1984, pp. 31-4.

17. Sir Halford J. MacKinder, *The Scope and Methods of Geography and the Geographical Pivot of History*, reprinted with an introduction by E.W. Gilbert (Royal Geographical Society, London, 1951), pp. 41-2, 44. The lecture was given in 1904. MacKinder's 'pivot region' became known as the 'heartland' from 1919.

18. Population predictions from *Estimated and Projected Populations of Selected Countries* (Foreign Demographic Analysis Division, US Department of Commerce, July, 1980); disabled: Alastair Henderson, 'Just Another Human Being', *World Health* (the magazine of the World Health Organisation), January 1981, p. 7; China's Army reduction: Gordon Jacobs, 'Streamlining China's Army', *Jane's Defence Weekly*), 31 May 1986, pp. 998-1001.

19. Gilbert Kütscher, *The Impact of Population Development on Military Manpower Problems: an International Comparison* (Industrieanlagen Betriebsgesellschaft mbH (IABG), paper presented to the Inter-University Seminar on Armed Forces and Society, University of Chicago, October 23-25, 1980.

20. Ibid., pp. 10-11.

21. Ibid., p. 11.

22. Ibid., pp. 12, 29. M. Feshbach and S. Rapawy, 'Soviet Population and Manpower Trends and Policies', *Soviet Economy in a New Perspective* (Joint Economic Committee, Congress of the United States, Washington, DC, 1976), p. 151; *Süddeutsche Zeitung*, 4 August 1980; G.R. Whitney, 'The Soviet Racial Balance Dramatically Changes', *International Herald Tribune*, 13-14 October 1979; G. Baldwin, *Projections of the Population of the USSR and Eight Subdivisions, by Age and Sex, 1973 to 2000* (US Department of Commerce, Series P-91, Washington, DC), June 1975.

23. Increases 1990 to 2000, 'Estimated and Projected Populations' table: Jim Crace, 'How many people can the world feed?', *Telegraph Sunday Magazine*, August 1984, p. 17: *Human Numbers, Human Needs*, (IPPF, 1984).

24. Christopher Duffy, *The Army of Maria Theresa* (David and Charles, London, 1977), esp. pp. 18-19, 167.

25. William Craig, *Enemy at the Gates: the Battle for Stalingrad* (Hodder and Stoughton, London, 1973), p. 236.

26. Gilbert Kütscher, *Ubersicht Frauen in Streitkräften*, research papers, 1978.

27. 'Why the girls queue four-deep to join up', *The Times*, 7 September 1984, p. 16; Nicholas Harman, 'Women at Arms', *Telegraph Sunday Magazine*, 8 December 1985, pp. 14-21.

28. Philip Finn, 'Russia "calls up" the girls in army crisis', *Daily Express*, 2 April 1985, p. 7.

29. Kütscher, *The Impact of Population Development*, p. 15; Ekkehard Lippert and Tjarck G. Rössler, *Mädchen in Waffen? Gesellschafte-und sozialpolitische Aspekte weiblicher Soldaten in der Bundeswehr*, Report of the Sozialwissenschaftliches Institut der Bundeswehr (Munich, February 1980).

30. Kütscher, *Frauen in Streitkräften*, Developing countries covered are Egypt, Algeria, China, India, Indonesia, Iran, Israel (not 'developing', in this author's view), Japan, Jordan, Malaysia, Pakistan, Korea, Singapore, Thailand.

3

Nuclear, Biological, Chemical or Conventional?

Biological weapons are living organisms, can be transmitted by 'vectors', like the fleas which carried Bubonic Plague, and are therefore unpredictable and capricious in their effects: probably too much so for immediate battlefield use. Whatever their potentially cataclysmic effect on civilian populations, biological agents are hardly a rational battlefield option, and will not be considered further here. Toxins of biological origin may be sufficiently quick acting and precise to have a battlefield role, and are considered as chemical agents. This chapter concentrates on the two other weapons of mass destruction — nuclear and chemical.

BATTLEFIELD NUCLEAR WEAPONS

After the explosion of the first atomic bombs in 1945 there were those who thought that they would render traditional operations of war obsolete. Even if not actually used, the mere prospect or threat of their use could profoundly affect military operations. As early as October 1945, Sir George Thompson, participating in the revision of the Tizard report on future warfare, foresaw that the new weapon's very potency might preclude its use. Whereas the tendency had been to wage war more and more unrestrictedly, he wrote, it was 'just possible that the nuclear weapon might reverse this trend'. Therefore, Britain should 'keep pre-atomic defence forces'.[1] The first atomic bombs were very large, because of their primitive construction and could thus only be delivered by large aircraft. They were also extremely expensive and fissile material was very scarce.

64

Therefore they were only suitable for use against strategic targets. As Tizard's revised report on the nature of future war of 30 January 1946 noted, 'the most obvious result is that the bombing of towns and industry now give a far greater return for war effort expended and may therefore become the most profitable type of war'.[2] By contrast, the effect of a Hiroshima or Nagasaki type bomb on army targets appeared to offer little return on the investment. It was estimated that when detonated at 300 feet above the ground it would disable tanks and guns out to 400 yards and soft-skinned vehicles out to 800, while in average battlefield conditions it would disable troops out to 1,200 yards immediately and 1,800 yards with delayed action. This appears to underplay the bomb's power somewhat: nowadays, it is assessed that a 20 kiloton (Hiroshima sized) bomb would probably destroy troops in the open out to 2,000 metres and those well dug in out to 1,000 (see Table 3.1).[3] However, evidence considered by the Tizard committee during the revision of its report in late 1945 was undoubtedly right in assessing that armies in the field and even concentrations of guns and vehicles before an offensive were not profitable targets, but that the infliction of heavy casualties on troop concentrations would be of serious importance. The density of troops on the ground had in recent wars been greater before an attack than on any other occasion and in those circumstances an army did present a profitable target. Against this, however, the danger from atomic weapons detonated close to one's own troops needed to be assessed. Finally, base areas with large depots, dependent on low-grade labour would be particularly vulnerable to attack with atomic bombs and in future no invading army should be allowed to depend on two or three large ports.[4] The vulnerability of ports, airfields and staging areas, rather than dispersed and dug-in fighting troops, is of recurring importance.

The shift away from almost exclusive emphasis on the strategic use of nuclear weapons had begun as early as 1951. A typical assessment of the effect of nuclear weapons on the battlefield from 1953 noted that their destructive power fell off rapidly with distance, regardless of the projectile's size. Field fortifications would also greatly mitigate the effect: dug-outs with the occupants' heads a metre below the surface would provide protection unless extremely close to ground zero — 700 to 1,000 metres. Radiation would 'be sufficiently absorbed by the intervening earth to ensure no more than delayed sickness'. Bridges were not especially vulnerable, only lateral blast from a direction approximating to the course of the stream being likely to demolish them. Highways would not be particularly affected by air bursts and where their destruction was a matter of necessity, ground bursts had to be used. Large-scale movements on roads were not a very rewarding target, because of their linear character. 'All that is likely to be achieved is the destruction of 120-140 vehicles over a length of four miles (six kilometres) or so. Of course, such action does throw the whole column into chaos.' Atomic weapons would tend more to create obstacles in front of marching columns than to destroy them. Rather than direct attack on columns, the authors therefore recommended attacking important crossroads, which tended to be situated in built-up localities. 'To destroy and infect them with residual radio-activity entails the blocking of vital communication centres. The effectiveness of such obstacles is still greater in towns divided into two parts by a river, which is often the case.' The recommended method of nuclear bombardment was to start at depths of 100 miles (160 kilometres). As the principal directions of the hostile concentrations became more clearly defined, the strikes were brought closer to the front, thus drastically reducing movement between front and rear. In all cases, nuclear attacks had to be supplemented by continuous attacks by tactical air forces. Finally, the potential of guided missiles to replace manned aircraft was noted.[5]

The first nuclear weapons were pure fission devices. To make a fission weapon the fissile material containing the isotopes — uranium 235 or plutonium 239 — has to be kept divided up into sub-critical masses until detonation, and then brought into a critical mass quickly. The first atom bombs illustrated the two broad ways of doing this. The first ever nuclear device, called the Gadget, detonated at Alamogordo in 1945, had a plutonium core weighing about 6.1 kilograms which was imploded by about 2,270 kilograms of high explosive to compress it to critical density. In order to prevent the weapon exploding too soon, before a reasonable portion of the fissionable material has had a chance to undergo a nuclear chain reaction, the fissile material is surrounded by a heavy material called a tamper. If the tamper itself is fissionable, such as uranium-238, it will then contribute to the fission yield as it will be fissioned by the fast neutrons coming from the interior initial explosion. The

Gadget's tamper was made of uranium. The Gadget gave a yield (size of the explosion) of about 22 kilotons (Kt) equivalent to 22,000 tons of TNT. Devices with a yield up to 0.9 Kt are referred to collectively as 'sub-kiloton'; above that and up to 0.99 megatons (Mt), as kiloton weapons, and above that as megaton weapons. Fat Man, the weapon dropped on Nagasaki, was based on the same design as the Gadget: a plutonium implosion weapon with a yield of about 22 Kt, again, and a yield to weight ratio of 0.0045 kilotons per kilogram of fissile material, a very low efficiency by modern standards.

The second type of device is exemplified by Little Boy, the bomb dropped on Hiroshima. This used the gun technique: two sub-critical spheres of uranium, one of which is fired at the other down a gun-type barrel. Little Boy contained 60 kilograms of highly enriched uranium giving a yield of 12 to 15 Kt, a much less efficient weapon than Fat Man. Although implosion devices are unquestionably more efficient than the gun type, and do not almost inevitably require high-grade uranium, they are more complex in their design and more delicate, which makes them unsuitable to withstand the shock of being fired from an artillery piece in a shell, for example. In the context of operational-tactical employment in land warfare, gun devices retain their importance. The W-33 nuclear artillery shell (Artillery Fired Atomic Projectile — AFAP) in the US Army's inventory is a gun assembly device. Gun assembly devices almost inevitably require high-grade uranium alloys. That used in many American weapons is called Oralloy (Oak ridge alloy).

In addition to being more efficient, the implosion device is also ideal to act as the trigger for fusion (thermonuclear) or 'hydrogen' weapons. Nuclear fusion is a much more efficient energy source than nuclear fission, but requires enormously high temperatures to initiate it — temperatures that are currently only attainable through nuclear fission. A fusion device typically contains a fission trigger in the centre, the fusion material round that, then the tamper, and then explosive round the outside which when detonated will compress the whole lot, initially giving rise to a fission reaction as the centre attains critical mass, then fusion. The most commonly used fusion material is likely to be lithium-6 deuteride. It is theoretically possible to repeat this process again and again, and there is no theoretical limit on the yield of a fusion weapon although in practice the amount of conventional explosive required would limit it.

67

By incorporating thermonuclear fuel, typically deuterium and tritium gas, into or next to the core of a fission weapon, the efficiency of the fission bomb can be improved, giving rise to so-called 'boosted fission' weapons. The fusion process itself adds only a little to the yield of the device. It is probable that the first British 'H-bombs' were in fact boosted fission weapons, and the distinction between fission and fusion weapons clearly begins to break down. Some variants of the W33 US nuclear artillery shell and the W70 warhead for the Lance battlefield missile both contain fusion components.[6] The fusion element is even more directly utilised in the Enhanced Radiation Weapon (ERW) (see below).

Present nuclear weapons release a vast quantity of energy in a very short time. This produces a very hot, incandescent compressed gas known as the fireball. This rises rapidly, in the case of a ground or low air-burst sucking up soil to create the characteristic mushroom cloud. Ground bursts are less efficient in disseminating flash and blast effects but produce more radioactive fall-out (see below). Air bursts maximise the former but produce negligible fall-out. Sub-surface bursts are particularly useful for creating very deep craters and would be primarily of use as demolition charges.

Nuclear weapons release energy in five different ways, all of which are militarily significant:

— Heat, causing ignition of inflammable material far from the explosion, skin burns and eye damage or 'flash'.
— Blast, caused by a shock wave moving outwards from the fireball at about the speed of sound.
— Immediate nuclear radiation. Neutron radiation predominates at shorter ranges, while dangerous gamma radiation travelling at the speed of light and with very high penetrating power travels further out. Most of the latter is generated after the explosion, about 50 per cent of the total dose being delivered in the first five seconds. Therefore, even after the explosion a dive for cover may be well worthwhile.
— Residual radiation. This consists of Neutron Induced Activity (NIA), where bombardment with neutrons from the explosion turns some material into radioactive isotopes, and fall-out, which is radioactive debris from the explosion which falls back to earth. Residual radiation decays with time, but its extent varies considerably according to the design and yield of

the weapon, the height of the burst and the strength and direction of the wind.
— Electro-magnetic pulse (EMP) and Transient Radiation effect on Electronics (TREE). There are two different types:

— Endo-atmospheric, which is generated by kiloton range yield weapons, usually low airburst, and which extends at most some tens of kilometres from ground zero,
— Exo-atmospheric pulse. This is generated by a multi-megaton yield weapon burst high above the earth, over 35 kilometres, where its flash and blast effects are not perceptible but its EMP alone can have a dramatic effect.

EMP was found to be more dangerous to transistors than to old fashioned valves, but the fibre optics which are increasingly being used do not pick it up and therefore do not transmit it to fragile semiconductors such as integrated circuits. On the other hand, while resistant to EMP, fibre optics are particularly vulnerable to radiation (see also Chapter 7).

A couple of nuclear explosions high above the earth could knock out power grids and damage electrical equipment over wide areas, perhaps an entire continental theatre of military operations. The potential of EMP to paralyse Command, Control and Communications and other military equipment including vehicles without ostensibly using nuclear weapons for 'hard kill' is obvious, and is discussed further in the chapters on Electronic Warfare and C_3I (Chapters 6 and 7). A massive EMP wave could create temporary mayhem and thus achieve massive operational and strategic surprise without itself justifying a nuclear response. The EMP effect of endo-atmospheric bursts on the battlefield also has to be considered, as this compounds their other effects and works far beyond the range of flash, blast and immediate radiation.

The effects of nuclear weapons depend on all kinds of factors including climate (see Introduction) and the weather on the day. Approximate effects on battlefield troops and equipment are shown in Table 3.1 and the graph (Figure 3.1). The effect of blast varies with the cube root of warhead power, so that a 160 kiloton bomb only has twice the lethal blast radius of a 20 kiloton burst. The heat effect varies roughly with the square root, so an 80 kiloton warhead causes lethal burns at twice the range of a 20 kiloton. The equation for radiation is very compli-

69

Table 3.1: Effect of nuclear weapons of various yields in battlefield conditions. Radius of lethal or immediate damage (metres):

Yield	Tanks and APCs	Troops in open or light cover	Aircraft	POL
0.01 KT	—	300	—	—
1 KT	450	700-900	900-1,200	—
5 KT	500-600	775	1,500-1,800	—
10 KT	750	1,000-1,100	2,100-2,400	—
20 KT	800	1,100-1,300	2,700-3,000	1,500
50 KT	900	1,900	3,700-4,200	—
100 KT	1,000	2,000-3,000	5,000-5,400	—
1 MT	—	5,500	—	—

Long-term effects are not taken into account, but may occur considerably farther away.
KT = Kiloton, equivalent to 1,000 tonnes of TNT; MT = Megaton,equivalent to a million tonnes of TNT.

Sources: Sidorenko, *The Offensive*, pp. 40-41; Reznichenko, *Tactics* (1984), p. 15; Jones, *Small Nuclear Forces*, pp. 68-9; Reinhardt and Kintner, *Atomic Weapons in Land Combat*, pp. 105, 169-75.

cated, but ionizing radiation (gamma rays) increase their lethal range only about 10 per cent with a doubling of yield. For this reason, smaller-yield fission weapons do damage to battlefield forces primarily with immediate radiation, whereas in the case of the larger-yield weapons flash and blast do the damage first.[7] Figure 4.1 only shows the effects of ordinary fission weapons: weapons with a fusion component and enhanced radiation weapons behave differently with regard to radiation.

Enhanced Radiation Weapons ('Neutron Bombs')

The effects of straightforward nuclear weapons are somewhat clumsy and indiscriminate. A refinement with particular battlefield applications is the Enhanced Radiation Weapon (ERW) or 'Neutron Bomb'. The ERW is a thermonuclear device designed to maximise the effects of high energy neutrons produced by the fusion of deuterium and tritium and reduce the blast from the explosion. Such weapons are known more precisely as Enhanced Radiation/Reduced Blast (ER/RB). The W-79 203mm (eight inch) artillery fired ER/RB projectile has variants with between 50 and 75 per cent of the yield provided

Figure 3.1: Effect of nuclear bursts in battlefield conditions

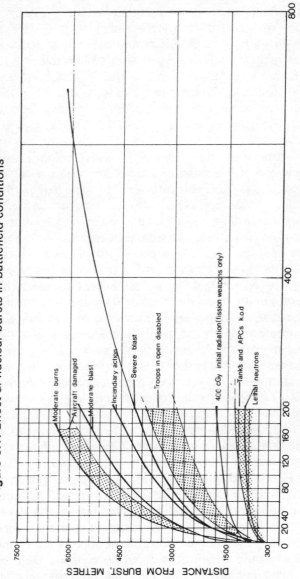

Armoured vehicles are well protected against heat and blast and are mainly affected by radiation. Other targets will be damaged by heat and blast before immediate radiation strikes. Radiation is now measured in cGys (centiGrays), which are the same as the former unit rads. The curve for immediate radiation is for fission weapons only; most in fact have a fusion element (see p. 68).

by fusion. The burst of prompt nuclear radiation (neutrons and gamma rays) is enhanced by minimising the fission yield relative to the fusion yield. This is done by eliminating or substituting for the U-238 components, particularly the tamper. Typically, a tungsten alloy with nickel, iron and rhenium is used, so that there is no 'dirty' third stage fission and consequent fall-out. The ER/RB weapon uses deuterium with tritium rather than lithium-6 deuteride as the fusion material to maximise the release of fast neutrons. These may be up to six times as numerous per kiloton of energy than are those escaping from a fission bomb. Roughly speaking, an ER/RB weapon of 1 Kt yield will produce the same level of immediate radiation as a 10 Kt fission weapon. A dose of 5,000 cGys radiation will incapacitate a man in five minutes and kill him within a day or two, so a dose of 8,000 cGys is sufficient for immediate battle-field impact. The 1 Kiloton ER/RB weapon will produce this at a range of between 700 and 1,600 metres: estimates vary, but in all cases the dose is the same as with a 10 Kt fission weapon. The distance from the ER/RB weapon which will cause severe damage to buildings and trees to blow down is correspondingly estimated at between 550 and 900 metres. In contrast, the 10 Kt fission weapon will do this damage at 2,800 metres, well outside the prompt radiation killing zone. Furthermore, the ER/RB device will create little or no residual radiation, unlike the ordinary fission weapon. It should be remembered, however, that the relationship between heat, blast and radiation is complex and that at some ranges, for example, a straight fission weapon of less than 50 Kt will produce more casualties among troops in the field by radiation than by blast and heat. It is in the area of the 1 Kt ER/RB weapon and the 10 Kt fission weapon that the comparison is most interesting. If the height of burst is very carefully selected (between the maximum range of blast and heat damage and the maximum range of immediately incapacitating radiation), a ER/RB weapon could kill by radiation without producing any blast damage on the ground at all. Because there is little or no residual radiation friendly troops would be able to operate in the area of the target very soon after the strike, and because there will be much less collateral damage to bridges, buildings and terrain their mobility will be less inhibited.

There are a number of obvious military advantages with ER/RB weapons. In addition to the reduced collateral damage and negligible residual radiation, the size of the neutron emission can be controlled precisely enough to enable it to be used against targets of varying size such as troop formations, enemy supply centres and so on. The strength of the neutron wave falls off rapidly away from the epicentre of the explosion, again adding to precision. The most effective protection against the neutron wave is provided by moist earth or concrete. A thickness of 25 centimetres of concrete or 35 of moist earth will reduce the strength of the neutron wave 10 times and double that thickness, 100 times. Against tanks, however, only 20 to 30 per cent of fast moving neutrons will be stopped by 100-125 millimetres of armour. In addition, the neutrons will react, with the shielding materials in the armoured vehicle to produce second-order activity and gamma radiation as well. The ER/RB weapon therefore undoubtedly favours the defence, and is particularly lethal against the crews of armoured vehicles.

There are complex problems with ER/RB weapons. For example, the long-term effects of neutron radiation are about six times as severe as those of gamma radiation, and have not been fully assessed. Therefore, one ought to ensure that no neutron radiation at all reached friendly troops — not too difficult, given the bomb's precise nature. Many ethical and moral arguments have been advanced against it, but all nuclear weapons kill in one way or another and the ER/RB weapon does so more precisely, and does a lot less collateral damage in the process. It has been argued that because of the lack of thermal and blast effects in certain circumstances an ER/RB burst might not be regarded as a nuclear weapons detonation and that this, combined with the reduced damage to surrounding territory, makes it more usable than ordinary nuclear weapons. However, ER/RB weapons are nuclear weapons and their use could equally precipitate a response with ordinary nuclear armaments, possibly not confined to the battlefield, and thus to unacceptable escalation. For this reason, other specialised area weapons such as fuel air explosives (see Chapter 5) will probably be preferred to ER/RB weapons.

In considering nuclear weapons technology, there are a number of 'third generation' weapons in the pipeline. These include: diverting X-rays from a nuclear explosion and pumping them out in a beam; ER weapons of very low yield (0.05 to 0.1 Kt) to knock out incoming missiles by radiation high in the atmosphere; and EMP weapons designed to generate directed

EMP, also referred to as a radio frequency weapon. These new forms of weaponry are examined further under Electronic Warfare in Chapter 6.[8]

Modern operational-tactical nuclear systems

The difficulty in separating land warfare from broader strategic considerations or the influence of air power, noted in the Introduction and Chapter 1, applies with particular force in the case of nuclear weapons. The Tomahawk cruise missiles and Pershing II ballistic missiles (ranges 2,500 and 1,800 kilometres, respectively) recently deployed by the Americans in Europe transcend the bounds of a straightforward land conflict and their appelation as 'intermediate' or 'medium' range suggests a level between operational and strategic. The Soviets' SS-22/Scaleboard and SS-23/Scud (ranges 885 kilometres and 500/300 kilometres, respectively) fall nicely within the Soviet definition of operational but between Western 'theatre' and 'tactical' weapons, the next of which is the Pershing 1A with a range of 160-720 kilometres, the American Lance, range 110 kilometres, and Soviet SS-21, range 100 kilometres, fall together in the same operational-tactical bracket. The characteristics of the two pacts' systems reflect their differing concepts of the levels of conflict to a considerable degree. In addition, the United Kingdom has Lance missiles and the French the 120 kilometre range Pluton. The latter will be replaced by the 350 kilometre range Hades. All other NATO nations' nuclear capable missiles are under American control and all Warsaw Pact systems are under Soviet control. Red China only has strategic missiles such as the DF-2 medium range missile with a range of 1,800 kilometres. No Chinese operational-tactical nuclear weapons have been identified at the time of writing.

Nuclear warhead designers prefer missiles for delivery because they enable implosion warheads to be used without too much difficulty. Artillery-delivered shells also have advantages, however, particularly their virtual pinpoint accuracy, crucial to the successful employment of small-yield nuclear weapons. The range, circular error probable (CEP) and yield of these various systems are shown diagramatically in Figure 3.2.[9] New and threshold powers systems are discussed below.

Figure 3.2: Ground-based operational-tactical nuclear delivery systems (mid-1980s).

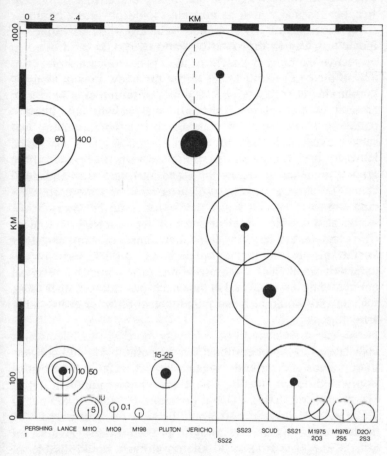

The vertical scale on the left shows the systems' maximum range: the horizontal scale at the top indicates the scale of the circular error probable (CEP) and the effect of the burst against troops in the open or light cover. Thus the Lance can fire nuclear warheads of 1, 10 or 50 kiloton yield. These would destroy troops as described out to 700-900, 1,000-1,100 and 1,900 metres, respectively. The dark circles show the CEP, which is the *radius* from the burst within which 50 per cent of missiles fired at a target are expected to fall. Thus Pershing 1 has a CEP of 400 metres, which gives an 800 metre diameter circle. Jericho-2 is reported to have a range of 700-1,000 kilometres, a low yield warhead and a CEP of up to a kilometre, and is represented as such here. SS-23 represents a dramatic improvement in accuracy over Scud, but Scud is shown as it may still be employed in the future by Third World nations. All yields are shown in kilotons. Gun and howitzer systems have virtual pinpoint accuracy, and no CEP is shown.

The nuclear battlefield

In order to protect against the immediate effects of nuclear weapons, as many men as possible should obviously be under cover in trenches or armoured vehicles when an attack is imminent. Any in the open or trenches should be dressed in protective clothing. If caught in the open, troops are taught to fall on their faces with hands under the body, thus minimising the burning effects. Even so, as a rule of thumb one 20 kiloton airburst would almost certainly incapacitate an infantry battalion. If the battalion is in march column formation, two such bursts would be required. Exposed infantry would be killed up to 1,100 metres from ground zero (the point on the ground immediately below the explosion), and tank and APC crews 800 metres away. Severe burns, blinding from flash, sickness and shock would injure many troops further away. EMP would also disable the electronics of sophisticated equipment (for example, artillery fire control systems, anti-tank and anti-aircraft missiles) still further out. A battalion might seem a comparatively small bag for the use of one or two nuclear weapons, but in forcing dispersal and in the knock-on effect on other units, such a strike would be a sharp and violent blow for even a large army to sustain.[10]

Nuclear strikes would be relatively more worthwhile against installations in the operational depth: ports, bases and concentration areas and airfields. Against a port, a 20 kiloton explosion would destroy loading and maintenance equipment out to 800 metres and Petrol, Oil and Lubricant (POL) facilities out to 1,500 metres. Ships in port would be sunk or incur irreparable damage up to 500 metres away from such a burst. Against an airfield, the blast from a 20 kiloton airburst would disable all exposed aircraft and helicopters out to about 3 kilometres, helicopters being slightly more vulnerable. Of course, this would not necessarily disable airfield runways, but, in contrast to other airfield denial weapons a 50 kiloton *ground* burst would excavate a crater about 85 metres in diameter and 20 metres (three storeys) deep. A hole this size in the right place could put an airfield completely out of action and take inordinate time and effort to repair.

Another potential use for nuclear weapons on the battlefield is as nuclear mines or Atomic Demolition Mines (ADMs). This may be more likely as a belligerent might consider that using them to create an obstacle without killing many enemy troops was less likely to provoke retaliation or international reprobation, and that it could act as a useful warning. A single 20 kiloton *sub*-surface burst would excavate a crater, some 120 metres in diameter and 35 metres (five storeys) deep, a formidable hole that could completely block a mountain pass or defile. Surrounded by radioactive debris, it would be dangerous and time consuming to clear a path around it or bridge it, and almost impossible to fill it in. Nuclear mines could also be used to create landslides, again blocking mountain passes, or to breach dams flooding thousands of square kilometres, an instant and reliable version of the famous Dambusters' raid of 1942.[11]

The use of atomic weapons to sculpt and tear apart the landscape has many advantages over their direct use against personnel and vehicles. Even if not deliberate, this is likely to result in large measure from their use anyway. As Colonel Sidorenko, one of the most eloquent portrayers of the nuclear battlefield, put it in 1970:

A new characteristic feature of the offensive in nuclear war is the *conduct of combat actions under conditions of the presence of vast zones of contamination, destruction, fires and floods.*

As a result of the mass employment of nuclear weapons by the warring sides, tremendous areas will be subjected to radioactive contamination; populated places, bridges and other structures will be destroyed; and big centres of conflagration and inundation will be formed. The sub-units will not only be forced to fight on contaminated terrain, but also to overcome destruction, rubble, and other obstacles which may also be contaminated with radioactive substances.[12]

Although the Soviet Union was initially behind the United States in the development of nuclear weapons, they caught up very rapidly, exploding their first fission bomb in 1949 and claiming to have exploded a hydrogen (fusion) bomb before the Americans in 1953. During the late 1950s, the Soviet Union accepted the idea that a 'revolution in military affairs' had taken place, which led to a shift in emphasis away from conventional forces towards nuclear and rocket armament. The Soviets would claim that their ideas on the employment of nuclear weapons as part of battlefield operations were in response to those of the

West. However, their particular emphasis on surface to surface missiles for delivery, which has its origins in their traditional expertise in rocketry and in Tukhachevsky's ideas in the 1930s, and the quality of their analysis of battlefield nuclear operations, suggest that their thinking in this area has for a long time surpassed that of the West in depth and coherence. Marshal Sokolovskiy, writing in the first edition of *Soviet Military Strategy* in 1962, had clearly formulated a picture of the future Theatre of Military Operations (see also Introduction and Chapter 4) which envisaged the use of nuclear forces and conventional in mutually supportive and complementary roles. Surface to surface missiles offered the most effective way of delivering nuclear warheads:

> The defeat of the enemy's ground troops, the destruction of his rockets, aircraft and nuclear weapons in carrying out any operations, will be achieved mainly by carrying out nuclear rocket strikes. This will lead to the formation of numerous zones of continuous destruction, devastation and radioactive contamination. Great possibilities are created for waging extensive manoeuvrable offensive operations with the aid of highly mobile mechanised troops. Trench warfare is obviously a thing of the past [see below!]. It has been replaced by rapid, manoeuvrable fighting operations carried out simultaneously or consecutively in individual regions at different depths of the zone of military operations.'[13]

Sokolovskiy stressed that the offensive zones for units and formations were expanding. He cited the example of the United States Army's view that an infantry division could attack along a 10-20 kilometre sector and a field army a 100-160 kilometre sector. The offensive, opined Sokolovskiy, would be effected along the lines with great gaps. Enemy groups would be destroyed by nuclear attacks by rocket forces and aviation and, in a number of cases, by the concentrated fire of conventional weapons. 'A characteristic feature of the battlefield is the considerable dispersion of troops, the relative sparseness and the possibility of wide manoeuvring'. Because of the nuclear environment, the offensive should be mounted primarily on tanks, APCs and helicopters. Dismounted attack would be a rare phenomenon. The fire and manoeuvre of vehicle-mounted troops would now reign on the battlefield, a philosophy which undoubtedly shaped the design of the very successful BMP infantry combat vehicle, which was designed as a nuclear and chemical tight fighting machine rather than as a 'battle-taxi'. Gaps and breaks in the enemy formations had to be sought, strikes had to be made on the flanks and rear of the enemy troops to cut them off, surround them and rapidly annihilate them or take them prisoner. If pockets of enemy resistance could not be overcome, nuclear strikes or concentrated fire from conventional rocket or gun artillery should be used.[14] Sokolovskiy clearly envisaged that the dispersal necessitated by the use or threatened use of nuclear weapons and the very rapid rates of advance which would be possible if huge gaps were blasted in enemy deployments would combine to produce a massive extension of the battlefield, like that produced by the introduction and assimilation of long-range small arms and artillery at the beginning of this century. This has undoubtedly helped create the enormous scope and sweep of the Soviet view of the theatre of war. The only problem is whether there would be room for these offensives 'with great gaps', for 'sparseness' and 'wide manoeuvring', especially in a European context (see Chapter 8). Furthermore, the nuclear weapons themselves could have counterproductive effects:

An advance will be hindered in a number of sectors because of high radiation levels and destruction. Zones with a high radiation level must be crossed by troops. When it is impossible to by-pass these zones they must be crossed in tanks and closed vehicles with the necessary shielding measures or overcome using helicopters and airplanes. It is not impossible that certain regions can be crossed by troops only after a drop in the radiation level with the appropriate antinuclear and antichemical measures being taken.[15]

Sokolovskiy's view that future European warfare was almost bound to take this form has been sharply modified (see Chapter 4); however, if tactical nuclear weapons were to be used on any scale, his view of an enormously wide ranging, swift and violent conflict may be right. A totally opposite view was put by the eminent and imaginative military writer Ferdinand Otto Miksche in the mid-1950s. Miksche cited the example of winter manoeuvres conducted by the Soviet Army in February 1954. An attacker succeeded in penetrating the high Carpathian mountain passes near Czernowitz. Both sides were assumed to be using nuclear weapons and to be about equal in strength. Each side concentrated its nuclear strikes on the lines of communication and supply centres of the opponent. The umpires declared that because of this, operations had ground to a standstill. Because of strong air opposition, air resupply of the forward troops cut off from their bases was not fully effective. Miksche reminded his readers that throughout military history the growth of firepower tended to increase the strength of the defence. Nuclear weapons had increased instantaneous firepower thousands of times while the means of movement — lorries and tanks — remained unchanged. Other factors favour the defence, too:

> The attacker is compelled to operate in the open whereas field fortifications offer, to a certain degree, shelter against atomic weapons. The defender can also protect himself more easily by camouflage. His strength is mainly based on concentric fire, whereas success in the attack largely depends on physical concentration of forces ... every concentration inevitably becomes a highly vulnerable target for atomic weapons. Furthermore, an offensive can only be deployed from depth, and it is precisely there that atomic weapons exert their maximum effect.
> Without concentration in attack, there can be no piercing power. Fire alone can hardly decide the issue, while without movement there can be no manoeuvre — consequently no decision. Could not all this again lead to a bogging down of the fighting?[16]

Miksche noted that within 6 kilometres of a burst all high-frequency apparatus would burn out, and that messengers would have to be employed. Nuclear weapons might give rise to a development 'entirely different from the one foreseen by armies at present'. The simpler weapons and equipment would be more dependable than complex systems which are powerless without extensive rear services. It might be that in nuclear warfare 'only material and tactical methods of the simplest kind will retain their value'.[17]

Miksche tested his theory by analysing what would have happened if nuclear weapons had been available to both sides during the German attack on France on 1940. Used initially by the Allies against Aachen and important communications centres, the effect was to stop the *Blitzkrieg* and strengthen the defence based on the Maginot Line and dug-in tanks. Battlefield use of the new weapons was followed by strategic bombardment, atomic bombs being used on London, Paris, Berlin, Düsseldorf, Cologne ... Here, of course, lies the greatest problem and danger with nuclear weapons in land warfare: the risk of escalation. In the author's view, it would be extremely difficult to restrict the use of nuclear weapons to the battlefield. The very scope of modern military operations (see Chapter 4) means that in Europe the operational depth embraces ports and staging areas in Britain on one side and Poland on the other. A future war using nuclear weapons would probably comprise classic land operations entwined with nuclear bursts, perhaps racing ahead as envisaged by Sokolovskiy, perhaps bogging down as Miksche thought, perhaps both, extending into the hinterland of the combatants. Endeavouring to escape or discourage nuclear strikes, forward units would hug the enemy very closely, perhaps accepting heavy casualties from conventional weapons as the lesser evil. The modern Soviet Operational Manoeuvre Group (see Chapter 4) is in part a reflection of the needs of the nuclear or potentially nuclear battlefield, with its emphasis on getting in among the enemy. Second echelons would be staggered at intervals, wide enough to enable a nuclear weapon to explode fairly harmlessly in between: Miksche reckoned about 6 kilometres. Generals commanding nuclear-equipped formations would be closely controlled by national governments, and any nuclear strike would probably have to be approved at the highest level. The time taken to get approval in a theatre disintegrating into vast zones of destruction and swept by fires and floods might delay operations, adding to the bogging down effect. Troops would be oppressed and paralysed by the fear of nuclear attack, either on them or their families back home. While nuclear weapons would not necessarily be used against major centres of power and population, medium-sized towns and large military bases would be hit, with massive loss of civilian life and collateral damage. At this stage, frantic diplomatic activity would probably succeed in curtailing hostilities.

Although the threat to use nuclear weapons either to avert conventional defeat or in response to an enemy's use of them is crucial to the structure of deterrence, what would happen if conflict were to break out in Europe is a rather different matter. Whatever their peace-time statements, it is likely that both sides would consider it against their interests to use battlefield nuclear weapons. In Europe the shadow of escalation and the direct involvement of both superpowers with their enormous arsenals, not to mention the unpredictable response of the British and French, would, in the author's view, tend to keep the conflict conventional and (possibly) chemical (see below). Because China also has the ability to inflict unacceptable damage on the Soviet Union, the same goes for the East Asian theatre although in the vast expanses of Mongolia and Siberia it is possible that the use of nuclear weapons could be constrained within the theatre of land operations more easily. The most likely setting for nuclear land war is probably among the emerging or 'threshold' nuclear powers in the Middle East and South Asia.

The new and threshold nuclear powers

In May 1974, India detonated its first nuclear device deep below the Rajhastan desert, near the Pakistan border. Besides the political desire to demonstrate that India was the dominant power in South Asia, nuclear devices have to be tested. Although this was declaredly for peaceful purposes, there could be no doubt that India with her population of nearly 800 million and the third or fourth largest army in the world (see Chapter 2) could also build a bomb.

One or two nuclear warheads are not enough to make a nation an operational nuclear power. In order to ensure redundancy and provide a second strike capability to deter other emerging nuclear powers from reciprocating in kind, a minimum of about six would be required. Other prerequisites are that the warheads be reasonably compact and the possession of a suitable delivery system, although even a big bomb like that used by the United States in 1945 could, *in extremis*, be rolled out of the back of a transport aircraft. Because of the availability of nuclear technology and expertise generally nowadays, it is likely that once in possession of a workable device a threshold power could refine it and make it more compact fairly quickly, and all the likely nuclear powers possess combat aircraft capable of delivering nuclear bombs (Phantoms, Mirages, F-16s, MIG-23s). Making warheads smaller so as to fit into tactical rocket warheads or artillery shells may take a while longer. When Miksche wrote about Europe in the 1950s, he was thinking in terms of 280 mm monster artillery pieces to deliver them, but noted that warheads fitting into 203 mm and 155 mm shells would be available fairly soon. Modern threshold powers have probably nearly reached the same stage of development. Finally, a new nuclear power needs to develop a Command, Control and Communications (C^3) system suitable for controlling their delivery and fighting a nuclear war. This would include target selection, hardening facilities against nuclear retaliation, training and so on.[18] As previously in Europe, the rarity and size of nuclear weapons would initially make them suitable for use against strategic and economic targets, and a battlefield capability would follow on later. All the threshold states could develop the infrastructure described fairly easily, and the main problem is the supply of enough fissile material. Nuclear warheads can be made either from enriched uranium or plutonium. The latter is produced as a by-product from nuclear reactors and is therefore more readily available although Pakistan, for example, has taken an interest in uranium enrichment.

Of all the nuclear or potential nuclear powers in these regions, Israel is clearly the most advanced. She undoubtedly has nuclear bombs and probably has them deployed in surface to surface missiles (Lance and reportedly the missile named, perhaps with grim humour, Jericho-2). The existence of Jericho-2 has not been acknowledged by the Israeli government at the time of writing, but various foreign sources claim that it is a two-stage missile with a range of some 700-1,000 kilometres and an inertial guidance system. It is believed to be an improved version of the Jericho-1 which has been deployed since the 1970s, but the deployment is unconfirmed. Israel can also deliver nuclear weapons by aircraft. Because of her small size, the Israelis believe that any conflict involving nuclear weapons would be total, and stress the impossibility of separating operational-tactical from strategic nuclear war, a function of geography as much as doctrinal disputation. In the event of massive success by neighbouring countries threatening Israel's survival, she would probably unleash nuclear weapons against the limited number of Arab cities presenting targets or against command and control facilities behind advancing Arab forces. Use against forward attacking formations would be suicidal.

Unlike other states in the region, Israel has the technological expertise to develop cruise missiles as a means of nuclear delivery in the future, and a sophisticated C^3I system based on an airborne warning and control system (AWACS) aircraft. By the year 2000 Israel might have a force of some 100 warheads. A force of about 300 surface to surface missiles might be equipped primarily with conventional warheads, but ten to twenty nuclear warheads could be stored in hardened sites and carried by helicopter to missile units.[19]

Iraq and Iran probably do not have a nuclear capability at the time of writing, but could have arsenals of maybe 25 warheads by 2000. Before that, Iraq might use a warhead as a last resort against Tehran in the event of Iranian forces carrying out their oft-repeated threat to cut the Baghdad-Basra road and threatening Baghdad itself. A mass of Iranian forces concentrating for a decisive breakthrough would probably not be seen as a worthwhile target initially, but if they attained an arsenal of 25 warheads it might be. However, nuclear warheads are most likely to be used first in a warning role, or against a key economic target like Kharg Island.[20] Given that the Iranians have a great superiority in manpower on the ground, and that they have of late been on the offensive, concentrating for attack whilst the Iraqi defence has been dispersed, identifying main thrusts and then manoeuvring reserves to defeat it, there would seem little point in the Iranians using an atomic weapon to blast a hole for an advance, especially as the Iraqi defence is so much deeper (see Chapter 1) than the lethal zone of a typical 20 kiloton warhead. Also, the relatively poor training of the Iranian forces makes them unsuited to manoeuvre through the results of a nuclear strike, although the Iranians do have a limited ability to 'chopper' elite troops over a nuclear strike zone. If Tehran were to acquire a limited nuclear force in the near future, its best bet would be to use it strategically, which its current leadership would probably do.

The most advanced thinking on operational-tactical use of nuclear weapons in this region has been done by the Indian and Pakistan armed forces. India of course fought China in 1962 and her desire to become a nuclear power probably owes a lot to this. An Indian nuclear force would probably emerge on two levels: a short-range force to counter Pakistan and maritime threats along India's long coastline, and a long-range force as a deterrent against China. The former might include surface to surface missiles: the latter intercontinental ballistic missiles, which would be well within India's capabilities to build, given her successful space programme. By 2000 India could have 200 to 300 nuclear warheads in service. A Pakistani force would be smaller, perhaps 50 warheads by 2000. Pakistan might obtain help with missile construction from China, but even so, it is unlikely that Pakistan would have many missiles available for nuclear delivery before the turn of the century. Turning to the specifically battlefield aspects of these forces, there Pakistan clearly takes the nuclear threat very seriously. This is seen as two tiered: that from super-power involvement and that from India. Turning to the likely battlefield threat specifically, published assessments by Pakistani officers portray a potent and diverse threat. Although these are declaredly unofficial and may incline to the pessimistic, they must present a credible estimate for military readers. According to one, by the late 1990s, India might deploy at most 250 to 300 gun-delivered nuclear warheads of 0.5 to 5 kiloton yield and 50 to 75 medium-range ballistic missiles of 5 to 200 kiloton yield, as well as 35 to 50 aircraft delivered weapons and cruise or ballistic missiles fired from submarines. At worst, the Pakistani Army is likely to be subjected to 15 to 20 tactical nuclear strikes on the first day of a nuclear war in the region followed by up to eight strikes per day thereafter. Indian thinking in fact is far more defensive: when the Indian Army began to discuss nuclear weapons openly in the mid-1970s the first major topic of discussion was nuclear mines (ADMs) with their ability to create barriers against major ground forces' invasion through choke points such as mountain passes or valleys. Their use in this role is more likely than straightforward attacks on armoured formations which are not necessarily profitable targets. Nevertheless, in the Indo-Pakistan war of 1971 there were large tank engagements including some 100 tanks on both sides at the battle of Shakergarh at the northern tip of India just below the beginning of the Himalayan range (see also Chapter 4). India's I Corps attacked the Pakistanis in a battle covering an area about 40 kilometres square. In such circumstances, army targets could be very attractive, especially in desert and mountain regions away from densely populated areas. If you take two one millionth scale air charts, which cover the 1,500 kilometres of the India-Pakistan frontier, they spread out over a large dining room table. The maximum destructive area of a battlefield nuclear weapon, a 4 mile (6 kilometre) circle is the size of the flat end of a pencil, and a large number of nuclear strikes would therefore be required to have any appreciable effect on that theatre.[21]

Pakistani officers clearly plan for operational tactical use of nuclear weapons by India, emphasising the need for hardening of equipment against nuclear effects, including EMP, and for thorough training. They have also taken a leaf out of the Soviets' book in concluding that the principal arm providing protection against blast, flash, radiation and contamination and retaining mobility on the nuclear battlefield is armour:

> The greatest requirement of troops on a nuclear battlefield ... dispersion ... affords protection from all the effects of a nuclear explosion, viz: blast, heat and nuclear radiation. However, for a body of troops to achieve dispersion for protection and concentration for attack at the beck and call of its commander, four factors have to be kept in mind, viz, mobility, communications, efficient logistic support and firepower. Are these not the characteristics of an armoured force? ...
>
> The atomic bomb does not, in any way, invalidate fundamental principles of war. The atomic bomb being just a powerful form of fire support, the importance of the forces of manoeuvre remains undiminished. Concentration of force will have an additional, nuclear, element to be considered. So will economy of force, logistics, surprise, etc.
>
> Armour with all its apparent characteristics will continue to be ideally suited for atomic warfare, having the ability to protect itself as well as exploit success in the face of a nuclear holocaust.[22]

When considering the use of battlefield nuclear weapons by new and threshold nuclear powers, there is also the possibility that they may be used against United States or Soviet intervention in a non-European theatre. The creation of the US Rapid Deployment Force (RDF) in the early 1980s underlined the perceived need to be able to intervene in crises worldwide; but such intervention would be totally dependent on a few large ports or airbases, both for pre-positioning of equipment and for actual deployment. A small nuclear power might launch nuclear strikes to destroy stockpiles or render airfields and ports unusable, a task for which nuclear weapons are ideal. However, it might also attack superpower forces once deployed, perhaps judging that the superpower concerned would not retaliate in kind because of world opinion or because there was no worthwhile target for it except a strategic one. Such a calculation (or mis-calculation) is more likely in the event of US intervention than Soviet, but nothing is impossible. The vulnerability of a Soviet or American power projection force based on a few ports or airfields recalls the warning in the 1946 Tizard report: the Mantra wheel continues to turn full circle.

OBSCENE AS CANCER, BITTER AS THE CUD: CHEMICAL WEAPONS

The first large-scale use of chemical weapons in war was probably against the British at Neuve Chapelle on 27 October 1914 when the Germans bombarded them with 3,000 shrapnel shells containing the irritant dianisdine chlorosulphate. On 31 January 1915 the Germans fired 18,000 shells containing bromide (tear gas) at the Russians at Bolimov. The gas achieved some surprise but the extreme cold prevented it functioning effectively. However, the first spectacular demonstration of its potential was on 22 April 1915, against the British and French sector at Langemarck, when 171 tonnes of lethal chlorine gas were released causing 15,000 casualties of which 5,000 were fatal within half an hour. Although not exploited, this surprise use of chemical weapons *en masse* had created the potential for massive operational success. There can be few clearer examples of the effect of new technology employed *in sufficient quantities* and *with surprise* to make a dramatic impact on the conduct of war, but also of the need to employ it as *part of a plan which provides for the exploitation of its effects at every level* (see Figure 3.3).

From then on, chemical warfare became an intrinsic part of the conduct of the Great War. To chlorine was added phosgene, and in July 1917 the Germans employed a new gas whose effects were even more horrific than the aforementioned non-persistent choking agents, which worked by corroding the lungs. This was the persistent blister agent dichlorethyl sulphide — mustard gas.[23]

The Great War was the only major conflict in which chemical weapons have been employed on a massive scale for a long

Figure 3.3: The use of chemical warfare to achieve massive tactical and operational surprise, 22 April 1915

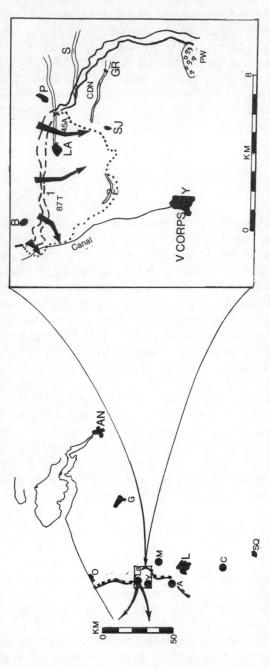

Right-hand diagram shows detail of the breakthrough near Langemarck. Left-hand diagram shows position of the breakthrough in relation to the sea and the potential to breakthrough to the coast further south.

A — Armentieres; AN — Antwerp; B — Bixschoote; C — Cambrai; CDN — Canadian Division; G — Gent; GR — Gravenstafel; L — Lille; La — Langemarck; M — Menin; O — Ostend; P — Poelcappelle; PW — Polygon Wood; S — Stroombeek ridge; SJ — St Julien; SQ — St Quentin; Y — Ypres; 1 — German and Allied lines, 17.00 hrs, 22 April; 2 — Limit of German advance, 22 April (midnight); 87T — French 87 Territorial Div; 45A — French 45 Algerian Div period, and remains the main source of wisdom for their effect on the conduct of troops and operations.[24]

Nerve Gas

The first nerve agent, tabun, was identified by Dr Gerhard Schräder, a German scientist, at the end of 1936, as a result of research into pesticides. A year later he discovered a related compound, almost ten times as lethal, which was christened sarin. A plant to manufacture tabun was set up with great secrecy at Dyhernfurth in western Silesia in 1940. This is how the principal modern chemical agents originated.

In a healthy person, nerves are stimulated by acetylcholine, to perform a given action. Acetylcholine (ACh) is then destroyed by choline esterase (ChE), allowing the nerves to come to rest. Nerve agents combine chemically with ChE preventing its normal action on ACh. This gives rise to involuntary nerve impulses, causing convulsions and death. Atropine will act as a partial substitute for choline esterase removed by the nerve agent and therefore neutralises the acetylcholine. Oxime tablets will decompose the nerve agent-choline esterase combination and restore the body's normal functions. These increase the body's resistance and are taken prophylactically. Atropine injections and oxime tablets are therefore the principal treatment for nerve gas victims. More recent pre-loaded syringes combine oximes with atropine. Care has to be taken in administering atropine as, like many drugs, it is itself a powerful poison. If excess atropine is given, atropine poisoning may result, although this is rarely fatal.[25] Nerve agents comprise the main 'super-toxic lethal' agents in use today. This heading, used in arms control negotiations, also comprises Lewisite and Mustard. The psychochemical 'BZ' (see below) is categorised as 'super-toxic', though not lethal.

Damocles' unused sword

The reasons why chemical weapons were not employed by or against the European belligerents in World War II are many and complex. They went to war infinitely better equipped to face the horror of chemical warfare, as far as they could tell, than any

89

nation today. In Britain alone 38 million gas masks and other pieces of anti-chemical equipment had been issued by the time of the Munich crisis. The reasons why chemical warfare was not initiated cannot be put down to moral scruples, either on the part of the creators of the concentration camps or the powers who incinerated Dresden. At every stage, both sides considered it against their interests to use chemical weapons at that time, for one reason or another. This applies particularly to battlefield conditions. The initial German victories were accomplished with speed and dash which would have been impossible had chemical warfare begun, and at that time they would have assumed that the Allies had arsenals of 'old fashioned' chemical munitions which equalled or exceeded their own. As the tide turned, the Germans concluded that they had more to lose from chemical warfare in the face of massive Allied air and, on the eastern front, artillery superiority, while the Soviets and from 1944, the western Allies, were fighting a manoeuvre war which they did not wish to see bogged down in a chemical swamp.

All assessments about both sides mirror Churchill's comment of July 1944: 'They have not used it [gas] because it does not pay them. The greatest temptation ever offered to them was the beaches of Normandy.'[26] The Normandy invasion was indeed the most obvious place for chemical warfare to be initiated. Despite the portrayal in popular films British and American troops went ashore thoroughly prepared in case chemical weapons and (although the troops themselves did not know it) nuclear radiation was used against them. General Omar Bradley confided that: 'When D Day ended without a whiff of mustard, I was vastly relieved. For even a light sprinkling of persistent gas on Omaha beach would have cost us our footing there.'[27]

As with nuclear weapons, isolated and confined beach-heads are particularly vulnerable targets for chemical. The potential effects of gas in the hinterland are less dramatic, but all experts agreed that they would have slowed down the tempo of operations. In Normandy or Italy, gas might create a very temporary advantage, but thereafter restrict the Allied advance.

On the eastern front, the Soviets were believed to be well equipped for the offensive use of gas and their overwhelming superiority in the air and in artillery and mortars would assure them a considerable superiority in chemical warfare as compared with the Germans. On the other hand,

The general use of chemical warfare would slow up Russian progress owing to contamination of important objectives, road and rail junctions and possibly water supply and also owing to the increased strain of moving large C.W. stocks over their lengthening communications. On balance, we believe that the Russians would lose more than they would gain were chemical warfare to start on the Eastern Front.[28]

The possibility of the Germans initiating gas warfare continued until early 1945, when the Allies believed that there might be plans to use gas as the Allies breached the Rhine in the west and the Oder in the east.[29] These fears, too, proved groundless. Military staffs on both sides clearly believed it would hamper rather than facilitate operations, given that the other side was believed to have a significant capability. Such considerations may not apply in a future war where one side's chemical armoury is very markedly superior to the other's, and one has a monopoly of delivering chemical at a time and place of its own choosing.

Modern chemical weapons and defence against them

The research effort which the Germans had put into developing nerve gas was therefore not used to defend the Reich. Instead, by early 1945 the factory at Dyhrenfurth had fallen intact into the hands of the advancing Red Army, along with the pilot sarin plant. The Soviets also captured the near complete plant at Falkenhagen, where the Germans had been planning to produce 500 tonnes of sarin a month. At this time the Germans were also working on a still more lethal agent, soman, later known as GD. The Germans had refined this but not manufactured it in quantity. All the documents relating to its production were captured by the Russians.

The German G agents — tabun (GA), sarin (GB), and soman (GD) — formed the basis of post-war Soviet chemical weapons. In 1952 ICI chemists, again attempting to produce a new pesticide, discovered a new agent. More viscous than G agents, it was roughly of the consistency of engine oil. This worked in the same way as G agents, interfering with the enzyme needed to control muscle movements. The first variant developed by American scientists was called VX. V agents have

91

also been developed by the Soviets, the two in use today being VX and VR-55.[30]

Modern chemical weapons contain the most lethal substances known, and create enormous problems for storage and transport. An idea which has recently attracted renewed interest is the so called 'binary' nerve gas weapon. Binary weapons consist of two separate components which are relatively safe or at any rate stable in themselves but which mix in the shell or rocket during flight to produce a nerve agent. One agent is stored inside the shell, the other stored and transported separately and only loaded into the shell just before firing. Interest in binary weapons originated in the US Navy, where there are particular problems with lethal agents stored in cramped conditions on warships, but by the mid-1960s a binary bomb had been designed and by the mid-1970s a binary 155mm shell. In the late 1970s a plan was produced for a US plant capable of producing 70,000 binary nerve gas shells each month, the agent being VX.[31] At the time of writing a final decision has still not been made, but the advantages of binary weapons are those of politics and safety. Although theoretically a binary weapon should be no less effective than one in which the chemical agent is already mixed, the need to mix two components in flight complicates the problem of construction and probably means that they are less effective, round for round, than less sophisticated chemical munitions.

The effects of modern chemical agents together with World War I vintage gases are shown in Table 3.2. The modern agents are very much faster acting, and are also far more potent and penetrative. A droplet of nerve gas the size of a pinhead can be lethal, and will soak through ordinary combat clothing or boots. A typical delivery system would be a US 155mm or Soviet 152mm shell, containing a substantial amount of explosive to make it burst and distribute the agent and about three kilograms of agent proper. Thus a single shell would contain enough soman to kill 150 men percutaneously or, theoretically, some 20,000 if inhaled.

The agent is not evenly distributed, but taking into account dispersion patterns it has been calculated that a 152 or 155mm howitzer battalion of 18 weapons (in fact, both NATO and Soviet battalions may now comprise 24) each firing only one round into a 2 hectare (100 metres by 200 metres) area could inflict 40 to 50 per cent casualties on fatigued troops in open

Table 3.2: Effect of selected chemical agents

| Agent | Type | Persistent/ non-persistent | Aerosol or vapour over target | | | | | Liquid sprayed on target | | |
| | | | To incapacitate | | To kill | | | | | |
			respiratory ID-50	time to effect	percutaneous LD-50 mg	respiratory	time to effect	density for area denial (kg/km²)	time to effect	percutaneous LD-50 mg
Phosgene	choking	non-persistent	1600	3-12h	na	3200	3-24h	—	na	na
Mustard	blister	persistent	200	4-6h	10000	1500	4-24h	10000	4-6h	4500
Hydrogen cyanide	blood	non-persistent	na	na	na	5000	½-15m	na	na	na
Sarin	nerve	semi-persistent	55	1-10m	12000	100	2-15m	na	na	1700
Soman	nerve	semi-persistent	25	1-10m	10000	70	1-15m	1000	½-1h	1000
VX	nerve	persistent	5	1-10m	1000	36	4-10m	300	½-1h	15

Note: Hydrogen cyanide and phosgene disperse rapidly and so cannot contaminate ground. Sarin also disperses rapidly except in cold weather. Persistency varies greatly; VX, for example, is effective for 1 to 12 hours in windy and rainy conditions, but for up to 16 weeks in calm weather with lying snow. LD-50 or ID-50 means the dosage expected to kill or incapacitate half those exposed to it. For aerosol this is given in milligrams per cubic metre per minute, for liquid milligrams per square metre.

Source: Charles Dick, 'The Soviet Chemical and Biological Warfare Threat', *RUSI Journal*, March 1981, p. 50; and David C Isby, *Weapons and Tactics of the Soviet Army* (Jane's, 1981), p. 214. VX is a Western invention but the Soviets have it also.

trenches and 15 to 20 per cent on fresh ones. In addition to wind, temperature and the degree of protection, even the victims' physical state can greatly affect the degree of impact of chemical weapons. One attractive non-persistent agent is hydrogen cyanide, which kills very fast but disperses almost as quickly. The problem in the past has been to deliver it in sufficient concentrations but the new Soviet BM-27 220 mm 16-barrelled rocket launcher might be a suitable method of delivering a significant dose. Almost immediately afterwards, perhaps ten minutes, advancing motor-rifle troops would not need to wear respirators.

Chemical agents would also be the most cost effective warheads for large operational tactical missiles like SS-21 with a range of 100 kilometres and presumably capable of carrying a warhead containing about 220 kilograms of agent like its predecessor, the Frog. A Scud or SS-23 could probably carry a chemical warhead about twice this size far into the enemy depth. With a circular error probable estimated at 300 metres, a couple of these could be fairly certain of spreading persistent chemical agent over an area target and denying it to an enemy for a long time.[32]

Choking and blood agents require a respirator to be worn for protection: blister and nerve agents require a complete nuclear, biological and chemical (NBC) suit. The main protective element in both is charcoal, which utilises the property of *ad*sorption, that is, retention of liquid, vapour or gas by strong chemical forces. The British NBC or 'noddy' suit comprises a layer of charcoal sandwiched between cloth. Normal clothing gives little or no protection so impervious overboots, hood and gloves also have to be worn. It is essential to maintain an airtight seal at the wrists, ankles, waist, neck and face. The respirator also includes a filter pad to trap contaminated particles and a filter against smoke. Even the British NBC suit will be penetrated in time by VX or VR-55, if it is splashed with liquid agent, and pads impregnated with Fuller's Earth are carried which can be used to powder affected areas and *ad*sorb concentrations of liquid. Even this outfit is tiring and uncomfortable to wear for any period of time and the effect on a soldier's feet of being encased in NBC overboots for any time is disgusting. A completely impervious (airtight) suit would be impossible to wear for any length of time without bringing on physical collapse. During exercise Lionheart in September

1984, a new NBC protection suit and respirator were first tested by the British forces, probably the best trained in 'fighting dirty' in NATO.

The Soviets also have an extensive range of decontamination equipment, for spraying vehicles, laundering clothes and so on. One of the most spectacular is the TMS-65, a modified aircraft engine which will blast a tank clean in three minutes. In the aftermath of the recent tragic incident at the Chernobyl nuclear power station, Soviet CW troops (*Khimzashchita*) were reported to have played a major role in the cleaning up operations. Soviet NBC equipment has been widely exported and full NBC treatment kits have been captured by the Israelis from the PLO.[33]

The alternative to dressing soldiers like divers to swim in a contaminated sea is to provide them with submarines. The modern tank and APC are well provided against chemical penetration, but there are limitations. Chemical weapons will generally be employed in conjunction with others, possibly penetrating a vehicle's skin. Troops cooped up in NBC-proof vehicles will become apprehensive and depressed, and resupply of NBC-proof tanks or self-propelled guns and personal communications between HQ vehicles will be impossible without breaking the NBC seal. On balance, however, it would seem to pay troops to stay in NBC-tight vehicles for as long as they can.

The chemical battlefield

If we first consider the possibility of Soviet forces in Europe using chemical weapons against NATO, this would certainly be a way of destroying, neutralising or at least severely inconveniencing a well-organised, in depth anti-tank defence based on anti-tank guided weapons. Chemical weapons would cause most casualties among infantry, and most of NATO's anti-tank weapons are infantry manned and are likely to be for some time. The combination of High Explosive and non-persistent chemical would have a synergistic effect while allowing Soviet forces to move through with relative freedom later. Hydrogen cyanide would also be of use in clearing areas for heliborne landings which would in turn provide stepping-stones to accelerate the main forces' advance. Persistent chemicals would be of particular value at the operational level. Besides causing heavy casualties and complicating NATO activities, they would be of particular use against airfields, supply bases (smothering pre-positioned stores with persistent chemical would make them useless for some time) and reserve areas. If the location of reserves is not known, then persistent chemical could be used to protect the flanks of an advance. NATO forces moving to counter-attack would not know the invisible barrier was there until they ran into it, and their movements would then be severely restricted. Such prophylactic treatment could be applied to especially likely axes for counter-attack, like defiles, bridges or gaps in hill features. Chemical could be used to throw a cordon around the bridgehead of assault river crossings, perhaps with a gap known only to the Soviets so that they could then move swiftly on their way. Finally, large chemical strikes would seem ideal for eliminating pockets of resistance or encircled forces, especially in built-up areas. As we shall see in Chapter 4, the Soviets place great stress on by-passing hard nuts, leaving them to be dealt with later, perhaps by a second echelon. If, as we shall see, there is no second echelon, there is no problem: plaster the besieged with chemical and leave them to die. Finally attacks on civilian targets would add to the general flood of casualties swamping medical facilities, create panic and a refugee problem which would further hamper NATO movements and create political pressure on the governments of nations affected, particularly Germany, Belgium, Denmark and Holland. The Russians might be chary about extending chemical strikes further into the NATO depth, that is, Britain and France, because they might get more back than they bargained for. The unilateral use of chemical weapons by the Soviets, at times and places of their own choosing, creating channels for their advance and eliminating by-passed enemy positions or denying large areas to the enemy would not slow down the tempo of their advance, indeed, it would almost certainly accelerate it. If NATO were able to respond in kind the situation becomes completely different. The Soviets would not know where or when they might be hit; which pieces of ground had been or were about to be saturated with VX. They would have to operate masked up, and be delayed with constant checks and decontamination. The effect would be as predicted in World War II: a slowing down of the tempo of operations. As noted in Chapter 4, the Soviets believe that a European war must be won very quickly indeed, and their entire concept of operations is tailored to a rapid and decisive advance. If bilateral chemical warfare were initiated, this would be impossible. Indeed, a slowing down of operations might be very much to NATO's advantage in giving time to bring up reinforcements, exploiting strains in the Soviet political system, and perhaps persuading an attacker that his gamble had failed and that a negotiated peace was desirable. If the Soviets wanted a swift victory, therefore, they would not initiate chemical warfare if they knew that a response in kind was likely. As proved in World War II, the stultifying effect of bilateral chemical warfare on military operations is a first rate deterrent against its use.

Such considerations led General Rogers, Supreme Allied Commander Europe, to press for a resumption of chemical weapons manufacture from 1980. In spring 1984 the British Cabinet's Joint Intelligence Committee (JIC) reported that the Soviets had some 300,000 tonnes of chemical weapons, and in August a number of articles reported NATO generals' renewed interest in acquiring a chemical arm. The British Prime Minister attended a series of briefings on chemical warfare, while in October a pamphlet by Manfred Hamm on chemical warfare added to public and official interest. The JIC report had apparently also identified a new 'slippy' chemical agent, capable of penetrating NBC suits more easily and creeping round seals. It is not clear from unclassified sources whether this is the same as VX or VR-55; other reports speak of 'thickened soman (TGD)'. General Rogers reiterated his request strongly in September 1984.[34]

From a military viewpoint, acquisition of new chemical weapons by NATO makes sense. They are comparatively cheap and simple to make and suitable delivery systems exist in profusion. They can be seen as a logical bridge in the ladder of deterrence: without them, the only way of upping the ante in the face of massive chemical attack would be with nuclear weapons. However, as this chapter has shown, it is the particular effect of chemical warfare on the nature of military operations which has been the most effective deterrent against chemical use.

Persian poison

One of the reasons for the upsurge of interest in chemical war-

97

fare in 1984 was the news that they were being employed in the long-drawn-out Iran-Iraq War. Chemical weapons have been used widely outside Europe before: by the Italians in Abyssinia before World War II, and chemicals were used by the United States in Vietnam, most widely for defoliation although tear gas was also used for tunnel clearing. Egypt employed mustard and phosgene in the Yemen in 1966, and it appears that Vietnam used mycotoxins (see above) in Laos in 1979, while the Soviets used them in Afghanistan in the early 1980s.[35] Chemical weapons are much more readily used against those who not only lack the capacity to retaliate but also lack sophisticated medical and detection facilities to report what is happening. The use of mustard gas on a large scale in a conventional war by the Iraqis represents a qualitatively different development, especially as the Iraqis appear to be able to produce the agent themselves. On 11 March 1984 it was reported that there was 'no doubt' that chemical had been used and that the Iraqis had been producing mustard gas for 18 months. There was also some evidence that the Iraqis had been using nerve gases as well, since some bodies had no trace either of bullet wounds or the characteristic blistering caused by mustard. Pre-loaded syringes of atropine were also found on the battlefield in the Gaziel sector, 50 kilometres north of Basra. The Iranians apparently bought them on the open market some months before. Some sources alleged that the Iraqis had built a plant at Akashat, a remote desert location 290 kilometres west of Baghdad, which could produce nerve gas. Like the first German nerve gases, this is apparently based on research into pesticides.[36]

Given the length of the Iran-Iraq War, its bitter nature and the infantry-heavy nature of the Iranian forces, it is perhaps inevitable that hard-pressed Iraq saw in chemical weapons which are relatively cheap and simple to manufacture a means of compensating for Iranian numerical superiority. Chemical weapons would also be particularly effective against troops who were poorly equipped and trained, as many of the Iranians are. The thought of kitting out all Iranian troops on that front with full NBC gear and of wearing it in the desert heat boggles the imagination.

By the end of March 1984, Iran was hinting that it might use chemical weapons in retaliation against Iraq. This may have been bluff, but Iran's oil industry has made it the most powerful country in the Middle East for chemical processing (except perhaps Israel). Chemical weapons like mustard would be very easy to make indeed, and Iran may have initiated their manufacture. However, once again, Iran is unlikely to initiate chemical warfare knowing that the Iraqis would retaliate immediately, because the better equipped and trained Iraqi army would undoubtedly get the better of them in a chemical conflict and Iraq is also better off for artillery, rockets and aircraft, all chemical delivery systems. In the next few years it is possible that many Middle Eastern states will acquire chemical weapons, if they have not done so already. In 1984, United States Defence Department officials estimated that between 14 and 16 countries had recently acquired chemical weapons, and that US forces might have to face chemical attack in the Middle East, South East and North East Asia as well as Europe. Six or seven countries in Asia were equipped with chemical weapons including Egypt, Iraq, Vietnam and North Korea. Any countries which obtained arms from the Soviet Union were likely to have the weapons. It would be surprising if Israel, with her advanced industry and vulnerable position, did not also have some chemical as well as nuclear arsenal.[37]

Future chemical weapons

Research into chemical weapons continues, new discoveries resulting from attempts to devise countermeasures to existing agents as well as from the desire to perfect the means of chemical offence. There has been some interest in non lethal agents, such as hallucination producing substances like LSD. LSD has been ruled out as requiring too dense a concentration, and suffers from the same problem as all such drugs: in rendering the enemy delirious, it is totally unpredictable in its effects. To give an illustration, an enemy commander under the influence of LSD is just as likely to order a nuclear strike as to surrender. Unfortunately, for reliability and effect lethal agents continue to be the most promising for general battlefield use.[38] Development of chemical warfare agents in the next quarter century is likely to move towards mycotoxins of fungal origin, which have the advantage of being relatively easy and cheap to produce, difficult to detect, and of attaining precision and lethality close to that of nerve agents. Efforts to refine nerve gases of the G and V families will continue.

CONCLUSIONS

Because both sides in the potential European war possess operational-tactical nuclear weapons, and because of the risk of escalation, it is likely that every effort will be made to prevent their use. If they are used, they might accelerate the tempo of operations or cause it to bog down in a large-scale nuclear version of the Great War, with assiduous digging. Will the nuclear battlefield really be fast and focal, as Sokolovskiy argued? Focal positions are particularly vulnerable to nuclear strikes: linear ones are not, as Miksche pointed out. It could be linear, with the lines widely spaced and static.[39] Throughout military history, mobility has only been preserved or maintained when improvements in firepower have been matched by corresponding improvements in the mobility and protection of forces. Whether the modern tank, APC and helicopter have increased in agility and resilience to keep pace with the exponential increase in firepower provided by nuclear warheads is a question which, it is hoped, will remain academic. Chemical weapons offer the most probable option. Unilateral use could produce massive strategic, operational and tactical surprise and accelerate an attacker's advance. If they were immediately used in retaliation also, however, they would have the opposite effect and might give a future European battlefield a World War I character. If this were assessed as likely, that would in turn deter their use, as it did in World War II. In all theatres, nuclear and chemical weapons would be employed alongside and in concert with more conventional military activity in accordance with the participants' concepts of operations, which will now be examined.

NOTES

1. Public Record Office (PRO), *Defe II 1251* TWC (45) 38, 24 October 1945. Memorandum by Sir George Thompson, 'Effect of Atomic Bombs on Warfare in the Next Few Years', p. 4.
2. PRO Defe II 1252, *Examination of the Possible Development of Weapons and Methods of War*, TWC (46) 3 (Revise), 30 January 1946, part II, 'Effects on Warfare', p. 8.
3. TWC (46) 3 (Revise), Part I, 'Matters of Fact Relating to Atomic Energy', section B(e), 'Effect on Army Targets'. Modern assessment: Colonel A.A. Sidorenko, *The Offensive* (Moscow, 1970,

translated under the auspices of the US Air Force, US Government Printing Office, Washington, 1976), pp. 40-41.

4. Defe II 1252 TWC (46) 3 (Revise), Annex, p. 11.

5. Colonel G.S. Reinhardt and Lieutenant-Colonel W.R. Kintner, *Atomic Weapons in Land Combat* (Military Service Publishing Co., Harrisburg, PA, 1953), pp. 7-8 (training of troops with nuclear burst), 17 (Dean), 31, 61-2, 123. These conclusions are accepted by Colonel F.O. Miksche, *Atomic Weapons and Armies* (Faber & Faber, London, 1955), pp. 113, 137-9.

6. The best scientific introduction to the effects is S. Glasstone and P.J. Dolan, *The Effects of Nuclear Weapons*, (3rd edn., US Department of Defense and Department of Energy, US Government Printing Office, Washington, DC, 1977). Most useful practical guides are Thomas B. Cochran, William M. Arkin and Milton M. Hoenig, *Nuclear Weapons Databook*, Volume 1, *US Nuclear Forces and Capabilities* (Ballinger, Cambridge, Mass., 1984); Brian Beckett, *Weapons of Tomorrow* (Orbis, London, 1982); and L.W. McNaught, *Nuclear Weapons and Their Effects* (Brassey's Battlefield Weapons Systems and Technology Series, Vol. IV, 1984).

7. On nuclear weapons effects, rules of thumb and a useful graph, if out of date as far as fusion and boosted fission weapons are concerned, are in Reinhardt and Kintner, *Atomic Weapons*, pp. 103-8, 169-75. On EMP and TREE, see Dr. Kurshid Ahmad Khan, 'Electromagnetic Pulse', *Pakistan Army Journal (PAJ)*, June 1984, pp. 37-41, esp. p. 37; Major Muhammad Bashir, 'Communications-Electronic Operations in Nuclear Environment', *PAJ*, September 1982, pp. 38-44; Major Farrakh Alam Shah, 'Nuclear Hardening of Equipment', *PAJ*, March 1983, pp. 2-14, esp. p. 5: effect on fibre optics: McNaught, *Nuclear Weapons and Their Effects*, p. 57. Miksche had in fact noted the effect of low bursts on high frequency apparatus back in 1955 (*Atomic Weapons and Armies*, p. 18).

8. Enhanced radiation weapons: Cochran, Arkin and Hoenig, *Nuclear Weapons Databook*, pp. 14-15, 19, 28-9, 55, 57, 72, 73, 278, 300, 308; McNaught, *Nuclear Weapons and Their Effects*, pp. 20-22; Michael A. Aquino, *The Neutron Bomb* (PhD, University of California, 1980: University Microfilm International, 1983), esp. pp. 39-51; Sam T. Cohen, *The Neutron Bomb: Political, Technological and Military Issues* (Institute for Foreign Policy Analysis, Cambridge, Mass., 1978) and *The Truth about the Neutron Bomb* (William Morrow, New York, 1983); Lieutenant-General V.G. Reznichenko, *Taktika (Tactics)* (Voyenizdat, Moscow, 1984), pp. 16-17. Cochran, Arkin and Hoenig, *Nuclear Weapons Databook*, give the range of 8,000 cGys immediate radiation from a 1 Kt ER/RB or 10 Kt fission weapon as 690 metres (p. 28); McNaught, *Nuclear Weapons and Their Effects*, as 1,600 metres (p. 21).

9. 'Nuclear Capable Delivery Vehicles: World Wide', *The Military Balance, 1984-85* (International Institute of Strategic Studies, London, 1984), pp. 130-36; French Hades, *International Defense Review (IDR)*, 8/1985, p. 1,301; the author's *Red God of War: Soviet Artillery and Rocket Forces* (Brassey's, Oxford, 1986). The CEP is the area

within which *half* of a number of missiles or shells fired at a target will fall, statistically.

10. Rodney W. Jones, *Small Nuclear Forces* (The Washington Papers/103, Center for Strategic and International Studies, Washington, 1984), pp. 68-9.

11. Ibid., pp. 64-8.

12. Sidorenko, *The Offensive*, p. 61.

13. Marshal of the Soviet Union V.D. Sokolovskiy, *Soviet Military Strategy* (3rd ed., Voyenizdat, Moscow, 1968, translated and edited by Harriet Fast Scott, Macdonald & Jane's, London, 1975), pp. 202-3.

14. Ibid., p. 293.

15. Ibid., p. 294.

16. Miksche, *Atomic Weapons and Armies*, p. 15 (exercise, pp. 17-18).

17. Ibid., p. 18.

18. Indian nuclear test: Dr. Khurshid Ahmad Khan, 'India's Atomic Programme', *PAJ*, December 1983, p. 9; requirements for a viable nuclear force: Jones, *Small Nuclear Forces*, pp. 9-11; Miksche, *Atomic Weapons and Armies*, p. 133.

19. Jones, *Small Nuclear Forces*, pp. 12-15, 42-3. The original Jericho was developed from a late 1960s model of Marcel Dassault (France). Reports of its range vary from 400 kilometres (*Pakistan Army Journal*, 1977) to 1,000 kilometres (a 1981 report). On Jericho 2, 'Jericho II and the Nuclear Arsenal', *Defense and Foreign Affairs Daily*, 9 May 1985, pp. 1-2; Judith Perera 'Israel's bomb heads for the hills', *New Scientist*, 23 May 1985, p. 8. The latter is the source of the 1 km CEP. It also claims that the Jericho 2 is called *Zeev* (wolf), but other reports indicate that this is the name of an anti-radiation missile.

20. Jones, *Small Nuclear Forces*, pp. 43-4; effect of a 70 kiloton nuclear explosion on Ras Tanura and Kharg island: Zivia S. Wurtele, Gregory S. Jones, Beverly L. Rowen and Mary Agmon, *Nuclear Proliferation Prospects for the Middle East and South Asia* (Pan Heuristics, Marina del Rey, 1981), pp. 7-7 to 7-10.

21. Jones, *Small Nuclear Forces*, pp. 44-5 and 68 for Indian ADMs; Farrakh Alam Shah, 'Nuclear Hardening of Equipment', p. 7, for expected nuclear threat; Shakergarh, Ravi Rikhye, *The Fourth Round: Indo-Pak War of 1984* (ABC Publishing Co., New Delhi, 1982), p. 102; Major General Sukhwant Singh, *India's Wars Since Independence: Volume Two: Defence of the Western Border*, (Vikas, New Delhi, 1981), pp. 87-109.

22. Second-Lieutenant Muhammad Tahir Naveed, 'Armour in a Nuclear Environment', *PAJ*, September 1982, pp. 27, 29.

23. The title is from Wilfred Owen's poem *Dulci et Decorum Est*; Ypres, 1915: Brigadier-General J.E. Edmonds and Captain G.C. Wynne, *History of the Great War Based on Official Documents, Military Operations, France and Belgium, 1915* (by Direction of the Historical Section of the Committee of Imperial Defence, Macmillan, London, 1927) (Official History), pp. 176-94. A general history is Sterling Seagrave, *Yellow Rain (Chemical Warfare — The Deadliest Arms Race)* (Abacus, London, 1981); David Rosser Owen, 'NBC

Warfare and Anti-NBC Protection', *Armada International,* 1/1984, pp. 78-90; Stockholm International Peace Research Institute (SIPRI), *The Problem of Chemical and Biological Warfare,* Vol. II, *Chemical Weapons Today* (SIPRI, 1973). Robert Harris and Jeremy Paxman, *A Higher Form of Killing: The Secret History of Gas and Germ Warfare* (Paladin, London, 1983), pp. 1-4; earlier use: Rosser-Owen, 'NBC Warfare', p. 78. Mustard gas: Harris and Paxman, pp. 24-8.

24. See the vivid quotation from Erich Maria Remarque, *All Quiet on the Western Front* (translated by A.W. Wheen, London, 1929), p. 79, 'Those first few minutes ...'

25. Discovery of nerve gas, Harris and Paxman, *Higher Form of Killing,* pp. 53-6; CW defence: Rosser-Owen, 'NBC Warfare', pp. 89-90.

26. PRO *PREM 3/89,* Prime Minister to Ismay, D 217/4, 6 July 1944.

27. Precautions against radiation: Harris and Paxman, *Higher Form of Killing,* p. 124; Bradley quote from Seagrave, *Yellow Rain,* p. 80.

28. PRO *PREM 3/89,* 'Military Considerations Affecting the Initiation of Chemical and Other Special Forms of Warfare', 1944, pp. 1-4.

29. Ibid., JIC (45) 36(0) Final, 26 January 1945.

30. Capture of plants by Soviets: Harris and Paxman, *Higher Form of Killing,* pp. 138-9; modern agents: Charles Dick, 'The Soviet Chemical and Biological Warfare Threat', *RUSI Journal,* March 1981, pp. 45-51; Rosser-Owen, 'NBC Warfare', p. 80.

31. Harris and Paxman, *Higher Form of Killing,* pp. 231-2; 'Commission backs Binary Nerve Gas', *New Scientist,* 9 May 1985, p. 4.

32. Dick, 'Soviet Threat', pp. 48-9; Bellamy, *Red God of War.*

33. Dick, 'Soviet Threat', p. 49; new NBC suit and AR-5 mask: Duncan Mil, 'Noddy goes to War in a new Suit', *New Scientist,* 11 October 1984: Soviet kit: David C. Isby, *Weapons and Tactics of the Soviet Army* (Jane's, 1981), p. 214; capture of NBC detectors by Israelis: personal observation; Mr. Gorbachev's speech on the Soviet news programme *Vremya,* 14 May 1986.

34. Duncan Campbell, 'Thatcher Goes for Nerve Gas', *New Statesman,* 11 January 1985, pp. 8-10 (includes reference to 'slippy chemical'); 'Chemical Arms for NATO' and 'Chemical War Threat Scares NATO', *Sunday Times,* 26 August 1984, pp. 1 and 9, respectively (latter includes reference to 'thickened soman'); 'General Rogers returns to the charge', and others, 'General calls for chemical weapons', (Farndale, commanding BAOR), *Daily Mail,* 21 September 1984, p. 2; 'Rogers in Plea for chemical weapons', *Financial Times,* 22 September 1984, p. 2,; 'Heseltine differs on chemicals', and 'US General wants nerve gas for NATO', *The Times,* 22 September 1984, pp. 1 and 4, respectively; Manfred Hamm, *Chemical Warfare: the Growing Threat to Europe* (Institute for European Defence and Strategic Studies, 1984), reviewed in Roger Scruton, 'Investing in the Unthinkable', *The Times,* 16 October 1984, p. 16; 'Dirty Warfare', *The Times,* 14 November 1984, p. 13.

35. Rosser-Owen, 'NBC Warfare', p. 82, Harris and Paxman, *Higher Form of Killing*, Seagrave, *Yellow Rain*, for use of chemical in Vietnam, Laos, Afghanistan.

36. 'US Accuses Iraq of Chemical Warfare' and 'Chemicals Test on Iranian's Body', *Times*, 6 March 1984, pp. 1 and 6; 'Pandora's Poison Box' and 'Baghdad's Deadly Secret', *Observer*, 11 March 1984, pp. 10 and 11, nerve gas plant in the latter; 'Nerve Gas: the Evidence on the Iraqi Battlefield' and 'Why the Iraqis went into Chemical Warfare', *Sunday Times*, 11 March 1984, pp. 1 and 3; 'Poison Spreading from Iraq', *Times*, 12 March 1984; 'Evidence Mounts of Chemical Weapons use by Iraqis', *Financial Times*, 13 March 1984.

37. 'Iran warns Iraq of Chemical Retaliation', *Times*, 24 March 1984, p. 1; 'Iran Hints at Chemical Retaliation', *Daily Telegraph*, 24 March, 1984, p. 36. For the continuing saga see 'Baghdad "plans big nerve gas offensive"', *Guardian*, 31 March 1984, p. 1; 'Chemical Ban on Iran', *Daily Telegraph*, 31 March 1984, p. 34. The latter denies reports that there might be plans to bomb Iran's gas plants. 14-16 countries: 'World rise in chemical weapons', *Times*, 21 May 1984, p. 5.

38. BZ: SIPRI, *The Problem of Chemical and Biological Warfare*, pp. 46-47, 304-5; on toxins, Seagrave, *Yellow Rain*, pp. 174-89, Rosser-Owen, 'NBC Warfare', p. 86; Harris and Paxman, *Higher Form of Killing*, pp. 186-90.

39. Miksche, *Atomic Weapons*, pp. 132, 140-1.

4

The Operational Art of Major Land Powers

For centuries it was adequate to use the term 'strategy' for broad questions affecting the conduct of war in general and the way armies manoeuvered before actually meeting. 'Tactics' described the way a battle was fought when two armies actually met. The creation of mass armies and the industrial revolution of the nineteenth century, which vastly extended the range of weapons and means of transport, gave rise to battles of great spatial scope and long duration. Whilst the operations of such armies were not 'strategic', in that their objectives were purely military and directly aimed at the defeat of the other in battle, they were clearly more than tactical. The term 'grand tactics' was sometimes used to describe the intermediate level that had arisen, but during the Great European War of 1914-18 the Germans began to use the term 'operativ' — operational. This was subsequently adopted by the Soviets (from the late 1920s), the Israelis and, recently, the Americans and British.[1] This book concentrates primarily on the operational level of war.

SOVIET UNION AND WARSAW PACT

All Warsaw Pact armies practise Soviet military art, and control at the operational level is firmly vested in Soviet officers. Henceforward, the term Soviet can be taken as referring equally to other Warsaw Pact countries, although some of the latter, especially Czechoslovakia, Poland and East Germany, are evolving a certain indigenous style at tactical level and indigenous variants of equipment. This trend may become more apparent in the next quarter century. However, the master plan for fighting a future European war is unequivocally Soviet, and is a development of the concept of a swift, violent and immane offensive evolved by Sokolovskiy and Sidorenko in the nuclear context. Savkin's *Basic Principles of Operational Art and Tactics* (1972) represents a slight shift away from the predominantly nuclear vision of future war, and is in any case sufficiently universal to apply equally to a war in which new and potent conventional weapons only are employed. Since then the trend has continued, although the fact that the 1984 edition of Reznichenko's *Tactics*, first published in 1966, evinces few changes indicates that the Soviet view of the battlefield is not quintessentially different when nuclear weapons are not used. That said, Soviet military art as it evolved between 1978 and 1982 under the auspices of the far-sighted and talented Marshal Ogarkov now clearly plans to fight and win a war in Europe without nuclear weapons if at all possible. In a recent key work, the influential commentator Gareyev made a surprisingly sharp criticism of Sokolovskiy, saying that not all his propositions had survived the test of the last 20 years.

The Soviets have a new concept of a Theatre of War (TV) which embraces a large section of the earth's surface, oceanic and continental, and comprises a number of TVDs. This has been translated as Theatre of Military Operations (TMO) but some prefer Theatre of Strategic Military Action (TSMA). The latter transmits the same idea as TVD does to a Russian: it is a region identified for military action on a *strategic* scale. Interestingly, Soviet analysis of NATO concepts of operations refers to the European Theatre of War (TV) and to the three NATO commands, AFNORTH, AFCENT and AFSOUTH, as TVDs. In the immediate post-war period Soviet thinking centred on a single Western TVD divided into two 'strategic directions', and this has led to the Soviet defector now working as an analyst calling himself Viktor Suvorov to assert that this is still the framework for Soviet operations, but he is almost certainly out of date. Soviet TVDs in Europe are probably as shown in Figure 4.1. The Western TVD (TSMA) is probably divided into three strategic directions, two swinging north towards Denmark and to Britain via the Low Countries and the third across France into Iberia. The western TV is probably just a geographical expression. In the Far East, the TV and TVD are one, because of its remoteness from Moscow. In the west, control over the TVDs is probably exercised directly from the Stavka of

Figure 4.1: Soviet theatres of war (TV) and theatres of military operations (TVD)

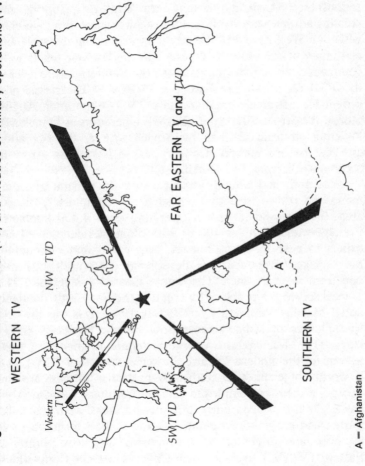

WESTERN TV

NW TVD

Western TVD

KM

800

SW TVD

FAR EASTERN TV and TVD

SOUTHERN TV

A

A — Afghanistan

the Supreme High Command in Moscow. Marshal Ogarkov was probably appointed to command the Western TVD after quitting his post as Chief of the General Staff, one of the three commanders in the Western TV.[2]

There has been much argument in the West about precise terminology, translation problems and the boundaries of TVDs. Suffice it to say that the Soviets have demonstrated great seriousness and vitality in long-term strategic planning, and creating a framework for it and for technological developments, while the West has had difficulty comprehending the scale and continuity of the process. Whereas in the last war fronts were commanded by the Stavka, there is now an intermediate level — the TVD or, in the Far East, the TV/TVD. The classic precedent for a strategic operation in a TVD is operation August Storm, the Soviet Strategic Offensive Operation in Manchuria. Styled a strategic Cannae by Soviet writers, the operation crushed the one million strong Japanese Kwantung Army in about a week, from 9 to 16 August 1945.

Geography had a major impact on the Soviet strategic command and control structure. In such a geographically diverse area, the three Soviet fronts operating on a 4,400 kilometre frontage with objectives 400 to 900 kilometres deep could not expect to keep in direct contact. Major and minor mountain ranges, lakes, rivers, marshes, deserts and space itself separated one front from another. The whole theatre was remote. The Soviets solved the problem by creating the Far East Command under Marshal Vasilevskiy on 30 July 1945. This was the first true Theatre of Military Operations, as the Soviets acknowledge. The Manchurian operation contains many cardinal lessons for the modern Theatre Strategic Operation (TSO), and is worthy of exhaustive study. Of particular interest are the deception measures employed and the resultant surprise at all levels, the use of apparently difficult and therefore unexpected routes, and imaginative operational and tactical techniques.[3] It has even more direct lessons for a possible offensive in the Far Eastern TV/TVD, against North China. The three fronts which might be employed bear the same names as those of 1945, the Transbaikal front assaulting the Beijing Military region, the 2 Far Eastern attacking the northern Shenyang Military region, and the 1 Far Eastern, the Eastern Shenyang (see the reorganisation of China's military regions below).[4]

The evolution of Soviet military geographical concepts is

Figure 4.2: August storm: the Soviet strategic offensive in Manchuria, August 1945. The prototype theatre strategic operation

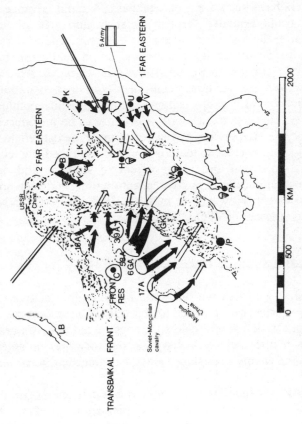

For simplicity, only component armies of Transbaikal front are shown in full, plus 5 army mentioned in the text. Dark arrows indicate advance by Soviet forces to 14 August: light arrows indicate subsequent advances. Parachutes indicate main airborne landings.
B – Blagoveshchensk; C – Choybalsan (Mongolia). GA – Guards Army; GK – Grand Khingan range; H – Harbin; K – Khabarovsk; L – Lesozavodsk; LB – Lake Baikal; LK – Lesser Khingan range; M – Mukden; P – Peking (Beijing); PA – Port Arthur; U – Ussuriysk; V – Vladivostok

clearly linked with, and a prerequisite for, that of strategic and operational command and control. In the past it could perhaps be said that the Soviets had C^2I — Command, Control and Intelligence, rather than C^3I (see Chapter 7), the weak link being communications. The lack of automated data links in the civilian network has reduced the back-up available to Soviet military communications as well as making them more easily identifiable. Digital switching technology and links between computers have been areas of weakness. A rapid advance into Europe could flounder through isolation and lack of information after the loss of relatively few communications links. At present the Soviet strategic command structure has 36 to 40 satellites in circular orbit, plus others in elliptical orbit with apogees over the western hemisphere and in geo-stationary orbit, and 26 VLF radio stations. A new satellite communications system — *potok* (flood) — is likely to be introduced in the late 1980s. Expanding Soviet concepts of the battlefield and emphasis on increased tempos will be followed by corresponding expansion and improvement of strategic and operational communications, increased automation and high-speed data processing. However, it may be 1990 before the Soviets can match present NATO C^3I systems.[5]

The Theatre Strategic Operation (TSO)

> The strategic offensive operation is the main, decisive form of strategic action by armed forces; only as a result of this is it possible to defeat strategic groupings of the enemy's armed forces in the theatre, occupy his territory and completely break the enemy's resistance and guarantee victory.'[6]

Whereas a normal Front (Army Group) pattern of operation, based on Great Patriotic War experience, might be a 600 kilometre advance in 12 days, a six-day pause, and then another 600 kilometres in 12 days, a TSO might aim to cover the full 1,200 kilometres in 22 days maximum, without pausing. The Soviets seem to be committed to a violent and total struggle of unprecedented scope. '*Regardless of the way it starts*, both sides would deploy multimillioned armed forces and mobilise all their economic and moral forces.'[7] This recalls the Schlieffen Plan which by its structure led the Germans to attack France even though from a political viewpoint they could conceivably have confined the war to the eastern theatre. Similarly, the internal dynamics of military art would today induce the Soviets to conduct a gigantic operation whose scope and violence possibly exceeded the political aim. Suppose their aim was a shallow envelopment inside West Germany, 300 kilometres deep, which would be sufficient to tip the economic and political balance of forces in Europe and the world in their favour. How could this be done without provoking a response from NATO which the Soviets might regret? If NATO responded as one, an operation conceived by the Soviets as limited, geographically, would swell to an undesirable level. In order to be sure of winning, the Soviets would have to attack to a depth far greater than the 300 kilometre wide strip of West Germany, attacking British territory and American carrier battle groups far out in the Atlantic. This reflects Clausewitz's understanding of the dialectic of war tending to extremes, and has a clear precedent in the Great War when the requirements imposed by battle actually exceeded the efforts justified by the political aims of the protagonists. As a result, in some countries political collapse preceded actual military defeat. Similarly, the Soviets would regard any element of moderation as a threat to the success of their operation. 'To introduce the principle of moderation into the theory of war itself would always lead to logical absurdity', as Clausewitz observed.[8] The principle of moderation has been introduced in practice in war, many times, in 'limited wars'. Might the Soviets conceive of a limited war in Europe? And might NATO concur? The thrust of Soviet military writing suggests, however, that in a campaign in the western TV or TVD the principle of moderation would be difficult to apply, except possibly at the conventional nuclear threshold.

On the basis of the dynamics of military operations, it would seem that even if Warsaw Pact ground forces were only required to execute a shallow envelopment inside West Germany, at least as a first strategic objective, the campaign would nevertheless be conceived as a TSO. Within the TVD, a TSO would comprise four overlapping strategic operations:

— an air operation
— an anti-air operation
— a theatre land (ground forces with air support) operation
— a naval or coastal operation

111

Each of these operations would involve the integration of all types of weapons, including artillery, missiles, air and electronic warfare. Broadly, the air operation seeks to degrade enemy air defence and close support aircraft, the anti-air operation to create conditions favourable to the movement of Warsaw Pact aircraft and ground forces. Both of these therefore contribute to the success of the theatre land operation. The latter might comprise three or four fronts within the TVD. The theatre land operation naturally includes a critical air component. Close air support is given by army aviation with helicopters at division and army level (each ground forces division has an organic helicopter squadron and an army a unit of regimental size), and fixed-wing aircraft such as the specialised Frogfoot ground attack plane at army and front.[9] The current and evolving Soviet concept of operations is therefore very much an air-land battle, as is the American. It must be emphasised that the discussion of these ideas in the open military press does not mean that the Russians could do it next month, or next year. These are concepts for the 1990s and beyond, and they are therefore very much *the future of air-land warfare*, rather than the present.

The Theatre Land Operation

As seen in Chapter 3, the nature of the theatre land operation is conditioned by the possible use and threat of nuclear weapons. The whole thing takes place in a 'nuclear scared' posture. Partly to prevent nuclear use, the Soviets would aim:

— To destroy or neutralise as many NATO air and nuclear assets as possible.
— To keep attacking forces as dispersed as possible.
— To make a number of penetrations so as to confuse the enemy as to the direction of the main thrust.
— Especially in nuclear conditions, to induce the enemy to strike dummy formations rather than real ones.
— To get their own forces as close as possible to NATO's and centres of population, so as to discourage the use of nuclear weapons.
— To paralyse NATO's ability to make the political decision to use nuclear weapons by striking deep, particularly at political targets.

All these require the Soviets to shift the centre of gravity of operations to NATO's operational depth as quickly as possible. By 'operational depth', we understand the entire depth of West Germany, at least. This has meant the resuscitation of the 'deep operation', first mooted in the 1930s and itself based on the earlier Soviet scheme of consecutive operations. Like all Soviet operational concepts, the deep operation has a microcosm at the tactical level: the deep battle (*glubokiy boy*).

The Operational Manoeuvre Group (Operativnaya manevrennaya gruppa) (OMG)

This aspect of the new Soviet concept attracted much attention in the early 1980s although it is important to see it as part of the overall picture. The OMG is nothing new: the Soviets acknowledge explicitly that it is based on the Great Patriotic War forward detachment and mobile group, and the action of cavalry armies in the Russian civil war 1917-22. There are also parallels with Imperial Russian practice.[10] In the immediate postwar period the Soviets envisaged launching front mobile groups consisting of mechanised armies after the enemy's tactical zone (then only 8 to 12 kilometres wide) had been broken, that is, they reckoned, on the morning of the second day of operations. The mobile group would be heavily reinforced, especially with engineer assets, and would rapidly be severed from the main forces. When the term OMG appeared in the Polish military press in 1982, therefore, nobody should have been surprised. The modern term OMG was initially identified from the Polish, but it is clearly a Soviet idea. A Soviet army might launch a division-sized OMG and a front possibly a larger ('corps') sized OMG. An OMG breakthrough is shown schematically in Figure 4.3 and 4.4. However, the difficulties of pushing a whole division through a NATO defence, if not an Iranian, Pakistani or Chinese one, and of controlling it in the enemy depth are obvious enough. A front OMG might therefore differ from a division's in function rather than in size. An army OMG might operate up to 70 kilometres ahead of the main body of the army and a front OMG, 150 kilometres or more ahead (see Figure 4.5). The OMG is not the same as the familiar second echelon, but it may have replaced it in some circumstances for two reasons. Firstly, in order to ensure that an

113

OMG breaks through, a strong first echelon is needed. If the penetration is carried out successfully, the enemy defence will be thrown off balance and there is no need for a second echelon. Secondly, much NATO thinking in recent years has sought to defeat a Soviet attack by striking with long-range weapons at the Soviet second echelon as it is moving up behind the first. The Soviets now know this. If the OMG passes quickly through the first echelon, the NATO forces' deep battle will be conducted against thin air. It must be stressed, however, that there is no standard organisation for armies and fronts; within them there could be any combination of OMGs, echelons and special reserves. Nor is the OMG concept completely accepted within the Warsaw Pact. Some Polish officers pointed out that in the last war the technical differentiation of different formations and units made it appropriate to use the rare fully mechanised formations to manoeuvre ahead of the main body, but that now all formations have much the same ability to manoeuvre. The introduction of helicopters and air assault brigades has however perhaps created a situation analogous to that in the war, forming a discrete super-mobile element. The same officer also criticised the tendency to 'write in' OMGs into the plan for every operation, without analysing whether it was really needed, as a sort of 'operational fashion'.[11]

The OMG concept must be constantly developing, and the vision of a reinforced armoured brigade or division being 'shot' through a hole in the defence like the super-hard penetrator of an armour-piercing round and advancing in one lump with a major-general at its head may be naive and oversimplified to the point of absurdity. The OMG would almost certainly only coalesce within the enemy depth, both for practical logistic reasons and also for concealment. Now that all Soviet forces are mechanised and have the potential to act as 'mobile groups', OMG components would be indistinguishable from those of surrounding formations, except perhaps for the presence of long-range communications systems (which would be switched off at this stage anyway). The best way of hiding an elephant is in a herd of trumpeting elephants and telling it to keep quiet. Figure 4.3 endeavours to show the subtle and insidious process of coalescence. It might not be controlled by one man in its van at all, but perhaps by the commander of the rear services of the army or front, who would be able to direct supplies and resources from a vantage-point in the rear. It is a variant of

Figure 4.3: Coalescence of Operational Manoeuvre Group
(OMG): illustrative

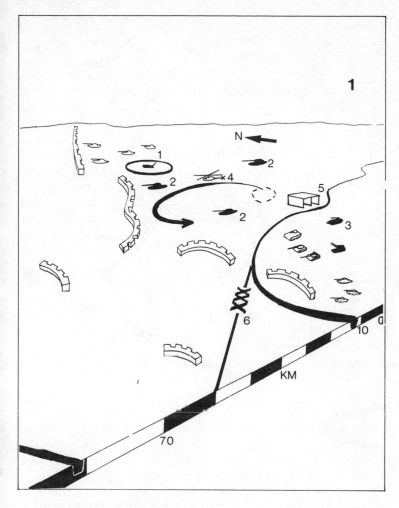

Frame 1 1. Special heavy artillery, exemplified by 240mm SP mortar, showing
range as circle
2. Tank regiments
3. Motor Rifle regiment (in a different division)
4. Assault helicopter squadron and supply helicopters
5. Special engineer elements; bridging and obstacle crossing
6. NATO Corps boundary

115

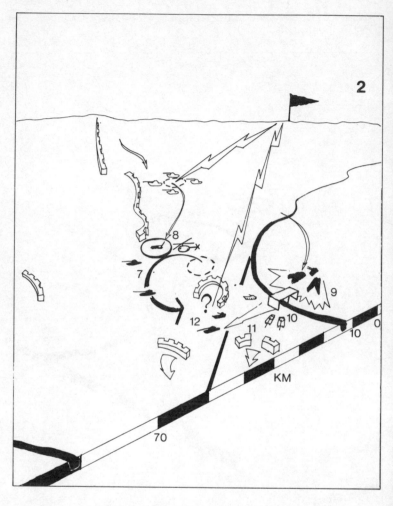

Frame 2 7. Two tank regiments aided by assault helicopters penetrate weak
            spot between formations in northern corps
         8. Heavy artillery moves on orders of OMG commander in the rear
         9. Soviet forces effect major breakthrough in southern corps
        10. Bridging unit moves up to push forces over river line
        11. Southern corps begins to withdraw
        12. One tank and one motor rifle regiment move through on rear
            commander's orders into flank of nothern corps

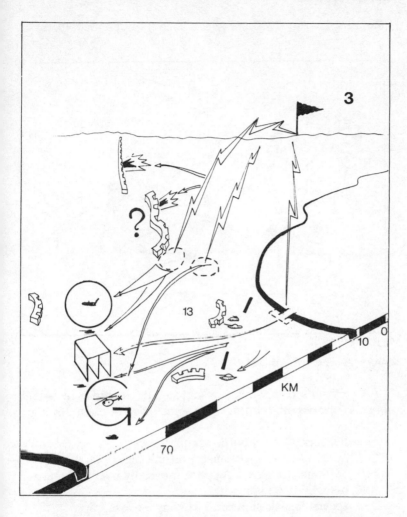

Frame 3 13. Two surviving tank regiments and one motor rifle, special artillery, engineers and helicopters coalesce on rear commander's orders to form OMG. To the north, surviving NATO units continue battle against main forces.

Napoleon's concentration of forces on the actual field of battle, but subtler: a concentration of forces within the body of the opponent, recalling oriental practice. It would require sophisticated tactical and operational communications and a high degree of reliance on the subordinate unit commanders, and is more a thing of the future than of the present.

117

Figure 4.4: Army OMG after severance from the main forces

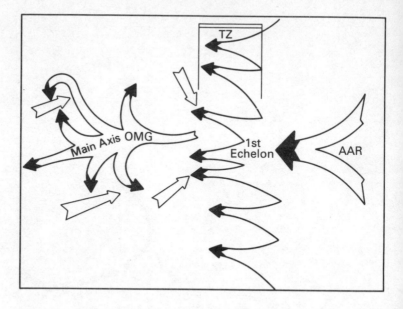

AAR — Soviet all-arms reserves

An OMG's components would equate to those of a tank brigade or division, reinforced by some or all of the following:

— helicopter or heliborne assault forces
— an air element (presumably assault helicopters)
— additional engineer support, especially river crossing and demolition equipment
— special logistic support, including air resupply
— additional air defence assets.

The dominance of air elements reinforces the analogy with the more than usually mobile forward detachments and mobile groups of the last war. The airmobile and air assault brigades which have recently been deployed would probably support OMGs. These are probably held at front or TVD level, and give those commanders the ability to strike at targets 20 to 100 kilometres deep without having to call on the Guards airborne divisions, who may be required for strategic tasks. The air-mobile brigades were founded in the early 1970s, are lightly

Figure 4.5: Two front OMGs converging on a major population centre

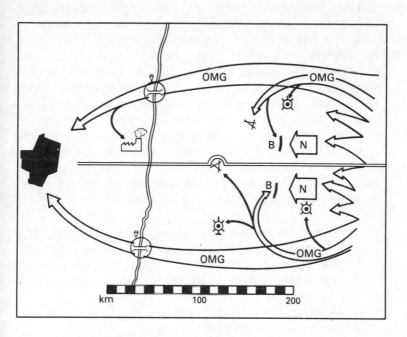

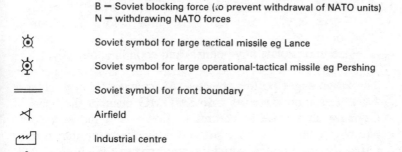

Army OMGs move to objectives closer to Soviet main forces
B — Soviet blocking force (to prevent withdrawal of NATO units)
N — withdrawing NATO forces

☒   Soviet symbol for large tactical missile eg Lance

☒   Soviet symbol for large operational-tactical missile eg Pershing

═══   Soviet symbol for front boundary

✑   Airfield

⌐   Industrial centre

⚲   Objective captured by airborne forces

equipped, comprise 1,700-1,850 men, and are based away from the central front facing NATO. They are clearly intended for use against, perhaps, Turkey, Iran, Pakistan or China. The air assault brigades are larger (over 2,000 men) and more heavily equipped. These are suitable for deep operations on the European battlefield. One air assault brigade has been deployed in Afghanistan since 1980, and has apparently seen extensive combat.[12]

There has been debate about whether the heliborne forces and fighter helicopters should be incorporated into the OMGs and move with them, or fly missions from the main deployment. An obvious compromise would be to start from the main deployment but land in the middle of the OMG and operate from there. It would be in the Soviets' interest to keep the OMG and supporting elements separated for as long as possible, and for it to coalesce inside the enemy defensive zone, so the air element would certainly move independently for much of the time.

An OMG would be given broad directives but the way these were carried out would be left to the discretion of the commander. The OMG would move fast and far into the enemy depth and might:

— destroy, disrupt or capture enemy nuclear weapons, HQs, airfields, Command Control and Communications (C^3) installations, logistic support and the lateral communications needed to move NATO troops to counter a Soviet breakthrough
— destroy enemy reserves in meeting engagements
— prevent withdrawal of NATO units
— pursue withdrawing NATO units in parallel and destroy them,
— seize NATO rear defensive lines before they can be occupied
— seize or isolate key political and economic objectives.

The latter might be the objective of front OMGs (see Figure 4.4.). The appearance of a Soviet OMG deep in the heart of Germany and close to centres of power and industry could paralyse political will to resist and convince some that further resistance was futile. It could fragment parts of the NATO Alliance. Strictly speaking, a manoeuvre group launched with this prime aim would be strategic rather than operational. A good precedent for this is Sherman's march through Georgia in 1864. One suitable objective might be the Liège-Arnhem road network. If seized with a force strong enough to hold for a few days, up to four divisions, possibly less, that would completely frustrate NATO reinforcement.

The most delicate and sensitive phase is the committal of the

OMG through the window of opportunity. Warsaw Pact authorities openly acknowledge that OMGs would be regularly exposed to counter attack and that OMGs and raiding detachments require more support and protection than those in the first or main echelon. In the Great Patriotic War, as much as 70 per cent of frontal aviation was allocated to support of mobile groups being inserted, and a modern OMG might have a similar amount of air and artillery support.[13] Modern Soviet front artillery has the range to support the OMG through its passage across the main defensive zone, while the OMG itself would solve the target acquisition problem. This would be supplemented by the activities of air assault brigades and independent battalions (see below). Before being committed, the main landbound elements of an OMG would probably be held in concentration areas 30 to 50 kilometres behind the forward Soviet troops. Every possible deception measure would be employed. Given that the OMG would be inserted on the first or second day of hostilities, if the TSO went well, the deception would not have to be kept up for that long. With the general confusion occurring on the outbreak of European hostilities and the massive air operation which would swamp NATO air assets, it is possible that an OMG might not be detected until too late to prevent its insertion. Against Iran, Pakistan or China the Soviets would enjoy an enormous advantage in space, the air and in electronic warfare, and they might hope completely to mask the operation unless American surveillance warned the intended victims.

Soviet principles of operational art and tactics

In 1979 the Soviet Army newspaper *Red Star* published an important exchange of correspondence on the question of whether military art was lagging behind the development of its material-based technology. A number of Western analysts have posed the same questions, alleging that military men are envisaging the employment of new weapons within World War II-type operations. This is an oversimplification; as the Russian debate concluded, for example, the principle of *aktivnost'* — drive, activity, aggression in combat — had often been in evidence during the Great Patriotic War. Modern weapons and platforms gave units increased opportunities for *aktivnost'*, by increasing the depth of strikes inflicted on the enemy simultaneously, and in swift manoeuvres by troops not only on the ground but in the air, a reference to the importance of helicopters in facilitating greater *aktivnost'*. They also allowed swifter transition from one kind of combat to another, an increase in the pace of troops' advance, the continuity and power of fire effect on the enemy. The principle of concentrating main efforts was only the same in form; in practice, instead of concentrating masses of tanks and guns in a very narrow area, as in the war, such concentration now had to be achieved by using the greater manoeuvring power and range of modern units and weapons. Similarly, the principle of co-operation between different arms had to be applied in an environment where the intensity of the struggle on the ground and in the air, for seizing and maintaining initiative, for achieving fire superiority and the spatial limits of the battle, were all increasing. The amount of work imposed on headquarters was therefore growing while the time in which to do it was reducing. The availability of computers and data processing might compensate for this. Lastly, there was the principle of surprise. In modern conditions the opportunity for inflicting unexpected and swift strikes had grown. Helicopters particularly had given units greater mobility and thus greater opportunity to carry out swift moves and concentrate their efforts in order to inflict sudden attacks on the enemy from any direction, from ground or air, front, flanks or rear. A surprise air *desant* was especially effective in intensifying the effect of a similarly unexpected frontal attack. As Vorob'ëv pointed out, these principles are of little importance in themselves: their significance lay in commanders' ability to put them into practice.

The Soviets have stated categorically that the lessons of the Great Patriotic War are now of renewed importance: that the former 'nihilistic attitude' to past experience should be deprecated; that modern weapons of greatly increased accuracy which may have effects analogous to small nuclear weapons have helped alter the nature of war; and that one cannot count on a future war being short. It may be long and bitter as never before. Because changes may occur more rapidly, there must be less reliance on the flawless execution of plans made in advance and more on 'operational questions'; being able to respond to changed circumstances quickly. Penetration of forces to a great depth presents many problems. Breaking through a defence saturated with anti-tank weapons, organising reliable fire destruction of the enemy, especially armoured targets, and the co-ordinated use of airborne desants, forward detachments and the vigorous exploitation of success, and defeating 'reconnaissance-destruction complexes' (see Chapter 7) were identified as the main ones in 1985. Particular attention was focused on the difficulty or carrying out encirclements. Soviet forces possess much greater manoeuvrability than before, but so do their potential opponents who will have correspondingly greater potential for 'organising shock groups' and breaking out of encirclement. Against this, modern forces are more dependent than ever on fuel and resupply, and on roads, and this may paralyse encircled forces, perhaps to a greater extent than the enveloping force. Finally, it is stressed that forces will not move consecutively from one bound to the next, but that there will be a determined, simultaneous attack on the enemy throughout his entire depth.[14] These Soviet views are not only of interest as those of a potential 'threat', but as perceptive insights into the nature of future war generally.

In 1981 the Soviets conducted exercise 'Zapad (west)-81', which clearly marked the end of a period when new ideas had been tested. It did not apparently include the simulated employment of nuclear weapons, although the threat of their use was a constant influence on the conduct of operations. 'Mobile groups', airborne, airmobile and amphibious forces all helped project the centre of gravity of combat into the enemy rear in order to prevent lateral reinforcement, while the Soviets strove to concentrate their own forces swiftly. It is confirmed that Zapad-81 also involved air, anti-air and naval operations. In other words, it played out the new Soviet Theatre Strategic Operation, with its four component 'strategic operations'.

Conclusion

Nothing said above indicates that the Soviet Union is planning to start an offensive war now or in the foreseeable future. However, if war breaks out or if she perceives that someone else is about to start one, then she plans to win it, win it quickly, and begin with surprise and initiative on her side. Whether those plans would succeed against NATO or China is debatable: traditionally, Russian and Soviet forces, while having a splendid

123

military tradition, have tended to perform less well than their physical toughness, equipment and formidable military theory would suggest. On balance, the risks of failure would seem to be too great to make military action an attractive option. In the case of Iran or Pakistan, the situation may be rather different. Within the Soviets' new concept, there are also many unquantifiables: would the OMG really work in practice? It has worked in the past, though it has had far from a smooth ride. At least it must force those who persist in the delusion that the Russians are solid and unimaginative to revise their views: it is a daring and audacious concept. The Soviet visions of the air-land battle and deep attack are also remarkably sophisticated, and have many similarities with the American. The Warsaw Pact enjoys commonality of operational thinking, horizontally, since all Warsaw Pact states practise Soviet military art, and vertically, since the same principles apply at all levels. Although Soviet tactics are less flexible than some Soviet commanders would wish, this reliance on Standard Operating Procedures (SOPs) and drills at the tactical level paradoxically gives Soviet operational commanders more flexibility in switching their main effort from one axis to another and in moving large formations swiftly over large distances, a function of Russian and Soviet geography and military experience.

NATO JOINT (COMBINED) DOCTRINE

The Warsaw Pact enjoys commonality of strategic, operational and tactical thinking. NATO, its most formidable if not, therefore, its most likely potential opponent, does not, although an embryonic framework of common tactical principles now exists and unified operational level plans are taking shape. The divisions of responsibility for defence of the key central front area are shown in Figure 4.6 and the peacetime locations of the various corps in Figure 4.7. Co-operation between NATO's different nations depends on a *combined* doctrine, in American English. In British English, *combined* usually refers to the interoperability of different arms and services and *joint* is normally used to refer to international activity. NATO defines doctrine as fundamental principles by which the military forces guide their actions in support of objectives.'[15] Doctrine is authoritative but requires judgement in application. In setting broad guidelines,

Figure 4.6: Corps divisions of responsibility on NATO's Central Front

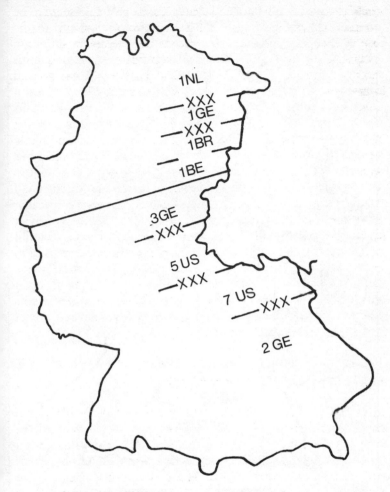

BE = Belgium; BR = British; GE = West German; NL = Netherlands; US = United States

what NATO calls doctrine is not, therefore, dissimilar to Soviet *doktrina*. However, it also lays down principles for the execution of what the Soviets would call military art. The unified NATO doctrine is set out in *Allied Tactical Publication (ATP)- 35(A)*, covering land operations and associated air support. The original *ATP-35* appeared in 1976, but a substantial review was completed by the beginning of 1983 and the resulting document

125

Figure 4.7: Peacetime deployment of NATO corps in Germany

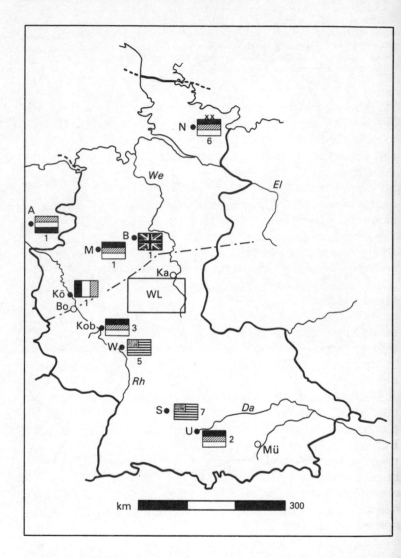

A — Apeldoorn (1 Dutch corps); B — Bielefeld (1 British corps); Bo — Bonn; *Da* — River Danube; *El* — River Elbe; Ka — Kassel; Kö — Köln (1 Belgian corps); Kob — Koblenz (3 West German corps); M — Munster (1 West German corps); Mü — München; N — Neumunster (Detached division); *Rh* — River Rhine; S — Stuttgart (7 US corps); W — Wiesbaden (5 US corps); *We* — River Weser; WL — approximately the area where exercise Wehrhafte Löwen took place; Dotted line — approximate boundary between NORTHAG and CENTAG

IMPORTANT: There is considerable speculation about the deployment of a third US Corps into NORTHAG in time of transition to war or war. Such a corps could well be deployed, but it is likely to be part of the Rapid Deployment Force and could equally be elsewhere. It would be deployed at the discretion of the US. If deployed into NORTHAG, it would form a valuable blocking force behind the forward corps. It is also likely that the French would put a corps into CENTAG, giving added depth there in a similar way.

ATP-35(A) may be regarded as a completely new publication. *ATP-35(A)* is declaredly a tactical doctrine but it explicitly aims to define doctrine for combined arms operations at brigade level and above and therefore deals with what the West Germans and Americans call the operational level. The publication itself does not acknowledge the existence of the third dimension of war.

It is of course understood that the land force doctrine of any nation may go beyond and expand on *ATP-35(A)*. However, the latter stresses that this must not lead to a decrease in the ability of their land forces to work effectively together. In addition to providing a common doctrine and vocabulary, *ATP-35(A)* aims to facilitate the identification of areas where additional standardisation is required. This is most important since, as *ATP-35(A)* points out, in the event of an attack, formations of different NATO nations will deploy alongside or pass through one another's area of responsibility or even be grouped in multinational formations.[16] Whilst the present peacetime deployments of NATO formations appear unlikely to change, *ATP-35(A)* is designed to facilitate changes which may well take place in the next quarter century. There is of course a precedent for a multinational formation in the Allied Command Europe (ACE) Mobile Force (Land) (AMF)(L). This comprises forces from seven NATO countries and is of reinforced brigade strength (see below). The main problem with interoperability will remain, however, on the boundaries of different nations' formations and in their perception of the whole operational-level battle.

ATP-35(A) regards manoeuvre as a key principle of defence. It is the decisive element at all levels. At the tactical level, defending forces make the best use of terrain assigned to them in order to concentrate combat power and inflict maximum losses on the enemy.[17] The same would apply at the operational level. *ATP-35(A)* also stresses that the effectiveness of defence is based primarily on the carefully planned fire of all weapons. The fire of manoeuvre forces, conventional and

127

nuclear artillery, armed helicopter support and that of tactical air forces must be complementary, carefully co-ordinated and brought to bear with the maximum effect at the right time and place. This is in fact similar to the Soviet view of Integrated Fire Destruction. Most importantly, *ATP-35(A)* insists that whilst the initiative is generally with the attacking force, the defender must not remain passive and wait to react. He must seize and create any opportunity to surprise the enemy and force him to part from his plans. At every level, the defender must take offensive action to harass the enemy. The defensive battle should therefore be fought with 'imagination, energy and aggressive spirit and with the aim to seize the initiative wherever and whenever possible'.[18] It is recognised that where the majority of the force available is armoured the defence can be conducted with greater flexibility and full use can be made of mobility. In this context, airmobile operations are particularly important. These are defined as operations where combat forces and their equipment move about the battlefield in air vehicles, normally helicopters, under the control of a ground force commander. An airmobile force can attack from any direction, striking objectives in otherwise inaccessible areas, overflying barriers, bypassing enemy positions, and thus achieve surprise. Airmobile forces can permit quick concentration of combat power at key places, and rapid dispersal to reduce vulnerability. They give the commander the ability to reinforce or relieve his forces quickly and over long distances and possibly enabling him to commit a larger part of his force than would otherwise be prudent, relying on a small airmobile reserve. Finally, they enable operations to be conducted independently of a ground line of communications (but they are not completely independent of terrain — see Chapter 1). *ATP-35(A)*'s emphasis on the aggressive energetic and elastic defence reflects the Iraqi conduct of defence at the operational level (see also Chapter 1), and Clausewitz's graphic description of the defence as 'a shield made up of well-directed blows'.[19]

ATP-35(A) recognises that any use of nuclear weapons represents a qualitative change in the nature of warfare. In this, it differs rather from Soviet doctrine which still tends to regard nuclear weapons as extremely powerful and efficient artillery shells. Use of nuclear weapons will, in *ATP-35(A)*'s admission, entail grave political, military and psychological consequences. If released, nuclear weapons will become the most important factor in operational plans. *ATP-35(A)* does not represent any change to national policies on the storage and employment of such weapons and, after acknowledging their importance, concentrates primarily on conventional operations.[20]

The Northern Army Group concept of operations and the counterstroke

During the second half of 1984, various European defence planning groups questioned the wisdom of the doctrine of follow on forces' attack and the relevance of emerging technology to meeting defence needs. In the second half increased emphasis was placed on the conventional option, the ability to sustain forces over a prolonged conflict (see Chapter 8), while FOFA was accepted as a long-term planning framework. These developments placed renewed emphasis on medical support, fuel, spares and readily usable reserves. It was admitted that reserves would have to be manoeuvered across corps boundaries, and thus national boundaries of responsibility, and by early 1985 it was admitted that a Northern Army Group concept of operations was being produced. The NORTHAG concept is designed to enable the defenders to seize the initiative from the attacker at the operational level. NORTHAG's commander, a Briton, would control a counter-stroke (see below) using reserves from the national formations under his command. Such a manoeuvre might be accomplished by a formation up to a full corps in size. Because reserves are obviously limited, the stroke would have to be accomplished with meticulous timing and accuracy, calculating precisely how much was needed to hold off the enemy at other points in order to allow maximum strength for the counter-move. Automated C^3I (see Chapter 7) would therefore be crucial to the successful accomplishment of this bold and large-scale operational counterblow.[21]

Alternative operational art

There have been a number of proposals for a unified NATO strategy which differ from the 'shield of blows' of *ATP-35(A)*. A purely defensive posture which eschews all offensive means in order not to appear provocative would theoretically be ideal for NATO, but in practical military terms the difficulties appear insuperable. One of the most radical ideas is that of the West German analyst Horst Afheldt, who would abandon tanks and, presumably, other mechanised vehicles, on the grounds that armies structured around armour are inherently offensive in configuration and are therefore destabilising. He would cover West Germany with a network of small units (about three or four men per square kilometre), causing a Warsaw Pact offensive to strike, apparently, at air, and then wear it down by slow attrition. This concept of a sea into which the enemy will sink may have some validity in circumstances like that of China, where there is vastly more space and people's lifestyle and expectations are not as advanced and therefore vulnerable to dislocation. Such a system would be unable to prevent an attacker seizing the immense wealth of West Germany and other parts of Western Europe and, having forsaken all the most potent means of offensive action, would be unable to recover them. Such guerrilla campaigns have without exception required a shift to conventional military operations to defeat an invader (the Peninsula, Vietnam), although they have been a valuable adjunct to them, and no one has ever won a war by purely defensive means. A third universal truth is that it is always cheaper not to lose something than to recover it later: the particular position of West Germany (see below) makes that of particular relevance there. Other schemes have a similar overall objective — 'non-provocative defence'. The originators of the British-based scheme called 'Just Defence' have understandably resorted to a time-honoured method of defeating an attacker efficiently, the stronghold strengthened by all the ingenuity of modern technology, in an updated electronic Maginot Line. Behind a 4 kilometre-wide wall of mines and prelaid sensors and a 2 kilometre-wide strip patrolled by motorcyclists and infantry armed with anti-tank guided missiles, an array of technological novelties such as precision-guided artillery shells (see Chapter 5), waits to destroy the oncoming Warsaw Pact forces, portrayed as tanks and APCs, inert targets waiting to be picked off like space invaders. The view of the potential enemy perhaps fails to recognise that 'war is not the action of a living force upon a lifeless mass but always the collision of two living forces': it also perhaps underestimates the pulverising, paralysing action of the attacker's artillery.[22] The declared aim of the

Soviet artillery force is to smash and suppress the defender's dispositions, with a crushing hail of high explosive and steel which would be particularly deadly against the delicate sensors and other equipment upon which so much reliance is placed, as well as against unarmoured anti-tank weapons. Reliance on the latter is in part a reflection of the out-dated belief, resulting from Yom Kippur, that ATGW had eclipsed the tank: improvements to tank armour, the lessons of Lebanon in 1982 and the logic of combined arms operations have combined to restore much of the tank's primacy (see Chapter 5). In particular, the tank with its heavy armour remains the only weapons system which has some chance of being able to fight and move under massive suppressive artillery fire. Finally, with some exceptions, men need comradeship and group solidarity to enable them to endure the horrors and exertion of war. Dispersed, in small groups or alone, morale and effectiveness would rapidly decline, especially as the outcome and goals of their continued efforts would be unclear. As also argued in Chapter 8, remote sensors, fortifications and other ways of substituting technology for flesh and blood have a great deal to recommend them, but it is unrealistic to envisage them substituting for mobile (counter) attack forces almost totally. Similarly, lightly equipped forces have proved to be too vulnerable on the mechanised high-intensity battlefield: two of the countries with most experience of recent war, the Germans and the Israelis, are in no doubt about that (see below), and the Russians are convinced of the value of mechanised armour. The new defence concepts are useful, and in combination with more conventional (counter) attack forces could help reduce casualties and employ less well trained troops effectively. The 'alternative' defence concepts and time honoured experience of war are not alternatives: they must be combined intelligently.

THE UNITED STATES

The United States continues to face the conflicting and competing demands of preparing for conflict either in the major land theatre of Europe, or elsewhere in the world using more mobile power projection forces, or both. The army's 'major and most serious challenge' remains 'armoured, mechanised, combined arms battle', which would certainly characterise European

131

war and probably war in the Middle East and South Asia as well.[23] In Europe, the US Army has two corps stationed in Germany, both part of CENTAG (see Figure 4.7). V Corps is based at Wiesbaden and VII Corps at Stuttgart. It is often remarked that the two most technologically capable NATO corps — the two American — along with two of the three West German corps are based in CENTAG where a main Warsaw Pact thrust might not be directed. On the other hand, the shortest route to the Rhine and a major strategic objective, Frankfurt, lies through CENTAG. NATO's peacetime deployments are not necessarily immutable, and the Soviets themselves concentrate on the West Germans and Americans as principal potential land opponents.[24]

In a future major war the US Army would fight in accordance with the August 1982 version of *Field Manual (FM) 100-5*. There are many similarities between the latter and *ATP-35(A)*, although *FM 100-5* is a doctrine for worldwide application. The US Army is emphatic that where there is any potential inconsistency between the two for a European conflict, *FM 100-5* would be modified in accordance with the NATO doctrine.

The July 1976 edition of *FM 100-5* had taken to heart the lessons of the 1973 war and stressed the demands of the 'first battle of the next war' on a battlefield where the tempo of combat and destruction of material would exceed that of previous wars dramatically. It stressed better training, the use of terrain, fire suppression and all arms co-ordination to counter the increased lethality of 1970s weapons. Then in 1977 General Donn A. Starry took over command of the US Army's Training and Doctrine unit (TRADOC) at Fort Monroe, Virginia, and began a series of initiatives which led to the doctrine now enshrined in *FM 100-5*, known by the fused syllables of AirLand Battle. Starry was the main intellectual force behind AirLand Battle, significantly aided by his deputy Lieutenant-General William Richardson, and a number of other officers. In November 1978, a TRADOC planning document called the Battlefield Development Plan was issued, which analysed fundamental components of the central battle such as 'target servicing' (a phrase borrowed from mathematical queuing theory), suppression and counterfire and air defence. Simultaneously, a study called Division 86 examined the optimum organisation not only for heavy (European) divisions, but also

132

light divisions, corps and echelons above corps.

Army 86 increasingly began to explore the idea of a deeper battlefield or, as it was formally called from 1980, the extended battlefield. It became progressively more obvious that commanders would have to see deep into the enemy's rear to delay, disrupt and destroy enemy follow-on forces while simultaneously fighting those in contact. A brigade commander needed to influence events up to 15 kilometres in the enemy's rear, a divisional commander 70 and a corps commander up to 150 kilometres. 'Deep' also extended to the time dimension: not only was it no longer sufficient to react after the event, or even immediately in 'real-time'. Commanders had to see ahead in time: 12 hours for the brigade, 24 for the division, 72 for the corps. At the same time, the Soviet invasion of Afghanistan at the end of 1979 led to demands for a long-range power projection force. TRADOC's light division study of 1979 was modified by the February 1980 decision to form such a force after experiments carried out with the US 9th Infantry Division.

The idea of the 'extended' and 'integrated' battlefields were concisely summarised in the phrase AirLand Battle, formally announced in March 1981, and embodied in the September 1981 draft of the new *FM 100-5*, the final version of which was published in August 1982.[25] The most contentious element of the doctrine concerns the attack of enemy follow on forces (FOFA) and second echelons (if there are any). In Europe, because of the political constraints which would apply in a European war conducted under the constant threat of nuclear use, attack by manoeuvre forces against objectives east of the intra-German border is precluded. A revised version of *FM 100-5* is in draft at the time of writing this book, and will probably be disseminated in late 1986. It is understood to contain no doctrinal changes but aims to remove the scope for misunderstanding of US Army doctrine by the United States' NATO allies, which happened with the earlier versions. *FM 100-5* provides for three types of battle:

— the deep battle (against enemy follow-on forces)
— the close-in battle
— the battle in one's own rear against Soviet special purpose forces (*Spetsnaz*), OMGs, etc.

Whereas elsewhere in the world the US might employ

133

manoeuvre forces deep in the enemy rear, thus mirroring Soviet military art, they have said they would not do so where this would conflict with NATO doctrine. What would actually happen in a European war is left to the reader to judge. As noted in the section on Soviet military art, the emphasis on attacking the second echelon may be misplaced if Soviet forces are not configured that way. This has been criticised as a 'lemming like rush to find and destroy nonexistent second echelons while Soviet/Warsaw Pact front ranks tear through NATO territory', but that is an oversimplification.[26] Detailed computer studies have shown that interdiction of follow-on forces, whether a true 'second echelon' or something else, combined with the contact battle should substantially reduce the Warsaw Pact's rate of advance (Figures 4.8 and 4.9). Nevertheless, common sense says that *in extremis* one must worry about the immediate threat first. Critics of the doctrine from a purely military viewpoint also point out that it depends too much on

Figure 4.8: Advance of Warsaw Pact forces on a piece of German territory, without interdiction (US computer modelling, 1982)

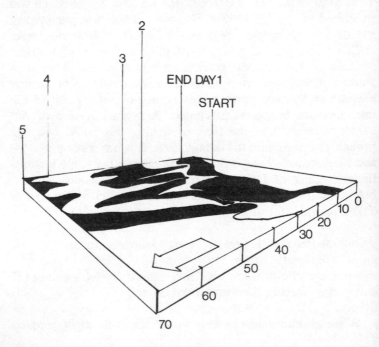

Figure 4.9: Advance with interdiction. Although Warsaw Pact success is reduced, they still penetrate to 70 kilometres by day five

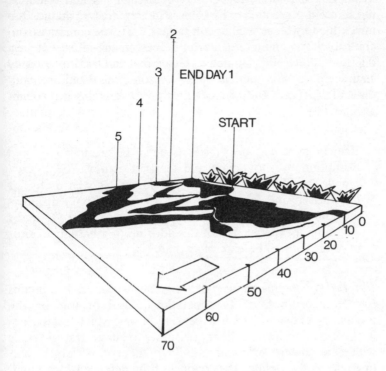

air and space systems for intelligence gathering vital to the location and identification of the most profitable targets, and that these are increasingly vulnerable to attack from Warsaw Pact ground forces (it is estimated that in the mid-1980s the Soviets had one tactical SAM system for each NATO aircraft!), and that many intelligence systems essential to the AirLand Battle were still under development (the Low Altitude Navigation and Targeting Infrared for Night (LANTIRN), the Joint Surveillance Target Attack Radar System (JSTARS) and the Navstar global positioning system). Although these may be in service by the early 1990s, there is a gap between the doctrine and the ability to execute it reliably. The same is true of the enormous intra-theatre airlift requirements necessary to deliver and support forces deep in the enemy rear. In the mid-1980s, the shortfall stood at 60 per cent.[27]

Although criticisms of the emphasis on attacking the second

135

echelon are valid, it is necessary to interpret the AirLand Battle doctrine flexibly and the same principles apply to, for example, identifying and disabling OMGs before they are inserted. A more recent presentation by General Starry stressed the need to attack the OMG, as well as soft targets, logistics, command and control, choke points and enemy forces on the move out to a depth of 200 to 300 kilometres. Given that an OMG might only coalesce inside the tactical defensive zone, this would be very difficult. AirLand Battle recognises that everything would not go smoothly.

Rear areas would be subject as never before to attack and disruption by subversion and terrorist actions and by air-mobile, amphibious and airborne forces, as well as by air interdiction and long range fires. Combat in built up areas including the extensive urbanized sections of West Germany would be inevitable. All of this adds up to a battlefield situation that would be extremely fluid.[28]

FM 100-5 contains many other significant points. It contains formal recognition of the operational level of war by the premier NATO and English-speaking power, which it describes as the use of available military resources to attain strategic goals within a theatre of war ... 'the theory of larger unit operations'.[29] It defines the conduct of the defence which might vary from a static positional one to a deeper, manoeuvre defence. It places greater reliance on reserves than the 1976 manual, indicating that about one third of formation (brigade and above) strengths would be held in reserve. Shifting forces laterally is discouraged, because it is extremely difficult physically and psychologically and is vulnerable to enemy interdiction. Finally, it dispels the simplistic view that there is a straightforward divide between 'manoeuvre' and 'attrition'. There is no necessary confliction between them: deep attack aims to increase the presentation rate of enemy forces by manoeuvre, thus increasing the rate of attrition. Conversely, 'firepower provides the enabling violent destructive force essential to successful manoeuvre. Manoeuvre and firepower are inseparable and complementary elements of combat.'[30]
    FM 100-5 enunciates current US Army AirLand Battle doctrine. It should *not* be confused with the futuristic study *Air*

Land Battle 2000. The semantic similarity has caused confusion not only among outsiders but within the US Army itself. Whereas *FM 100-5* deals with contemporary conditions, *Air Land Battle 2000* endeavoured to look up to 20 years ahead. The first version was dated 4 September 1981 and a revised version 10 August 1982. A subsequent study called *Focus-21* developed the air land battle theme further, and produced radical recommendations including, for example, the allocation of USAF assets to a corps commander or having an Air Force general in command of an army corps. This has now been modified and combined with *Air Land Battle 2000* to produce a new concept of future operations called *Army-21* with which the author had some indirect involvement in 1985. Like *Air Land Battle 2000, Army-21* aims most immediately to provide a framework for the development of equipment. The main problem about attacking follow-on forces is that where corps will have the means to see the follow-on echelons by the early 1990s, they may still lack the means to hit them. Too much reliance needs to be placed on non-army systems, principally those operated by the Air Force. The United States is therefore developing weapons which fit in with the deep attack philosophy, notably the Army Tactical Missile System (ATACMS) (see Chapter 5). There is apparently a shift towards doctrine driving procurement, rather than equipment driving doctrine, although the relationship remains as ever complex. There are also political problems with deep missile strikes. The plan developed under the auspices of the Supreme Allied Commander Europe (SACEUR), General Bernard Rogers, at the turn of the 1970s, was to mount a centrally-controlled strike of 1,200 to 10,000 missiles at Warsaw Pact rear echelons. This was approved as NATO policy at the end of 1984, but it poses many problems. How deep is deep? The Soviet Union itself? That would upset the Russians very much. Secondly, the Soviets might be unsure whether these were conventionally warheaded missiles, and might assume the worst. There are also problems with the great cost of such a system, and although much of the component technology is tried, the system as a whole is not.[31]

The American conduct of their sector of the air-land battle in the central region would be characterised by high mobility, massive firepower and airmobile operations. It is natural for the Americans to regard Germany as a land theatre in which military operations must be conducted in the way which will ensure

137

ultimate victory at least cost. It is war on land and in the air above, not war for land. The Germans see it differently.

THE FEDERAL REPUBLIC OF GERMANY

Because of its numerical strength, its commitment to defend its homeland and its military tradition, the West German Army (*Bundeswehr*) must play the major role on NATO's side in a future European land war. The Federal Republic (FRG) provides 50 per cent of land forces in the Central Region, 50 per cent of ground based air defence and 30 per cent of combat aircraft. Because of general conscription, the *Bundeswehr* is able to maintain total armed forces half a million strong in peacetime. In transition to war (TTW) reservists can be called up to bring the strength of the army to a million in three days. The army's reserves comprised 645,000 men in 1985 (see also Chapter 2). The *Bundeswehr* provides three out of the eight full NATO corps in West Germany as part of the NATO strategy of forward defence. These is I German corps, based at Munster in peacetime, which has a division detached to Commander Land Forces Jutland at Neumunster (see Figure 4.7), which comes within NATO's northern region (AFNORTH). Otherwise, I Corps is subordinated to the Northern Army Group (NORTHAG) of NATO's Central Region (AFCENT). AFCENT is commanded by a German general, but his subordinate, COMNORTHAG, is British. The other two West German corps are in central Army Group (CENTAG): III Corps, based on Koblenz, and II Corps in the south, based at Ulm. The Corps contain varying numbers of armoured (*Panzer*) and mechanised infantry (*Panzer-Grenadier*) divisions, except for II Corps, which because of the terrain in southern Germany has a quasi-mountain division (*Gebirgsdivision*) which includes a mountain (*Gebirgs-Jäger*) brigade. There is also an airmobile (*Luftlande-*) division, subordinated to III Corps but in fact deployed as three airborne (*Fallschirm-Jäger*) brigades, one to each German corps.

As the 1983 German white paper argued most convincingly, the FRG has no alternatives to the strategy of forward defence (*Vorneverteidigung*). This is 'cohesive defence near the border with the objective of preventing any loss of ground and preventing damage'.[32] Thirty per cent of the population of the FRG lives within 100 kilometres of the intra-German border, and this area also contains a quarter of the country's industrial capacity. The situation has many similarities with that of France in 1940: a strong shield is needed to hold forces on the border and allow reserves to be mobilised. Trading space for time is not an option.

The West German concept of land operations is set out in *Army Regulation (Hdv) 100/100*.[33] This dates from 1973, and explains that in the event of a Warsaw Pact attack, the *Bundeswehr*'s mission would be:

- to stop the attacker near the border and to destroy his shock forces
- to prevent him from sustaining his attack with fresh forces brought up from the depth of his deployment
- to recapture any NATO (i.e., German) territory he may have taken.

The first two objectives are clearly common to NATO. The recovery of lost ground is laid down as an aim of counterattack in *ATP-35(A)* but the Germans place more emphasis on this than other nations, for obvious reasons, and it permeates their thinking at operational and tactical levels. The Germans place great stress on *Beweglichkeit* which means both mobile operations and 'flexibility of mind'. As noted above, the Germans regard 'operational' as meaning the handling of divisions and corps. A possible corps layout is shown in Figure 4.10. This corresponds with the standard format for NATO Corps set out in *ATP-35(A)*.[34] There are two distinct zones: the delay zone (*Verzögerungszone*) and the main defence zone (*Verteidigungsraum*). The dividing line between them is the Forward Edge of the Battle Area (FEBA), in German *Vorderer Rand der Verteidigung (VRV)*. This is not the same as the Forward Line of Own Troops (FLOT), as the *VRV* need not be physically occupied by troops. The corps reserve may consist of an armoured brigade, an airborne brigade which might also be deployed with the help of the helicopters of the Army Air Corps Regiment, and an anti-tank helicopter regiment. The Germans see their defensive operations essentially as a battle against armour, and concur fully with *ATP-35(A)* that fully armoured forces offer the greatest flexibility. The only foot infantry is in the *Gebirgs-Jäger* brigade. Anti-tank helicopters

139

Figure 4.10: Bundeswehr Defence

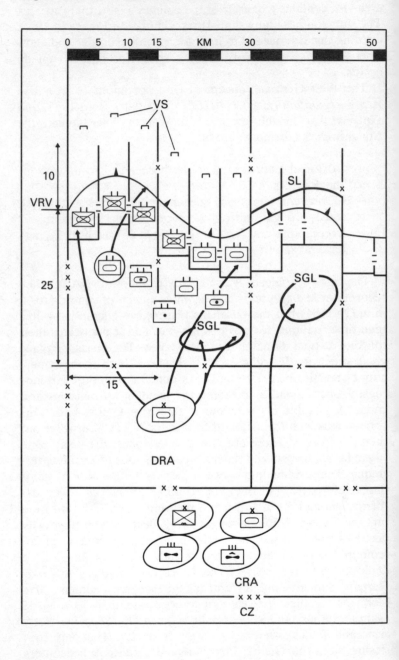

VS — Vorgeschobene Stellungen (Forward Positions); VRV — Vorderer Rand der Verteidigung (Forward Edge of Defence); SL — Sicherungslinie (Security Line); SGL — Schlüseel Gelände (Key terrain); DRA — Divisional Rear Area; CRA — Corps rear area; CZ — communications zone;

 Helicopter Regiment (transport);

 Helicopter regiment (Anti-tank)

are also crucial in the anti-armour battle, and here the Germans also clearly agree with *ATP-35(A)*. They stress that the fire-power of helicopters' long-range anti-tank weapons, their speed, manoeuvrability and independence of terrain conditions, enable them to establish or shift centres of anti-tank resistance very quickly. This is particularly important where wide sectors have to be defended with limited numbers of troops.

A typical armoured division consists of three brigades. The brigade is the main building block of the *Bundeswehr*. The division in Figure 4.10 has two armoured brigades and one *Panzer-grenadier*. One brigade might be deployed forward initially, as a covering or delay force. This would endeavour to delay the enemy for a set period of time, in order to give the rest of the division time to prepare its positions. It would also weaken the enemy's leading elements. Once the covering force has completed its task, it would withdraw through the main defensive area and become the divisional reserve, leaving two brigades forward.

The current brigade structure is the result of rethinking which began in the early 1970s in connexion with the introduction then of a new tactical defensive doctrine. This imposed the requirement to hold ground and to halt the enemy's attack either in front of the *Verteidigungsraum* or in the forward part of it. The new structure was tested in 1976-7, and formally announced on 7 November 1978 as Army Structure (*Heeresstruktur*)-4. The German field army was reorganised into 36 combat brigades, 17 *Panzer* and 15 *Panzer-grenadier*. The territorial army was strengthened by increasing the readiness of certain units including reorganising the old home defence commands (*Heimatschutz-kommandos*) into a structure more akin to a mechanised brigade. Although there was little change in regular divisional troops, corps troops were strengthened, losing their armoured regiments to divisions but acquiring an

141

anti-tank helicopter regiment with 50 BO-105 assault helicopters and 80 light and medium transport helicopters. Because of the greater power of modern weapons within the brigade, it was possible to have four smaller battalions (*Panzer* or *Panzergrenadier*) instead of three larger ones as previously.[35]

A brigade might be allocated an area up to 15 kilometres wide and 25 deep. Within this area the commander establishes where the main enemy thrust is to be expected, where obstacles and firepower would be most concentrated. However, the commander must be able to shift the 'point of effort' (*Schwerpunkt*) very quickly if required. The brigade commander must also determine key terrain (*Schlüssel Gelände* — SGL). This has to be retained against all attacks and must be recaptured if lost. Within the brigade area, individual battalions would be allocated specific areas in which to conduct their own mobile defensive battles. The brigade would, however, have a reserve, probably a tank battalion. This might have three pre-planned tasks:

— to reinforce a forward battalion if an enemy main axis through it had been identified
— to counterattack the enemy once his momentum has been lost or if ground has to be recaptured
— as a counter-penetration force

The brigade commander also lays down the areas which the artillery is to occupy. These should be sited away from the expected direction of the enemy's main thrust. Rocket artillery plays an important part in the German concept of operations. The Germans obviously wish to keep the nuclear threshold as high as possible in order to preserve their country. Rather than use nuclear weapons, they have the concept of *Raumverteidigung* — 'Area Defence', which relies on multiple rocket launchers (see Chapter 5) to deliver anti-personnel and anti-tank mines, thus creating an instant obstacle in the same way that a nuclear weapon might, but one which would be much more difficult for the Soviets to traverse subsequently.

West German tactical doctrine recognises that unarmoured combat units must defend their positions even if the enemy envelops them with armoured forces. The unarmoured units must separate enemy infantry from tanks, and using skilful fire and local counterattacks they must prevent the enemy getting a foothold in the tactical defensive zone. Armoured units will allow the enemy to run into their positions and then endeavour to destroy them with concentrated direct fire. If a brigade commander realizes that the forward defence unit alone cannot prevent an enemy advance, he must employ his reserve early in order to nip a threatening danger in the bud by reinforcing his forward defence elements or through a counterattack. If this fails, the division may act, but only when the enemy's objectives and the direction of his main thrust have become apparent.

In deciding when to counterattack, it is vital to know whether and when the impetus of the enemy attack is flagging and therefore whether the enemy is likely to be smashed before he can bring up fresh forces. However, the last possible moment is when the defence threatens to break up. Counterattacks will avoid strong or formed enemy units. German corps will support divisions' combat operations, primarily by allocation of artillery and engineer troops, plus of course the rapid and decisive intervention of air. Airmobile reserves will be deployed where a unit has to be reinforced very quickly or where a gap has to be closed, and will then be used against the enemy flank or rear. The German philosophy seems to regard corps troops' intervention very much as a last resort, and the conduct of the battle devolves very much on divisions and even more so on brigades.[36] Against a Soviet army which thinks very big indeed, this could be a disadvantage.

Exercise Reforger 74 (10 –20 October 1974)

In this exercise, the German Panzer Brigade 30 exercised under operational (in the German/American sense) control of the US First Infantry Division, in order to compare tactical doctrine and to test the ability of the two armies to co-operate.

German brigades are very much self-contained units. Nevertheless, cross attachment of German and US forces at brigade and battalion level proved feasible, although cross attachment below this level was not recommended. Panzer Brigade 30 carried out offensive operations under first infantry division's control without any significant doctrinal conflict. Defensive operations were more of a problem: although US and German doctrine is essentially similar, misunderstandings arose as the

Americans misconceived the purpose and nature of German deployments. For example, German doctrine, like American, emphasises the need to hold the enemy in the forward area, which requires strong reserves to be held by battalions. The Americans criticised this as possibly leading to the need for premature deployment of the division reserves. Similarly, they criticised the Germans for not holding key terrain. As seen above, the Germans place enormous emphasis on holding key terrain, and this impression probably resulted from the Americans' misunderstanding German map symbols. The exercise showed that there was more scope for misunderstanding in defence than attack, but that with practice formations of different nations can work together very well. Whether this will be possible in the confused environment of a future European war, with formations thrown together without any prior notice, is uncertain.[37]

Exercise Wehrhafte Löwen (Able Lions), 16-23 September 1983

This was held in the Fulda Gap area, south of Cassel, which might be the most attractive route for a Warsaw Pact thrust into CENTAG. A fuller account with maps is given in the author's chapter in the *RUSI/Brassey's Defence Yearbook* for 1985.[38] The main lesson in the realm of operational art concerns the air dimension. This was the first time that III German Corps had committed anti-tank helicopters in close formation in an exercise. The combination of high fire power and high mobility surprised many foreign observers, and was particularly gratifying to the *Bundeswehr* who are extremely proud to possess this versatile and potent weapon. Another facet of the air dimension was provided by fixed-wing air support. The main tasks of fixed-wing aircraft were Battlefield Air Interdiction, Close Air Support and Tactical Air Reconnaissance. Control of these aircraft by Army Forward Air Controllers (FACs) proved a great success. The *Bundeswehr* place great stress on the integrated nature of the AirLand Battle, as do the Soviets, NATO's common doctrine, and the Americans.

Conclusion

The *Bundeswehr* is clearly very adept at handling brigades and divisions. Some might find cause for concern in the apparently static nature of *Bundeswehr* defence at the medium and higher levels; divisions and corps seem to be wedded to areas of ground. However, it is clear from *Wehrhafte Löwen* that the *Bundeswehr* certainly envisage moving whole divisions over considerable distances, and this could be seen as a microcosm of a larger operational (in the Soviet sense) battle. Forward defence and the need to hold West German soil are not incompatible with *Beweglichkeit*, involving the manoeuvre of formations and aggressive counterattack on a large scale, fully reflecting the 'spirit of the offensive' philosophy of *ATP-35(A)*.

GREAT BRITAIN

Although Great Britain disposes of only some 56,000 troops in Germany in peacetime, the strength of this force would nearly treble to 150,000 in time of war and the commander of Northern Army Group (NORTHAG), as critical to NATO's survival as CENTAG, is a British general. In spite of their tradition as predominantly a maritime power, the British adapted to the demands of major continental war with remarkable speed and understanding during 1914-18, and today its senior generals understand its spirit remarkably well. The British Army is likely to be committed to the continent for the foreseeable future, and, like the American, regards major air-land warfare there as its most demanding potential task.

The British did not formally recognise the operational level of war for many years, but by 1985 they had certainly done so. In October 1985 General Farndale, commander of NORTHAG and the British Army of the Rhine (BAOR), addressed himself specifically to the operational level when talking about the counter-stroke (see below). He defined this level as division, corps and higher level operations. The British therefore see the operational level as lying somewhere between the German and Israeli interpretation of it — brigade/division — and the Soviet. However, the General was quite clear that the most spectacular results could be achieved at Army Group (equivalent to Soviet front) level, indicating an appreciation of

145

the need to think big.[39] It is uncertain how far the operational level has permeated ordinary British officer training at the time of writing.

In the mid to late 1970s, the first British corps — Britain's main land force on the central front — was reshaped from three large divisions with three brigades each to four smaller divisions, each with two less permanent field forces, in place of the fixed brigade. However, a number of exercises culminating in the 1980 exercise Crusader demonstrated that the loss of staffs below division led to a lack of flexibility, command and control. The British Army has now therefore returned to the idea of three divisions of 12,500 men in three brigades each, with a fourth stationed in Britain but ready to redeploy to Europe at the first sign of danger. Thus the reliance on the Territorial Army, which forms a crucial element of British front line strength, and the need to get both across the channel in an atmosphere of political uncertainty with refugees pouring the other way, are all disadvantages. Furthermore, Britain's abolition of conscription means that there are relatively few other men or women with military training available to form reserve armies in the event of a war dragging on.[40] Against this, the British Army of the Rhine (BAOR), which consists predominantly of first British Corps, plus TA reinforcements, are exceptionally well trained and motivated and, combatant for combatant, the British may well be the most potent force on the Continent. There may not be enough of them, however.

The British armoured division is a highly mobile formation, able to concentrate forces rapidly to attack and disperse just as rapidly. Its component brigades will in turn comprise battle groups, usually three in number. In conducting the defensive operational battle, the British, like the Germans, recognise the concept of key terrain, which is defined as an area the holding of which gives a marked advantage to either side. They also place great stress on the concept of the covering force, which is deployed by the highest operational commander to screen and guard the main defensive position. A screen means a force with the main aim of identifying and reporting on enemy movements, whilst a guard is deployed to delay them, usually for a fixed period of time. The terms counter-penetration, counter-attack and counterstroke also all have specific meanings: the first, to block an enemy incursion into a defended area, the second to retain lost ground vital to the defence, and the third (counterstroke) specifically to destroy moving enemy forces. The distinction between the last three terms is often misunderstood.

British defensive operations, like German and American, will be offensive in concept. All ranks are urged to be as aggressive as possible, constantly to shift positions in order to survive and keep the enemy guessing, and to keep up energetic offensive action. A covering force could be deployed ahead of the main defence in order to delay the enemy's advance long enough for a coherent main defence to be established. If the latter is completed before the enemy attacks, then the covering force will endeavour to destroy enemy reconnaissance and determine enemy thrust lines. Enemy reconnaissance and probing attacks must be held for long enough to force them into time-consuming deliberate attacks, but the covering force must avoid becoming involved in major fighting. It is recognised that there are unlikely to be sufficient forces to prevent the enemy from infiltrating between covering force positions, especially at night and in bad weather. These will have to be countered by small local reserves and artillery ambushes from the forward main positions.

The main defensive battle will make use either of positional defence or of mobile defence. The former comprises mutually supporting positions and obstacles in depth, and is considered appropriate when the enemy is unlikely to use tactical nuclear weapons, when the possession of the ground itself is vital, or when the defence lacks mobility or is pinned down by enemy air superiority. Mobile defence is used when a sector cannot be held in sufficient strength to allow mutually supporting positions in depth or where the imminence of nuclear use necessitates increased dispersion. It goes without saying that the distinction between the two types of defence is never clear cut. Commanders are encouraged to consider carefully what is and is not key terrain, and to accept gaps if necessary to achieve economy of force elsewhere.

The corps reserves must not be committed until the direction of the enemy's main thrust has been identified. Corps reserves will be used for counter-penetration, counterattack and counterstroke. In the former, timing is crucial, in order to be in place before the enemy forces arrive, and armed helicopters and heliborne troops may be the most suitable for this. Counter-attacks may be immediate or deliberate, the former offering the opportunity to dislodge an enemy before he has time to consolidate on captured ground. The counterstroke is mounted by concentrated armoured forces against an enemy which has achieved a penetration and is still on the move. The British also envisage the use of Army Group reserves in a major operational (in the Soviet sense) defensive battle. It is unlikely that Army Group reserves will be used in the British corps area until all corps reserves have been committed. The aim would be to counter enemy breakthroughs which cannot be contained within the corps main defence area, or to assist the corps in reestablishing the main defence line once enemy penetrations have been contained within the corps area. Army Group reserves may be used conventionally, but are particularly important for use in support of nuclear strikes. The reserves will not be committed early, but held back until really major threats have been assessed. This will depend on rapid movement and timely and accurate information, and is an area where automated C^3I (see Chapter 7) could be of critical importance. Corps assets must be used in close co-operation with the actions of Army Group reserves, including surveillance from behind the tip of an enemy thrust (a large-scale version of the Israeli strongpoints in Golan — see Chapter 1), continued containment of enemy breakthroughs, attrition of enemy formations, particularly second echelons which might be used to reinforce the enemy's operational breakthrough, and securing routes for counter-penetrations and strokes by Army Group reserves. Army Group reserves may have to pass through forces of a different nationality which are in contact with the enemy!

Like the Germans and Americans, the British are placing special stress on the use of armed helicopters and heliborne forces for rapidly countering enemy penetrations, and in exercise Lionheart in 1984 demonstrated their ability to do this with considerable success.[41] In their envisaged conduct of an operational level defensive battle with movement of brigades and corps reserves, and then with Army Group reserves moving through various nations' corps, the British evince a surprisingly broad operational vision. This is a tradition which goes back through Haig to Marlborough, and given the political and strategic influence wielded by Britain within the NATO alliance, could well work to the latter's advantage.

ISRAEL

Israel's very recent experience of major mechanised wars in 1973 and 1982 makes examination of her present concepts of operations both more difficult and less necessary than in the case of powers which have not fought such wars recently. Also, Israel's geographical situation constrains her to a very limited number of options, and the political factors at work in the Middle East also influence those. Israel is very small and narrow, so she must fight for every metre of ground, the more so as conflict is likely to be curtailed by superpower intervention which makes the acquisition of bargaining counters attractive. The Israeli Army began life based on the British, but the lessons of 1956, 1967 and, less obviously, 1973 and 1982 have caused it to regard heavy armour as the most effective battlefield force and least costly in human life. The Israelis are adamant that this is still the case. In spite of their British-influenced past, therefore, the Israelis set great store by German military experience. Some of the most influential books have been the World War II memoirs of von Senger and von Manstein, and Liddell Hart's *Other Side of the Hill* and *Scipio Africanus.* They believe, with some justification, that the German Army has had more influence on modern tactics than any other, and understand the concept of the operational (*Ma'archati,* in Hebrew) level in the same way as the Germans: brigade and division operations, primarily. Their use of the term appears to have evolved independently.

Israel's standing army of 104,000 is deployed in 11 armoured divisions, 33 armoured and 10 mechanised infantry brigades. The largest Israeli field formation is the division or *ugda* (plural, *ugdot*). This was originally tested in the 1967 war, and comprised all tanks, artillery, mechanized infantry and support on a given axis of advance. The tank battalions formed the metal point of this lance, two tank battalions from each brigade. After 1973, the *ugda* apparently became a regular formation like a western division. An *ugda* comprises three brigades, which are the principal operational formations of the Israeli army, the *ugda* commander exercising overall control.

Following the 1973 war, the Israelis endeavoured to develop a more balanced combined arms force, especially mechanised

149

infantry in APCs. The latter, the American M-113, a large thinly armoured shoe-box, proved vulnerable in 1982, and the Israelis, according to published reports, have modified old Centurion tanks to make very heavily armoured APCs. These would presumably be used in concert with their new Merkava (meaning 'chariot' in Hebrew) main battle tanks, which can also carry infantry. This concept, reminiscent of heavy cavalry and dragoons, is probably the result of bitter experience and the need to conserve precious manpower on the face of a battlefield which is 'saturated' (*revayah*') with fire. Movement is the decisive factor in major war, and its retention in the face of increased firepower is the greatest problem. The Israelis may be seeking to do this using the massively protected mobile elements described above at the tactical level. Like other countries, they will probably preserve operational mobility by using the helicopter. Thus, the transport helicopter will replace the lighter 'deep penetration' tanks envisaged by the armoured pioneers of the 1930s. At the same time, fixed-wing aircraft have become too costly for close air support, and the assault helicopter will fulfil this role. As fire paralyses movement on the battlefield, the atmosphere becomes the medium through which large-scale manoeuvre can take place, independent of lakes, seas, mountains and marshes. The problem is making a helicopter which is reliable, strong and simple. As we saw in Chapter 1, the complex facilities needed to maintain and repair helicopters, giving rise to the need for large fixed bases, offset some of their innate mobility. In this respect, Israeli thinking parallels that of NATO and the Warsaw Pact.

The need to support infantry in close country, and particularly the fighting in Lebanon may have led the Israelis to adopt artillery with more enthusiasm than before. Tube artillery may be too unwieldy for highly mobile operations in some areas, and the Israelis are also clearly aware of the potential of rockets. The limitations of the theatre and the very great numerical superiority of their potential adversaries, combined with the greater motivation and education of the individual Israeli, makes the Israelis' technological edge of even greater importance than elsewhere in the world. Their very considerable advances and experience in the fields of electronic warfare and C^3I will be discussed further in Chapters 6 and 7, but the value of these dimensions of warfare in getting the most out of an out-numbered force, and directing scarce resources to where they are most needed quickly, is obvious. Israel has the capacity to mobilise about 85 per cent of her manpower of military age, and a considerable proportion of women. Even so, in any conflict she has to win quickly, and with minimum casualties. How long could Israel sustain a war on all fronts if superpower interest did not conclude it?[42]

INDIA

The Indian subcontinent, like Russia and the Soviet Union, has found that division of its vast extent into geographically distinct commands is the most effective way of administering its defence. There are five commands: Central, Eastern and Southern Commands cover the heartland while the crucial strategic region of Kashmir and the northern Punjab is under Northern Command, and the west of Punjab and the area west to the Pakistan border lies under Western Command. The Army's operational formations; eight corps headquarters controlling 2 armoured, 1 mechanised, 18 infantry and 10 mountain divisions, plus independent brigades and other arms, are deployed into these commands.[43]

From the early 1960s until 1971 the Indian high command had to have contingency plans for defence against Pakistan in the west and east and China in the north. Because of China's active political support to Pakistan, which continues, the spectre of a three-front war was always, and to some extent still is, present. The Chinese did not come in on Pakistan's side in the 1965 India-Pakistan hostilities but India was forced to retain strong troops facing them. India also has to face the prospect of combat in three widely differing types of terrain. In the west, there is the sandy Thar or Indian desert, forming a band up to 400 kilometres wide running northeast between Jodhpur and the Indus. In the north are the Himalayas, the world's greatest mountain range. Here, India, Pakistan and China meet in the area of the Siachen glacier, and the boundaries are undefined. In the late 1970s India began to send military mountaineering teams into this area, which had previously only been ascended by teams from Pakistan. In 1982 the Pakistanis drove off an Indian expedition, but in 1984 the latter returned in brigade strength and occupied the northern end of the glacier under the shadow of the Indira Col. Here temperatures can reach minus 50 degrees Celsius — cold enough to freeze exposed skin to the consistency of metal. These conditions preclude very large-scale warfare here, and even further south terrain and weather will take a heavy toll. In 1965 and 1971 India held the initiative in the North Kashmir sector, which has tended to make the Indians complacent about their superiority in high-altitude warfare. India's ten mountain divisions are a reflection of this. Roughly speaking, North Kashmir, the area concerned, lies north and east of Srinagar. This is the most northerly major town with an airstrip, lying on a flat valley floor between the Pir Panjal and Great Himalaya ranges. West and south lies West Kashmir, which is much flatter with better communications. Operations in the former area would depend on roads passing through narrow defiles, giving earth-moving equipment an enhanced importance. They would tend to depend on artillery firing from focal firebases in support of infantry patrols, as often in Vietnam. Bad weather would severely hamper air operations and in the winter military operations would probably become impossible on any scale. Because of the terrain, relatively primitive aircraft, helicopters and engineer teams could do disproportionate damage by generating landslides.[44]

To the east lies the former East Pakistan, now Bangladesh. The Brahmaputra river (Jamuna) runs from north to south, cutting Bangladesh roughly down the middle. To the west, runs the Ganges (Padma), dividing the country again, while the Meghna flows in from the northeastern (Chinese) direction, joining the Brahmaputra south of Dacca. These three great rivers, which divide the country into four regions, are all so wide that it is difficult to see one bank from the other. Before they disgorge into the Bay of Bengal, they form vast watery deltas, a veritable watery maze. Most of the surface communication is by inland water transport: the road and rail systems generally run north-south and serve the main towns only. The countryside is generally flat, low-lying and waterlogged, with few bridges or good roads running west-east. Furthermore, this area is heavily affected by the monsoon which lasts from May to October. The latter will turn India's western and eastern potential theatres of war into a quagmire, further adding to the criticality of timing.

The geography of the East Pakistan/Bangladesh area led the Indians to exploit the potential of Soviet-made PT-76 light amphibious tanks in 1971. General Aurora, Commanding the Indian Eastern Command, disposed of two regiments of PT-76s; and such systems would be very useful in future operations in such terrain.

Indian represents the remarkable combination of a potential military superpower (as we have seen from Chapter 2, its army is the world's third largest, 1,100,000 against Vietnam's million). India's is an all volunteer, thoroughly professional army having a strong legacy from the British regimental tradition. The army's air assets, like those of the Soviet Union, are at the time of writing still flown by air force pilots, although the Indian Army is keen to have its own Army Air Corps. In previous wars, the Indian Army has shown many of the characteristics of its British forbear. India tended to emulate Montgomery in massing huge quantities of men and material to crush the enemy in a set-piece battle which some Indians have strongly criticised. The one exception to this so far has been the Bangladesh campaign of 1971, and its lessons have been taken very much to heart. Through a combination of numbers, manoeuvre and liaison with insurgent forces, India decisively defeated Pakistani forces in the area. In late November 1971, Indian forces conducted a number of set-piece attacks in the northwestern sector of Bangladesh with heavy casualties and little success. Whenever the Indians attacked fortified positions, the Pakistanis put up strong, brave and dogged resistance.

It became apparent that the orthodox concept of step by step reduction of fortified defensive positions would not only prove costly in casualties, but in time as well, and this was not acceptable in the context of the short war envisaged in the Indian operational plan ... for speedy victory bypassing fortified positions was imperative. The collapse of the Pakistani Army in the eastern wing could only be achieved by outmanoeuvring it, and not by set-piece battles.'[45]

The lessons were applied in Bangladesh, but not in the west where the significant battle of Shakergarh bulge was conducted against strong Pakistani fixed defences and minefields. However, the minefields were far from formidable, carelessly laid, and could have been cleared with much more speed and *élan*. The main reasons for the slow pace of the Indian advance have since been assessed as lack of sufficient strength in main thrusts and diversions of strength to clear villages some way from the main axes of advance. A rapid Soviet-style advance bypassing such areas would have given greater speed and thrown the enemy off balance. 'The Indian strike lacked spirit to force the pace

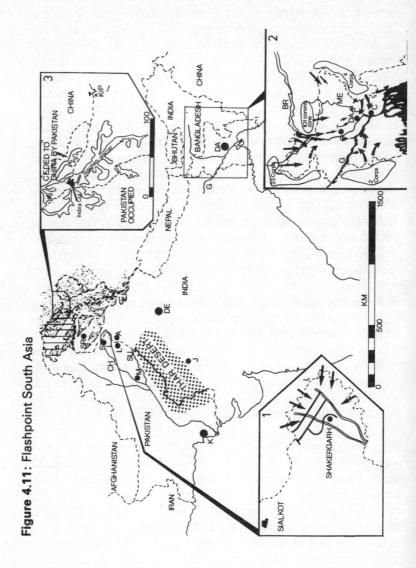

Figure 4.11: Flashpoint South Asia

154

Key areas mentioned in the text shown:
1. Shakergarh bulge battle, 1971.
2. Invasion of East Pakistan, 1971.
3. Disputed area and Siachen Glacier.

A — Amritsar; BR — Brahmaputra (river); C — Chandpur (river); CH — Chenab (river); DA — Dacca; DE — Delhi; G — Ganges (river); I — Indus (river); J — Jodhpur; K — Karachi; KP — Karakoram Pass; L — Lahore; M — Multan; ME — Meghna (river); S — Sialkot; SR — Srinagar; SU — Sutlej (river); T — Tangail

Vertical lines indicate Pakistan occupied area.
Black arrows indicate Indian attacks.
In Shakergarh bulge, black lines indicate minefields.
Double lines indicate rivers/nullahs (watercourses).

against the enemy and failed to imbibe the truth that "the best balance lies in unbalancing the enemy", as convincingly proved in Bangladesh.'[46] The sluggish advance was also the result of efforts to match the pace of the footsoldier with the armour or vice versa. The correct approach, according to the perspicacious Major-General Sukhwant Singh, would have been to let the armour and mechanised infantry go full tilt until they hit the enemy and for leg infantry to catch up later to reduce any strongpoints still holding out. He has therefore suggested reorganising striking formations into mechanised divisions with heliborne capabilities (a sort of Indian OMG?). The generalship of the battle has also been criticised: Indian generals lacked 'any feel of the pulse of the battle'. The lessons of the 1971 war have clearly been taken to heart and, in concert, perhaps, with Soviet ideas which the Indians may have imbibed along with Soviet equipment, suggest much more dynamic operations in future wars in South Asia. Indian military thinking, leadership and organisation need to be reshaped to introduce flexibility into their tactical plans and to achieve greater mobility and heavier punch. Particular stress is placed on the need to increase potential for the use of heliborne forces. Indian concepts, training and planning should, according to the late Major-General Singh, be oriented to achieve decisive and swift results in a short war. 'Slow, deliberate, cautious and time consuming operations do not fit the present [and future] context and need to be recast.'[47] The Indians may be expected to adapt new technology to the needs of their particular environment. In addition to the use of amphibious tanks, mentioned above, assault helicopters will be of great value in overcoming the terrain and weather of the Himalayas, and laser-guided bombs and shells would be of particular value in dropping the bridges or blocking the narrow defiles which form the principal means of communication for potential opponents in that rugged theatre of war. The desert to the west provides classic opportunities for wide-sweeping armoured operations, and possibly for the employment of nuclear weapons.

PAKISTAN

Pakistan's 450,000 strong army is deployed as seven corps in one territorial command, with two armoured and 16 infantry divisions, plus independent brigades and other arms. Like the Indian Army, Pakistan's owes much to the British military tradition, and is an all volunteer, formidably professional force. The Muslim tradition of highly mobile operations and traditional stress on the moral ascendancy of the fighter for Islam, combined with the traditional prestige of arms in Islamic society, have also given Pakistan's army an impressive twist. Pakistan has not the resources to match her main potential opponents — the Soviet Union in occupied Afghanistan on the one side and India on the other — in a long war. However, by judicious use of the defence which, like that of NATO, may be composed of many aggressive moves, she may be able to make aggression against her unattractive and unprofitable. Pakistani military writers constantly refer back to the Muslim military tradition, beginning with Muhammad's defeat of 1,000 opponents with 313 men at the battle of Badr. They also analyse American and European military thought, particularly British, German and Soviet, but do so critically with a keen eye for the requirements and limitations imposed by their own geography and economy.

> The dilemma of our defence is the direct result of our not too happy geostrategic environment vis-à-vis the hostile attitude of our powerful neighbours and the poor socio-economic conditions of the country.[48]

All Pakistani authorities agree that the country's strategic posture must be defensive. Offensive tasks are envisaged, but purely for the improvement of their defensive posture or 'seizing an opportunity', a statement which permits considerable latitude of interpretation. On the eastern frontier, with India, Pakistani units and formations are required to occupy extended frontages, giving rise to large gaps between positions, over-stretch of material resources such as minefields, and creating vulnerability to infiltration. The defence will be particularly vulnerable to tank attack, its anti-tank resources and artillery widely dispersed. Pakistani defence is also heavily influenced by terrain, in east and west, where in the mountains it is based on 'a linear series of heights, very close to the international border, due to political constraints overriding tactical considerations'.[49] No defence is impregnable: a determined enemy assault is bound to succeed in rupturing these thin cordons, and can only be countered by regaining local superiority by moving up reserves. However, very few lateral communications lines are available in the mountainous regions of Pakistan, and rear areas along the main supply routes (valleys) are very vulnerable to heliborne forces and paratroops.

Pakistani defence thinking has gone through three main phases since 1960. The first, from 1960 to 1965, was the so-called 'new concept', which envisaged a series of fortified parallel lines to wear down the attacker, with a mobile force dealing the final counterblow. These lines would be dug in advance but this posed the problem of when in a crisis they should be occupied, and the idea of manning a linear defence in equal strength all along its length was both inappropriate to Pakistan with her resource problems and a military nonsense anyway. The same considerations apply to modern proposals for Maginot Line solutions to Western European defence. As a result of the 1965 war, the Pakistanis adopted 'Area Defence', which, while correcting the faults of the 'new concept', came to place too much stress on holding ground. It recognised, correctly, that in certain areas, such as the west Punjab, tactical (or operational — the Pakistanis do not seem to differentiate at the time of writing) and strategic defence was one and the same: in other words, that main population and strategic centres were within a stone's throw of the enemy. This is much the same as the situation the French faced in 1940, and the West Germans and Israelis face now. The solution was the same, too: ground must be held at all costs. This not only robbed the Pakistanis of flexibility in conducting an operational defensive battle in the west; it also distracted attention from the different theatre of military operations, which was to be India's objective in 1971: East Pakistan.

The latest concept, which has still not gained official

approval, was adopted after 1971 and called the 'Limited Offensive'. This has much in common both with the Egyptians' limited advance in 1973 and in some ways with the US Army's current AirLand Battle doctrine. The idea is mainly to seize territory and retain it as a bargaining counter. In recognising that one cannot be strong or resist assault everywhere, and in deprecating passivity, this idea is an improvement, but it has been criticised, perhaps rightly, as being too terrain orientated and not fulfilling or misunderstanding the Clausewitzian idea of a shield of blows, to destroy enemy forces and throw the enemy off balance.[50]

Pakistani soldiers realise that the only viable defensive concept is that of a wide-ranging mobile defence forming an operational shield of tactical blows. Combined with their quantitative weakness *vis-à-vis* the USSR, India and (possibly) China, this has caused them to show great interest in the classic instruments of such a combat, as in Europe and the Middle East: the helicopter and the armoured counter-penetration/stroke/attack. The armed helicopter can

> Optimise the defence potential of the army. The Pakistan Army, when weighed against adversaries, suffers from a quantitative disadvantage, which can probably be balanced by a superior mobility and qualitative edge in armament. The armed helicopter is a viable solution.[51]

The Pakistanis have therefore devoted great attention both to their own use of attack helicopters and countering that by their potential enemies.[52] At the time of writing, the main likely adversaries (the Soviet Union and India) only have enough helicopters to use them in areas where a decision is to be forced. Pakistani formations in such sectors have to place special emphasis on anti-attack helicopter measures. They also place special emphasis on using deep patrols to provide early warning and to deny the enemy the bases he needs from which to operate helicopters, another manifestation of the integrated nature of the AirLand Battle as envisaged by NATO, the Warsaw Pact and others.

The other decisive arm in the shield of blows is the armoured counterforce. The Pakistanis' concept centres on the armoured regiment group, equivalent to a British battlegroup: the term regiment is used in the British sense of a battalion-level formation. The armoured regiment group is configured for the attack, and may be divided into a number of combat teams. Fire assets apart from the tanks will usually be deployed to form fire-bases, either for the regiment group or for individual combat teams, the manoeuvre elements sweeping round to a flank. The attack may not always succeed but its objectives must be selected with skill and it must be pressed forward with dash and *élan*. The concept has much in common with the British counterattack/counterstroke, albeit perhaps on a smaller scale than envisaged by some British commanders, which accords with the constraints of resources and terrain.[53]

The Pakistan Army clearly draws many ideas from NATO and Warsaw Pact thinking and also has original ideas of its own. It is extremely realistic in assessing how those ideas relate to its own circumstances. As one of their most eloquent commentators, Colonel Mohammed Yahya Effendi, reminded us,

The developments that are in the offing in the industrially advanced countries is a source of scant solace for the Third World. The development of lethal and accurate air and surface delivered precision guided weapon systems has made conventional warfare as deadly and destructive as nuclear, because of the assured destruction of the selected target ... Such advanced technology will be denied to the Third World. Already the technical disparity is immense ... the only answer for the Muslim World today is to acquire technology, simple military technology which could be applied in accordance with Lanchester's Law which, when simply stated, postulates that when the enemy has superior weapon systems, we should outnumber him with two to four times the number of systems of the same type.[54]

All military powers must trade different assets off against each other. It is not just a simple equation of quality versus quantity or machines against men: many Third World countries, including possibly Pakistan, might claim superior motivation or training against an opponent's numerical superiority. The Soviet Army has always stressed the need for a mass army of high quality: belt and braces. The ultimate value of numbers, and of a superiority in quantity ultimately becoming one of quality, has no more unambiguous advocate than the largest army on earth: The People's Republic of China.

159

THE PEOPLE'S REPUBLIC OF CHINA

Chinese military thought obviously owes a great deal to the thoughts of chairman Mao Tsetung, which in turn incorporate those of Sun Tzu and other military writers through Clausewitz to the lessons of peasant revolutions in eighteenth, nineteenth and twentieth-century China. Although many of Mao's thoughts are of universal application, they are primarily of interest to the student of guerrilla warfare, and since Mao's death in 1976 the trend, already present, for the Chinese to place more stress on conventional operations has become more marked. Although Western analysts have used much ink analysing Mao's thoughts and the theory of People's war, surprisingly little has been written on the world's largest army's likely conduct of large-scale classic military operations. Whereas the defence of China, with her 28,000 kilometre land boundary against outright aggression rests primarily on the concepts of nuclear deterrance on the one hand and people's war on the other, defence of the politically crucial and industrialised areas rests on a fairly conventional defence doctrine and there is a need for forces which can strike offensive blows, as in Vietnam in 1979, as a political instrument.

The People's Liberation Army (PLA) is a term encompassing all China's armed forces. The vast majority of the PLA (nearly three million — see Chapter 2) are ground forces, making the PLA the most significant force in land warfare on the face of this planet in terms of numbers and no mean one in terms of quality. The PLA was until recently deployed into eleven military regions (see Figure 4.12), but in mid-1985 a reorganisation was reported to be underway. This would transform the eleven military regions into seven. The three major ones — Peking, Canton and Shenyang — will continue, but the Wuhan military region (apart from the Hubei and Sanxia military districts which will be subordinated to the Wuhan and Canton military regions, respectively), will merge with the Jinan military region. The Lanzhou military region will merge with the Urumqi, the Chengdu with the Kunming and the Fuzhou with the Nanjing. Operationally, the Chinese have 35 armies (some 46,000 men each), encompassing 13 armoured and 118 infantry divisions. In spite of the introduction of new equipment, the PLA remains therefore an infantry-orientated force. Connected with the reorganisation of military regions is emphasis on a new

Figure 4.12: China: neighbours, land frontiers and military regions (pre-1986)

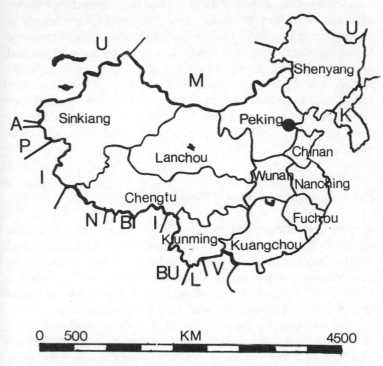

A = Afghanistan; B = Bhutan; Bu = Burma; I = India; K = Korea; L = Laos; M = Mongolia; N = Nepal; U = USSR; V = Vietnam

The military regions shwon are in the process of amalgamation into 7 (see text).

Military Regions	Front	Facing
Shenyang	North east (Shenyang)	USSR
Peking, Lanchou	Northern (Peking)	USSR, Mongolia
Sinkiang	Western (Sinkiang)	USSR, Mongolia
Chengtu	South West	India
Kunming, Kuangchou	Southern	Indochina
Nanching, Fuchou, Tsinan, Wunan	Eastern	Taiwan

style Army Group formation, the *jituan jun*, comprising a varied number of subordinate armies. This indicates that the Chinese are stressing the operational level in conventional war.[55]

Chinese military principles are encapsulated in the phrases 'one point, two sides' and 'divide and destroy'. The former is an envelopment in which the enemy's weak point is attacked simul-

161

taneously with feints and enveloping movements. 'One point' refers to the concentration of overwhelming strength at the weak point; 'two sides' refers to at least two supporting attacks, although there may be more than this. Divide and destroy is essentially an eccentric movement, used where it is impossible to envelop the enemy, and involves penetrating his position and destroying him in detail. The Chinese experience of guerrilla warfare has made them masters of envelopment from within, and it could be argued that this makes their theory of war three-rather than two-dimensional. This is borne out by their principles of combat, which are speed, secrecy, infiltration and night operations.[56]

The Huai Hai Operation, 1948-9)

In spite of their expertise in guerrilla operations, the PLA have the ability to conduct conventional operations at all levels, and clearly understand the operational level of war. Perhaps the most striking example is the Huai Hai operation of 6 November 1948 to 10 January 1949, named after two rivers and also known as the Xuzhou operation. This was the largest land battle in Asia of modern times. The PLA used operational level manoeuvre by a force of half a million men to defeat a Nationalist force of about the same size during the Chinese Civil War. The PLA penetrated Nationalist defensive lines, isolated Nationalist armies and achieved a decisive victory, in spite of the Nationalists' material superiority and the fact that the latter were operating on interior lines. By penetrating nationalist lines and destroying armies individually, the PLA were using 'divide and destroy' at the operational level. They also destroyed Nationalist lines of communication and used operational manoeuvre to counter Nationalist attempts to break out of encirclement.

The PLA captured 320,355 prisoners and killed or wounded 171,151. 155 generals were captured, killed, wounded or went over to the PLA. The booty gives an idea of the nature of the operation: 4,215 artillery pieces, 14,503 machine guns and 151,045 rifles, but only 215 tanks and six aircraft. In other words, it was an overwhelmingly infantry-heavy operation, relying extensively on foot mobility, although 1,747 trucks and 6,680 mules and horses were also captured. In terms of the

Figures 4.13 and 4.14: The greatest land battle of Asia of modern times: The Huai Hai or Suchow (Xuzhou) Operation, 6 November 1948 to 10 January 1949

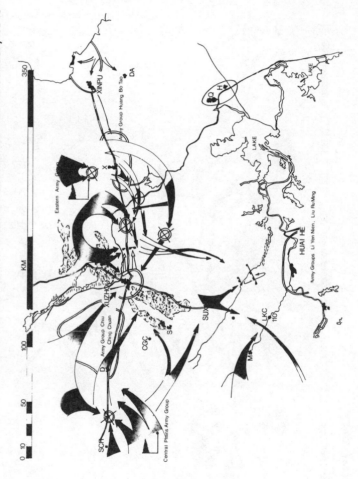

Figure 4.14

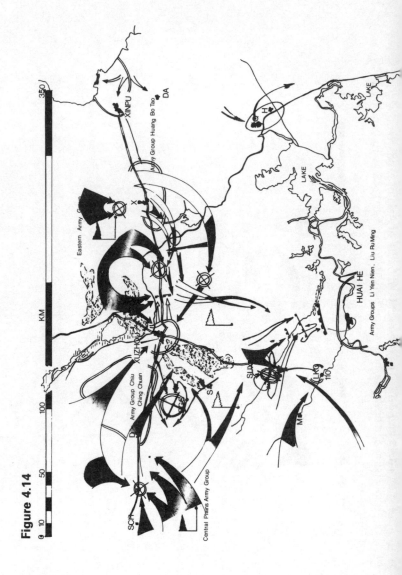

164

First map shows phase 1, from 6 November to 22 November. Second map shows second phase 23 November to 15 December superimposed. 16 December to 10 January were spent destroying the Nationalist pocket around Chen Guan Chuang.
CGC — Chen Guan Chuang; D — Dangshan (Tangshan); DA — Dayishan; H — Huai An; LKC — Lung Kang Chi. 110 indicates revolt of 110 division in phase two; M — Meng Cheng; P — Peixian; Q — Qingiang; S — Suixi; SCH — Shang Ch'iu; SUX — Suxian

Symbols are as in Chinese (PLA) original

Toned/dark arrows indicate PLA advances; thin arrows indicate Nationalist retreats; light arrows indicate Nationalist reinforcement in first map: subsequent PLA operations in second map.

▬▬▬ Fortified line

⬭ Enemy-occupied area

⊗ Destroyed enemy pocket

PLA Army Groups are translated: Nationalist have their original Chinese names. PLA Army Group Headquarters are shown with a fluttering banner, the same as the Soviet symbol for a front. Black banners original HQs; white banners for second phase.

composition of forces it represents a stage of development roughly equal to World War I. However, the PLA has made great strides in equipment and training since then, and is unlikely to have lost its genius for conducting immense and complex battles at the operational level of war. In a future major war in Asia, land operations like this involving a million men might well recur. The Chinese Army still studies the wars against Chiang Kai Shek for operational lessons, so the Huai Hai campaign is of current relevance.[57]

Modern Chinese Operations

Although China's land strategy may be defensive, operationally and tactically she acknowledges the primacy of the offensive. Offensives may be conducted by fronts, army groups or armies in order to break through the various echelons of an enemy's main defences. The offensive will use one of the forms of envelopment described above to isolate and destroy the main body of the enemy and, if possible, engage his reserve. A Chinese army should be able to reach objectives 20 to 25

165

kilometres behind the enemy FLOT in a single night. Attacks at this level are normally carried out in three echelons of roughly equal strength, called attack, support and reserve echelons. Alternatively, an army may be committed all at once, the rear echelons formed by other armies (as in the flexible Soviet view of echeloning). A Chinese front may be allocated an airborne division although the latter will usually operate in battalion or regiment sized parts. The PLA's airborne and airmobile forces are, like the Soviet, strategic in orientation and forming part of the air force. There are believed to be three divisions based in the Wuhan military region. The Chinese envisage bold use of airborne and airmobile forces although the numbers and types of aircraft available are limiting factors. They would be employed to seize important areas, routes and crossings in advance of major offensive thrusts and to protect the rearward movement of Chinese forces, to sabotage enemy nuclear delivery means, disrupt enemy command, control, communications and logistic support, support amphibious landings, assist allied guerrilla forces, and for internal security missions against renegade elements. The Chinese consider operations involving one or two airborne divisions as strategic, and those of regimental or battalion size as tactical; although they clearly have an expertise at the operational level, this is not enunciated formally.

Chinese geography and climate place special emphasis on fighting in special conditions. The Chinese clearly believe that large-scale land operations are possible in conditions which some Western armies would consider prohibitive. Winter can be very severe in north and west China, and the Chinese prepare for operations in these conditions extensively. Winter conditions increase the importance of shelter against the elements, hinder the construction of defences, make rivers, lakes and swamps passable, radically altering the nature and significance of terrain, and restrict air support. In fact, they play into the hands of the PLA's particular advantages. There are many parallels to be drawn with the Mongols' experience, and the same goes for fighting in built-up areas where, like the Soviets, the Chinese endeavour if possible to bounce or rush a town or city from the line of march, before the enemy can establish defences. If this fails, extensive air and artillery support is needed, and several converging attacks are then made to break up the enemy defence and destroy it piecemeal ('divide and destroy').

China's geography has caused the PLA to stress mountain warfare. In very high mountains, such as those on the Sino-Indian border, troops have to be acclimatised and specially equipped. The usual manoeuvre is frontal attack, with regiment and battalion sized units operating along roads and valleys. Enveloping forces are employed to seize commanding heights and passes. It would be surprising if the PLA, like the Soviets, did not make special use of heliborne forces to facilitate and accelerate such operations. In defence, Chinese would adopt focal positions on commanding heights, and stress the need for these to fight on even if enveloped. Finally, in southern China jungle predominates, and Chinese forces receive specialised training in the conduct of jungle operations. In Yunnan and Kwangsi provinces, and on the borders of Burma, Thailand, Cambodia and Vietnam, the terrain is both jungle covered and mountainous. Rugged terrain, dense primary and secondary jungle, small scattered villages, paddy fields, marshes and streams, but few metalled roads or railway lines, make this type of terrain particularly demanding. Chinese forces operating here would probably be stripped of armour and heavy artillery below divisional level. The conduct of operations would be devolved, with tactical units taking full advantage of natural cover, night and guerrilla warfare techniques.[58] However, some of the PLA's likely opponents may be even more adept at fighting under similar circumstances.

The Sino-Vietnamese War, 1979

The overall picture is still one of an old fashioned war, like the great battle of Huai Hai 30 years earlier, although the equipment used was more modern. It was a 'one-dimensional war with a smattering of tank and artillery support'.[59] Neither side used their air force and navy, partly to limit the conflict, partly because the Chinese could have little confidence taking on a Vietnam which had only recently made a strong showing against United States air power. In the mountain-jungle terrain and the 'horror of company sized action' in Lang Son and other cities, the Chinese' best fighting qualities were exploited; had they pushed on into the more open terrain of the Red River Delta their weaknesses *vis-à-vis* the Vietnamese would have undoubtedly become more apparent and the Vietnamese might

167

have used air power against the toiling ant-like columns. The Chinese wisely halted where they did.[60]

Future Prospects for the PLA

At the time of writing the PLA is undergoing a process of technical modernisation under the leadership of Deng Xiaoping. However, the influence of a generation of political commissars appointed during the Cultural Revolution and before, and the sheer size of the PLA, regardless of modern equipment, pose enormous problems. For example, Deng planned a reintroduction of a formal military rank structure, but at the time of writing this has still not been implemented, a distinction only being made between commanders (officers) with four pockets on their uniforms and others with two.

The Chinese perceive a lightning strike by Soviet forces as the greatest potential danger. There are 46 Soviet divisions in the Far East, including four in Mongolia, and they are all of good quality. The better equipped, mechanised forces now deployed by the Chinese are in fact less flexible than the guerrilla/infantry forces of former times: Chinese senior commanders have admitted that they are utterly dependent on their logistic bases. This has affected the old strategy of luring the enemy deep; after Mao's death it was recognised that 'the defence of the cities is of great significance to stabilising the war situation, preserving our war potential and supporting a protracted war'.[61] Luring the enemy deep no longer means engulfing the enemy wherever he is, it

> does not mean letting enemy troops go where they like, but we will force them to move as we want to key places where we will put up a strong defence, prevent them from penetrating inland unchecked and systematically lead them to battlefields of our own choice so as to wipe them out piecemeal.[62]

Until recently the Chinese believed that by the time an enemy reaches 'core China' — the key centres of population and industry — he will be overextended, although the Soviet OMG concept, especially with front OMGs and their emphasis on penetrating very far and fast, means that they now fear a

Soviet lightning seizure of the industrial northeast. The Chinese have, however, made ingenious use of the terrain in cutting gigantic canal-like traps in key mountain passes not only along the border but also inside China, north of Peking. This might slow down a Soviet *blitzkrieg*, although it might be impossible for Chinese forces to counterattack under the dominance of superior Soviet air power. Chinese Manchuria, which contains two-thirds of China's energy (oil and coal) and much of its heavy industry, is, however, vulnerable to attack on two sides, and its desert terrain favours Soviet mechanised operations rather than allowing the Chinese to use their best qualities. In the event of major conflict between the USSR and China, such an operation might be the most attractive one for the Soviet army, not least since they practised it in 1945, but even so it would be immensely costly and must always invite nuclear retaliation.

At a time when some Western commentators (see above) are suggesting that 'armoured' (often a form of shorthand for mechanised combined arms) forces are obsolescent or should preferably be replaced, it is illuminating that the Chinese are moving in the opposite direction. The PLA's history, and particularly emphasis on people's war, militated against development of armour and so does China's geography, 80 to 90 per cent of her terrain being 'poor' or 'unsuited' to armoured vehicle mobility. The Chinese have been working on the development of combined arms doctrine but still have to field a really modern main battle tank. The most noteworthy Chinese combined arms exercise took place to the northwest of Peking in September 1981, and since then regular regimental level exercises have taken place annually. In June 1982 an exercise in the Ningxia Hua autonomous region simulated battlefield nuclear conditions. Motor-rifle regiments are being included in tank divisions, but this is a slow process and in the interim the Chinese are forced to field sharply differentiated 'positional warfare' units, with artillery as a key component, and 'mobile warfare' units, based on armour. In 1979 the Chinese used massed concentrations of artillery in their attacks on fixed positions, a legacy of their former close relationship with the Soviets. Re-equipment is very high on the PLA's list of priorities but the problems are immense. Deng has admitted that re-equipment with 1980s systems will not be complete by the first decade of the twenty-first century, by which time China will still be 20 to 30 years behind the USA, USSR and Western Europe. It is estimated that the PLA urgently needs 3,000 modern tanks, 8,000 armoured personnel carriers and 20,000 trucks. Even so, these would only form the steel tip of a lance composed principally of older systems. Just as the Soviets optimised the use of a limited amount of armoured and motorised equipment within the context of a much larger army by creating special mobile formations which were expected to go much faster than normal ones, to penetrate deep and unhinge the enemy defence before the others caught up, so the Chinese might be tempted to do the same thing today, an extension of their pragmatic philosophy of 'the best weapons for the best fighters'.

The PLA clearly recognises that drastic reform is necessary in order to be prepared to meet future aggression, especially by an adversary like the Soviets. Elder officers of the PLA, reared on Mao's 'human sea' concepts, have difficulty in coping with this, and current articles stress the need for change. Nevertheless, human valour and clever tactics are still stressed: according to the Chinese, 70 per cent of a war is still won by superior tactics and human sacrifice (not so different from Napoleon's 'the moral is to the physical as three is to one').[63] China will continue to optimise her dominant military resource — numbers of people — over the next 25 years. This is not an extravagant or heartless philosophy.

The Chinese have often been accused of using 'human wave' tactics, including the invasion of Vietnam in 1979. This is journalistic oversimplification. Where important objectives had to be taken, the Chinese would endeavour to concentrate maximum force at the decisive point as in any military operation by any country — ideally, two to six times his strength. In China's case this more often than not means numbers of men. Chinese attacks were pressed home with fanatical enthusiasm, but the Chinese are not the only soldiers who have pressed on in circumstances which seem intolerable from a suburban armchair. The Chinese soldier is well trained in basic military skills, highly motivated and physically incredibly tough. Slowly but surely, the Chinese are improving their ability for combined arms, mechanised combat, and certain elements may be suited to carrying out limited offensive strokes, although forays beyond China's borders will be few and far between in the next quarter century. The Chinese are aware of their weaknesses: 'In war

numbers alone confer no advantage. Do not advance relying on
sheer military power'.[64]

CONCLUSION

Armies are not inclined to advertise their plans for fighting the
next war, and the information in this chapter has been influenced by what is available. It has not been possible to examine
tactics in detail, or to include all the major land powers. However, the selection here has enabled the reader to familiarise him
or herself with the full range of conditions and terrain likely to
be encountered in future major land warfare, in Europe, the
Middle East, south Asia centring on the Himalayan chain,
China's southern frontier with Vietnam and her northern one
with the USSR. The superpowers and European nations are
both developing new technology and then finding ways to use it,
and also developing it as a specific response to requirements.
That technology will be examined next.

NOTES

1. General Dr. Hugo von Freytag-Loringhoven, *Generalship in the
World War* (trans. US Army War College, Washington DC, 1934), p.
34; 'Grand tactics': Major-General J.F.C. Fuller, *On Future Warfare*,
(Sifton Praed, London, 1928), p. 104; Soviet adoption: *Soviet Military
Encyclopedia (SVE)*, Vol. 6 (Moscow, 1979), p. 55 and Vol. 7 (1979),
p. 264; A. Golubev, *M.V. Frunze o kharaktere budushchey voyny
(M.V. Frunze on the Character of Future War)* (Voyenizdat, Moscow,
1931), p. 8; W.D. Jacobs 'Tukhachevskiy Rediscovered', *Military
Review*, August 1964, pp. 68-9.

2. Colonel V. Ye Savkin, *The Basic Principles of Operational Art
and Tactics* (translated from the Russian of 1972 under the auspices of
the US Air Force, US Government Printing Office, Washington, DC,
1982); Lieutenant-General V.G. Reznichenko, *Taktika (Tactics)*
(Voyenizdat, Moscow, 1984); scope of TVs and TVDs; Binieda,
'Geografia wojenna ...' p. 3; Glazunov and Nikitin, *Operatsiya i boy*,
(Voyenizdat, Moscow, 1983), pp. 17-24 (see also Introduction); post-
war thinking: Major-General M. Cherednichenko, '*Razvitiye teorii
strategicheskoy nastupatel'noy operatsii v 1945-53 gg.*' ('Development
of the theory of the strategic offensive operation between 1945 and
1953'), *VIZh* 8/1976, p. 41; Viktor Suvorov's view, 'Strategic
Command and Control: the Soviet approach', *IDR* 12/1984, pp. 1813-
20. Terminology and significance: John G. Hines and Philip J. Petersen,

'Changing the Soviet System of Control: Focus on Theatre Warfare', *IDR*, 3/1986, pp. 281-9. The most recent key work is Colonel-General M.A. Gareyev, *M.V. Frunze — Voyenny teoretik* (*M.V. Frunze — Military Theoretician*) (Voyenizdat, Moscow, 1985), Sokolovskiy outdated, p. 239.

3. On the Manchurian operation see Lieutenant-Colonel David M. Glantz, *August Storm: the Soviet 1945 Strategic Offensive in Manchuria* (Leavenworth Paper 7, Combat Studies Institute, Fort Leavenworth, February 1983), and *August Storm: Soviet Tactical and Operational Combat in Manchuria, 1945* (No. 8, June 1983), esp. pp. 1-4 and 163-4 of the former, 1-6 of the latter; Army General I.M. Tret'yak, *'Razgrom Kvantunskoy armii na Dal'nem Vostoke'* ('Defeat of the Kwantung Army in the Far East'), *VIZh* 8/1985, pp. 9-19, in particular p. 12.

4. Hines and Petersen, 'Changing the Soviet System of Control', pp. 284, 285.

5. 'The Military Implications of Inadequate Communications', Soviet Intelligence Feature, *Jane's Defence Weekly* (*JDW*), Part 1, 22 March 1986, pp. 524-5, part 2, 29 March, pp. 569-71.

6. Cherednichenko in *VIZh*, 8/1976, p. 41.

7. Ibid.; Gareyev, *M.V. Frunze*, p. 237.

8. Clausewitz, *On War*, Howard and Paret edition, 1976, Book 1, ch. 1, p. 76.

9. See the author's 'The Operational Art of the European Theatre', *RUSI/Brassey's Defence Yearbook*, 1985, esp. p. 231, and 'Conventional Quick Kill', *JDW*, 19 May 1984, pp. 781-6.

10. See the author's 'Antecedents of the Modern Soviet Operational Manoeuvre Group (OMG)', *RUSI Journal*, September 1984, pp. 50-8.

11. Immediate post-war: Cherednichenko, 'Razvitiye', p. 44; Resurrection of the concept: Christopher Donnelly, 'The Soviet Operational Manoeuvre Group: a New Challenge for NATO', *IDR* 9/1982, pp. 1177-86, Charles Dick, 'Soviet Operational Manoeuvre Groups: a Closer Look', *IDR*, 6/1983, pp. 769-76; Philip J. Petersen and John G. Hines, 'Military Power in Soviet Strategy against NATO', *RUSI Journal*, December 1983, pp. 50-56, and the author's 'Operational Art' and 'Conventional Quick Kill'. Polish reservations: 'SZA', *'Operacyjne grupy manewrowe'* ('OMGs'), 'Military Thought' section, *Zolnierz Wolnośći* (*ZW*) (*Soldier of Freedom*), 26 October 1982, p. 4.

12. David C. Isby, 'Soviet Airmobile and Air Assault Brigades', *Jane's Defence Weekly*, Vol. 4, No. 11, 14 September 1985, pp. 561-5; Major Roger E. Bort, 'Air Assault Brigades: New Element in the Soviet Desant Force Structure', *Military Review*, October 1983, pp. 21-36.

13. Fire support: the author's *Red God of War* (Brassey's, Oxford, 1986); *LPZU*: Colonel Dr. T. Wojcic, 'Combat Vehicles and Helicopters on the Modern Battlefield', *ZW*, 4 January 1978, USA translation.

14. Major-General A.I. Vorob'ev, *'Razvitiye printsipov taktiki'* ('Development of the principles of tactics'), *KZ*, 5 December 1979, p. 2; principles of operational art: Savkin, *Basic Principles*, pp. 167-277; of tactics, Reznichenko, *Taktika*, pp. 51-70. Categorical 1985 state-

ments are from Gareyev, *M.V. Frunze* pp. 240-45.

15. *ATP-35(A), Land Force Tactical Doctrine* (2nd draft, January 1983), p. C-12.

16. Ibid., p. 1.

17. Ibid., p. 3-6; AMF(L), *RB 100-3, Interoperability of British, Canadian, German and United States Forces* (US Army Command and General Staff College, Fort Leavenworth, November 1983), pp. 1-1 to 1-16.

18. *ATP-35(A)*, p. 3-7.

19. Clausewitz, *On War*, Book 6, ch. 1, p. 357.

20. *ATP-35(A)*, p. 1.

21. General Burgess (then Deputy SACEUR), lecture to the RUSI, 24 January 1985.

22. See Hew Strachan, 'How should Nato fight?', *Times*, 23 August, 1-85, p. 10. Quote, Clausewitz, '*On War*', Book 1, ch. 1, p. 77.

23. John L. Romjue, 'The Evolution of the AirLand Battle Concept', *Air University Review*, May-June 1984, p. 9.

24. See the author's chapter in Philip A. Towle, *Estimating Foreign Military Power* (Croom Helm, London, 1982).

25. Romjue, 'Evolution', pp. 5-11.

26. See Major Jon S. Powell, 'AirLand battle: the Wrong Doctrine for the Wrong Reason', *Air University Review*, May-June 1985, p. 21.

27. Ibid., pp. 18, 19.

28. Romjue, 'Evolution', p. 12.

29. *Field Manual (FM) 100-5 Operations* (Headquarters, Department of the Army, Washington, DC, 20 August 1982), p. 2-3.

30. Ibid., p. 2-4.

31. Strachan, 'How should NATO fight?'; on Army-21, *Army-21 — US Army concept for the future*, Information Paper DAMO-PDQ (Department of the Army, Washington, DC, 12 April, 1984). *Army-21* begins with projections about the international environment, including the spread of nuclear and chemical warfare and sophisticated weaponry, and demographic problems in developed countries. It then covers technology, which will be exploited to multiply human capabilities and save manpower, together with the use of artificial intelligence. The third section covers potential adversaries, from the Warsaw Pact to terrorists, and the fourth the characteristics of future battlefields, which will be more lethal and sophisticated, have more intensive combat, be fought in a wide variety of environments, with the time dimension more crucial, and greater integration of the air-land-sea dimensions.

32. Federal German Republic, Minister of Defence, White Paper 1983: *The Security of the Federal Republic of Germany* (Bonn, 20 October 1983), p. 144.

33. *HDv 100/100 Führung im Gefecht (Command and Control in Battle)*, September 1973. This is referred to and cited in John J. Mearesheimer, 'Maneuver, Mobile Defense and the Central Front', *International Security*, Winter 1981-2 (Vol. 6, No. 3), pp. 104-22.

34. *ATP-35(A)*, Diagram 3-1-1, opposite p. 3-18.

35. *RB 100-3*, pp. 2-8 to 2-12.

36. Ibid., pp. 3-21 to 3-22. For a West German interpretation of

FOFA, see *'Das FOFA-Konzept* (Follow-on Forces Attack) *und seine Bedeutung für das deutsche Heer'* and *'Prinzip der Staffenbildung bei den Landstreitkräften des Warschauer Paktes'*, *Soldat und Technik* 3/1985, pp. 118-19. On the willingness or otherwise of the Germans to manoeuvre: Rodney Cowton, 'Give an inch and win the war', *Times,* 27 August 1984, p. 8, with the views of General Chalupa, the German commander of AFCENT.

37. *RB 100-3*, pp. 4-4, 4-13, 4-15.

38. 'The Operational Art of the European Theatre', *RUSI/Brassey's Defence Yearbook 1985* (Brassey's, Oxford, 1985), pp. 249-55.

39. General Sir Martin Farndale, *Counterstroke — future requirements*, lecture at the Royal United Services Institution, London, 15 October 1985.

40. Henry Stanhope, 'The ring of confidence around BAOR', *Times,* 7 September 1984, p. 15; Rodney Cowton, 'Today's Army' and 'Progress all the way in arms and firepower', *Times,* 7 September 1984, pp. 15 and 16. Otherwise, conversations with British officers.

41. See, for example, '"Enemy" flops in war game', *Daily Star,* 20 September 1984, p. 10, in which a Dutch heliborne desant is successfully ambushed, and 'Strike force gives the Army a boost — now American generals admit it ... the Tommies are tops', *Daily Mail* 23 September 1984, p. 17.

42. Conversation with Israeli generals and Dr. Martin van Creveld. *Ugda*: Edward Luttwak and Dan Horowitz, *The Israeli Army* (Allen Lane, London, 1975), pp. 176, 292-6, 363; Gunther E. Rothenberg, *The Anatomy of the Israeli Army* (Batsford, London, 1979), pp. 106, 120, 140-41. Divisions, brigades, etc.: *The Military Balance*.

43. Major-General Edward Fursdon, 'Indian Army divided into five commands', *Daily Telegraph,* 19 June 1984, p. 5; Michael Hamlyn, 'British military tradition is alive and well in India's modern Army', *Times,* 16 June 1984, p. 6. Deployment details from *The Military Balance*.

44. Three-front war: Major-General Sukhwant Singh, *India's Wars Since Independence*, Vol. 1, *The Liberation of Bangladesh* (Vikas, New Delhi, 1980), p. 58; glacier: Michael Hamlyn, 'Silence on the glacier war', *Times,* 18 September 1985, p. 6; Indian perceived superiority, firebases, etc.: Rikhye, *Indo-Pak War*, pp. 66-72. For a useful perspective on Indian assessments of Pakistan, see also Ravi Rikhye' Nine examples from recent Indian Experience', in Philip Towle, ed., *Estimating Foreign Military Power* (Croom Helm, London, 1982), pp. 194-236.

45. Geography: Singh, *Liberation of Bangladesh*, pp. 67-8; *PT-76s*, p. 67; tradition and helicopters: Fursdon, 'Indian Army'; lessons: Singh, p. 127. Concise account in E.R. Hooton, 'The Lightning Campaign: India's Victory in the East', *War in Peace*, Vol. 6, No. 72, pp. 1436-9.

46. Singh, *India's Wars since Independence*, Vol. 2, *Defence of the Western Border*, pp. 107-9; for a view of what might be happening, Rikhye, *Indo-Pak War*, pp. 101, 126, 129. Maps and Pakistani view:

Brigadier Nisar Ahmed Khan, 'Covering Troops Battle-Shakargarh 1971', *PAJ*, September 1984, pp. 49-51.

47. Singh, *Defence of the Western Border*, p. 109.

48. Brigadier Syed Khalid Mahmood, 'The Integrated Defence: an Indigenous concept', *PAJ*, December 1981, p. 9. Dispositions from *The Military Balance*. Battle of Badr: Lieutenant-Colonel Muhammad Afzal, 'Relative Strength in Modern Wafare', *PAJ*, December 1981, pp. 27, 30.

49. Offensive tasks as component of defensive and seizing opportunity: Major Khalid Anis, 'Integrating Helicopters with Artillery', *PAJ*, June 1983, p. 4; dispersion, linear series of heights, etc.: Lieutenant-Colonel Iftikhar ur Rehman, 'Defensive Battle in Mountains', *PAJ*, September 1984, pp. 30-31.

50. Major (retd.) Mohammed Saeed Tuwana, 'An appraisal of our Defence Doctrines', *PAJ*, June 1982, pp. 2-13.

51. Major Khalid Anis, 'Integrating Helicopters with Artillery', p. 4.

52. Threats to Pakistanis' helicopters: Captain Jamshed Iqbal Bajwa, 'Battlefield Threat to Gunship Helicopters', *PAJ*, June 1982, pp. 30-35; enemy threat: Major Saeed Ahmed Khan, 'Fighting Attack Helicopters', *PAJ*, December 1983, pp. 38-42.

53. Major Khalid Bakhtyar, 'Training an Armoured Regiment Group for Attack', *PAJ*, December 1983, pp. 43-7.

54. Colonel Mohammed Yahya Effendi, 'Technological Imperatives of Mechanised Warfare: Today and Tomorrow', *PAJ*, December 1982, pp. 12-25, quote on pp. 23-4.

55. 11 Regions, Defense Intelligence Agency, *Handbook on the Chinese Armed Forces* (US Government Printing Office, Washington, DC, 1976), pp. 1-7 to 1-13. This was published commercially as *The Chinese Armed Forces Today* (Arms and Armour Press, London and Melbourne, 1979); general issues are explored in Gerald Segal's excellent *Defending China* (Oxford University Press, 1985). On the reorganisation of military regions into 7: 'China Reorganising military structure', *JDW*, 29 June 1985, p. 1264, and G. Jacobs, 'Streamlining China's Army', *JDW*, 31 May 1986, pp. 998-1001, which also deals with Army Groups (*jituan jun*).

56. *Handbook on the Chinese Armed Forces*, pp. 4-1 to 4-7.

57. I am grateful to Gary J. Bjorge for giving me access to his research for his forthcoming Leavenworth Paper, *The Huai Hai Campaign: Chinese People's Liberation Army Performance at the Operational Level of War*, for giving me copies of Chinese sources and maps and translating them. Still studied today: Jacobs, 'Streamlining China's Army', p. 1001.

58. *Handbook on the Chinese Armed Forces*, pp. 4-47 to 4-48, 4-52 to 4-56.

59. Segal, *Defending China*, pp. 211-30, quote on p. 220.

60. Ibid., p. 220.

61. Claire Hollingworth, 'The PLA's long, slow haul to modernity', *Pacific Defence Reporter*, June 1984, pp. 17-22, quote on p. 20; Hugh Davies, 'China's New Model Army', *Sunday Telegraph*, 20 January 1985, p. 6; 'Confident Teng calls for younger blood in Army', *Daily*

Telegraph, 3 November 1984, p. 6; 'As China Grows Strong', *Economist*, 31 January 1986, pp. 13-14, 39-41, move to conscript from volunteer and improvements in officer training, p. 40.

62. Hollingworth, 'PLA', p. 20.

63. G. Jacobs, 'Training and Academy programmes changing for People's Liberation Army', *JDW*, 21 September 1985, pp. 633-4 and ibid., 'China's tank armies', *JDW*, 1 February 1986, pp. 159-61, armoured and combined arms warfare development, terrain and recent exercises in the latter. Latest is Jacobs' excellent 'Streamlining China's Army', *JDW*, 31 May 1986, including possible Soviet seizure of northeast (p. 1001); equipment requirements: Hollingworth, 'PLA', p. 20; Chinese style, Segal, *Defending China*, pp. 250-51.

64. Sun Tzu, *Art of War*, IX (Marches), p. 122.

5

Weapons, Platforms, Protection

The major battlefield of 2010 will at first sight look disappointingly familiar to today's readers. Major land weapons systems and platforms are surprisingly long-lived. The British Chieftain tank, the basis of the Challenger being introduced at the time of writing, first saw the light of day as a prototype in 1958, and was shown to the public in 1961. The Centurion, which did splendid service in the Yom Kippur War in 1973, and is still around, was designed as long ago as 1943, and prototypes appeared in 1945. Chieftain and Centurion have both been constantly developed and upgunned, and will continue to be so, but the basic design goes on, if not forever, at least for 30 years and more. The same is true of the Soviet T-62, still in service with some Warsaw Pact forces although being replaced, and likely to remain a numerical mainstay of Third World countries' armies for many years. This was developed in the late 1950s and entered full production in 1961. Improved ammunition (witness the Israeli APFSDS round in Lebanon in 1982 — see below), improved rangefinders and sighting equipment and additions to the armour, can increase the potency of an old design exponentially. Armoured personnel carriers can certainly carry more potent weapons than before, although perhaps giving less opportunity for other improvements. The American M-113 was developed in the late 1950s and produced from 1963; the British FV 432 entered production in 1962. A generation ahead of these in design, if only a few years in time, came the Soviet BMP, first viewed in 1967. The BMP 2 with improved armour protection introduced in 1982 was just a modified version of the same design. The APCs replacing the M-113 and the 432: the Bradley and the British MCV-80 ('Warrior'), respectively, presumably expect to enjoy as long a life, perhaps 20 to 25 years. Longest lived of all, but possibly presenting most scope for adaptation and modernisation, are artillery pieces. The Soviet M-1946 130 mm gun which has pulverised targets across the world was developed from a naval gun of the 1930s, and was being used with devastating effect in the Gulf War in 1984. Less exceptional designs, like the American 175 mm M-107, 203 mm M-110 and 155 mm M-109, were all developed in the early 1950s, and produced from 1961. They are still in service at the time of writing a quarter of a century later, although the first two are showing distinct signs of wear and the M-109 has been modified with a stretched barrel. Improved ammunition, including rocket assisted, extended range and improved conventional or 'smart' munitions (see below), combined with artillery's ability to fire indirect (that is, at targets which it cannot itself see), give almost limitless opportunity for adaptation, as long as the rifling is not actually worn out. Small arms are steadiest of all: the basic British rifle design, the Lee-Enfield, a development of the Lee-Metford, was still in use by its country of origin in the 1950s and by the Israelis in 1967. It would have been recognisable to a soldier of the Boer War (1899-1902). The British Self Loading rifle (SLR) replaced in the mid-1980s, was essentially the same as the 1950s FN rifle. The Soviet Kalashnikov AK series will probably kill, whether for legitimate governments or terrorists, to the end of the century and well beyond.[1]

A number of new and exciting developments are, however, taking place in the 1980s which will profoundly affect the conduct of major land warfare and are connected with the operational and doctrinal developments described in Chapter 4. The most obvious and prominent is the development of land-based multiple launch rocket systems and tactical missiles capable of striking deep into the enemy's deployment as part of the increased emphasis on striking deep and follow on forces' attack. Multiple launchers were first used on a large scale by the Soviets in the Great Patriotic War, while the Germans pioneered the large missile, but improvements to the power and accuracy of the former and the accuracy and battlefield agility of the latter constitute a 1980s weapons revolution. In particular, the large calibre of modern multiple rocket systems and the greater accuracy of modern single tactical missiles (see also Chapter 3) make them perfect vehicles for carrying the most ingenious new warheads which the wit of man can devise. Given the time in service of major weapons systems, and the lead times required to develop new ones, a survey of those systems being introduced or discussed at the time of writing will determine what will be available until 2010 and probably beyond. Electronic Warfare (EW) and Command, Control, Communications and Intelligence systems (C^3I) may develop more quickly, and are considered in their respective chapters. However, a weapon that does not get to the right target at the right time to do a specific job is useless, and the developments described in this chapter are totally dependent on the other developments described in Chapters 6 and 7.

MULTIPLE ROCKET LAUNCHERS AND THE NATO MULTIPLE LAUNCH ROCKET SYSTEM (MLRS)

The United States Army completed its first test firing of the Vought MLRS in September 1983.[2] The British Army has received four MLRS launchers at the time of writing (the end of 1985) direct from the USA for training and evaluation purposes. Britain is committed to a European collaborative development of MLRS along with Italy, West Germany and France. It is likely that a contract will be let during 1986 and the system might therefore be in full service from the early 1990s. The adoption of a multiple launch rocket system by two nations (the USA and UK) which had traditionally shown little interest in such systems was probably the most significant development in land weaponry of the 1980s, especially given the correlation between these and doctrinal developments. The West Germans, French and Italians have multiple launch rocket systems already, but the acquisition of MLRS, in German MARS (*Mittleren Artillerieraketen-system*), is still a major landmark.

Soviet interest in multi-barrelled rocket launchers has not diminished since the Great Patriotic War. Because there is no recoil to deal with, the launcher can be on an ordinary truck, thus facilitating the combination of high firepower and mobility which the Soviets seek. The latest is the heavy BM-27, estimated to have a range of 35-40 kilometres. In many ways it is comparable to the NATO MLRS, or rather the other way round, as the BM-27 antedates MLRS by at least six years.

Having experienced the effects of Soviet rocket artillery

between 1941 and 1945, and having deployed the *Nebelwerfer* then, it is understandable that the Germans have been NATO's most fervent advocates of multiple rocket launchers. In addition, the Germans' very natural desire to keep the nuclear threshold high has led to a search for alternative ways of denying areas to the enemy. This is the *Raumverteidigung* (area defence) concept. The Light Artillery Rocket System (LARS) has been in service for some time and will continue until replaced or supplemented by MLRS from 1987. LARS can saturate a distant area with mines very quickly, creating an instant obstacle, and the German MLRS will have the same ability (see below).[3]

The main reason why the British and Americans have eschewed multiple rocket launchers in the past is the difficulty of supplying ammunition. However, changes in the threat and the nature of the modern battlefield have forced them to revise their views. The same factors have also affected the Soviets' views. Soviet, US and West German forces are all almost exclusively mechanised, and both Western and Warsaw Pact artillery is becoming increasingly self-propelled. This means that the time available to engage, hit and destroy the opposition is reduced while the amount of ammunition needed to have any effect is correspondingly increased. Both the Soviets and the West have drawn the same conclusion; it is necessary to put down more rounds on the target in less time. Soviet Army studies have indicated that one way to do this is to make the battalion the usual unit of artillery fire, but NATO, which was at the time of writing outnumbered four to one in artillery pieces, has had to look for other options. The doctrine of Follow-on Forces Attack (FOFA) and the need to hit OMGs before they can rupture NATO forward defences necessitate striking deeply. However, the manned fixed-wing aircraft is rapidly ceasing to be cost effective as a platform for delivering conventional weapons on the battlefield. Once main axes are identified, it is essential to channel, halt and delay advancing Soviet forces. If nuclear weapons are not to be used, some sort of powerful area weapon is needed. All these factors predicate a long-range weapon able to deliver a dense concentration of powerful munitions in minimal time — like MLRS. Another problem is locating targets accurately beyond visual observation range. Target information will have to come from enemy electronic emissions and radio or radar direction finding. Such information may not be accurate enough for conventional artillery, but it could be for MLRS with its area coverage. MLRS is not merely a substitute for conventional artillery: the two types of system have very different characteristics and roles, and in future major land operations it is important that senior commanders understand the differences. MLRS is suitable for delivering area weapons (minelets) or warheads which require a given density within a given time (chemical), or 'smart' munitions against mass targets. Gun artillery has greater precision and greater regularity, and is thus suitable for use against accurately located targets, targets which need to be suppressed for a prolonged period rather than instantly paralysed, or for delivering high-value projectiles against precisely located individual targets (laser-guided shells).

The present MLRS Warheads are the M-77 bomblet and the AT-2 anti-tank mine. The former is intended for use against unprotected or lightly protected targets, such as enemy towed artillery, air defence assets, C^2 and supply installations, and infantry. The rocket warhead contains 644 bomblets with both shaped charge and fragment effect. The AT-2 anti-tank mine is specifically designed to defeat enemy armour in the forward areas of enemy deployment and to defeat enemy armoured breakthroughs rapidly. The rocket has a range of about 40 kilometres, and deploys 28 mines. A MLRS launcher can therefore lay 336 AT-2 mines, covering an area about 1,000 metres by 400. To be effective, one mine has to be placed every half metre of front, requiring five or six launchers to sow a dense 1,000 metre-wide strip.

INDIRECT FIRE ATTACK OF ARMOUR

In 1983 a Memorandum of Understanding was signed for the development of a terminally guided sub-munition rocket for the MLRS (MLRS phase three). This is designed to engage armoured targets which, because their armour is thickest at the front and their top armour thinnest, are most vulnerable to top attack. If this can be made to work on the battlefield — and there is every reason to believe that it will — it could have, must have, revolutionary impact on the conduct of battles involving massed armour, making that as vulnerable to indirect fire from all artillery in range as infantry in the open was to roughly directed shrapnel shells. The contract for the Terminally Guided Warhead (TGW) was won by an international consortium comprising prestigious electronics firms from the US, Britain, France and Germany. TGW is due in service in 1992 and will comprise six unpowered 100mm diameter sub-munitions in each MLRS rocket. As the rocket nears the target the sub-munitions are ejected and rear and forward wings are deployed. When the TGWs reach a pre-set height above the ground they commence a search from left to right across their path with a 94 GHz narrow beam millimetre wave seeker (see also Chapter 6). When the TGW recognises a tank it starts to count until it reaches the target number allocated to it before launch, presumably to stop all the TGWs homing in on the same tank. Then it goes into a steep dive to hit the tank on top with a shaped charge warhead.

A related system is the US Army's Sense and Destroy Armour (SADARM) which is being developed to fire from 203mm and 155mm artillery pieces. One being developed for the 203mm shell comprises three sub-munitions which are ejected and descend by parachute, spinning to search for the target in a spiral track. To complicate counter-measures the 203mm SADARM uses both millimetre wave and infrared seekers. The 155 shell SADARM uses infrared only, which would be easily fooled. Competitive engineering development began in 1985 with a proposed in-service date of 1990. Other NATO nations plan to use 203mm SADARM rounds from 1991. This places new emphasis on 203mm (eight inch) artillery, currently represented by the ageing M-110, and suggests that a new long-range heavy gun (rather than howitzer) is needed. The Soviets have recently introduced the highly mobile long barrelled 203mm gun, and if SADARM is to be exploited to the maximum NATO might well follow suit. MLRS TGW or SADARM would be used to best effect as far forward from the forward line of defence (FLOT or German *VRV*) as possible, thus implementing FOFA by wearing down enemy second echelon forces or OMGs moving up from the depths (see Chapter 4). The British Merlin 81mm mortar bomb, appropriately named, is designed for indirect fire anti-armour use at much shorter ranges, only out to 4 kilometres. Within that range, however, it will pick up any armoured target within a search area covering some 300 square metres with its millimetre wave seeker and then home in on it from above. Although the short range of the mortar and the great accuracy needed to get it within sniffing distance of the target limits its value, it is a start. Delivery will start in the late 1980s.[4]

Since the 1930s when tanks became a major force, gunners have dreamed of being able to deal with them with indirect fire. Technology is now turning this dream into reality. Although at present target acquisition problems would tend to focus attention on the shorter ranges — out to 35 or 40 kilometres for MLRS and long and extended range guns (see below) — there is no reason in theory why an accurate tactical missile with a CEP of, say, 300 metres should not deliver a load of smart anti-tank bombs capable of seeking out individual tanks and crippling a formation massing hundreds of kilometres behind the forward elements of an army. The effect would be to extend the battlefield again, forcing armour to operate as if within visual range of the enemy throughout the depth of the theatre. Except when moving, it would like overhead protection as infantrymen need overhead protection against shrapnel. In order to move openly, enemy surveillance would have to be blinded and artillery, rocket and missile positions suppressed. The classic tactics of fire and movement would have to be applied on an operational scale, and no-man's land and the battlefield would stretch accordingly. Top attack will also undoubtedly influence the design of tanks themselves (see below).

In the nearer term, another way of making artillery fire effective against tanks is the Copperhead laser-guided shell to be fired from tube artillery. The future of Copperhead is uncertain at the time of writing. The idea is at first sight excellent. It enables an observer with a fairly lightweight designator to guide a heavy artillery shell from any weapon within artillery's considerable range on to a resilient target which clearly adds to flexibility. However, an observer has to be within sight of the target, whether a man or woman on the ground or in an aircraft. Given the large number of other visual contact weapons, such as tank guns or anti-tank guided missiles, which may be available, the effort involved in guiding an artillery shell from far away on to the target seems considerable. The concept may be worthwhile with very large artillery shells which are unsuitable for deployment far forward, such as 203 mm, and increases in armour protection, or the use of prepositioned hardened fire positions may drive manoeuvre forces to invoke ordnance of this calibre. If, as seems likely, future war is characterised by enemy and friendly forces getting mixed up together, then the ability of an isolated unit to call on heavy projectiles from friendly forces far away and guide them in with precision would be of particular value.

LARGE OPERATIONAL-TACTICAL ROCKETS AND MISSILES

The increased vulnerability and cost of manned aircraft combined with improvements in guidance systems have placed and will continue to encourage more interest in the large rocket (unguided, like the Soviet Frog) or, more likely, missile (guided) as a means of delivering munitions to targets in the enemy depth. At present, the main Western system is the Lance, range about 100 kilometres (see Chapter 3), while the Soviets bracket NATO's operational depth with SS-21, 22 and 23. Although there have been liquid-fuelled battlefield missiles in the past, these are inconvenient and dangerous and future battlefield missiles are likely to be exclusively solid-fuelled. Improvements in guidance give them enough accuracy to deliver improved conventional munitions, fuel air explosives (FAE — see p. 186) and chemical warheads within a worthwhile distance of the target. Airfields, helicopter and Harrier landing sites are certainly worthwhile targets but if equipped with smart sub-munitions they could be used against large armoured concentrations, and give the possibility of remote mining of areas beyond the range of MLRS. At the time of writing the United States is developing the Army Tactical Missile System (ATACMS) as part of the FOFA concept. This was formerly known as *Joint* TACMS, but that designation has been superseded or possibly applied to a qualitatively different system. ATACMS is an operational-tactical weapon, and might therefore be assigned to corps commanders. If so, it would carry conventional or improved conventional, and possibly chemical, warheads only. ATACMS will be mounted on a MLRS launcher (TEL) and will look almost identical to MLRS. ATACMS will replace or supplement Lance in the conventional role, and will have an appropriate range, perhaps 150 kilometres. A contract was signed with Vought at the end of March 1986. Because ATACMS will be all conventional, this raises a question about the Lance replacement; a nuclear capable missile will still be required.

Using the MLRS TEL will make ATACMS cheap and commonality of command and control will further ease its integration into service. ATACMS might therefore be fielded in the early 1990s. The ATACMS missile will also be able to accommodate all the sub-munitions already developed for MLRS and Lance. It is envisaged that ATACMS will be of particular value against 'time sensitive' targets, because of the speed with which it can be deployed and reach its target.[15] The main problem, as always, is that of target acquisition. ATACMS will be fully integrated with emerging target acquisition and C³I systems (see Chapter 7), such as JSTARS and Aquila.

CRUISE MISSILES

The term cruise missile is an emotive one, but it designates any missile which is powered all through its flight. It can therefore follow a level or varying trajectory, which gives the opportunity to fit it with a terrain comparison (Tercom) guidance system. Cruise missiles can therefore be made very accurate; although precise figures are unavailable, an accuracy of within 12 metres is claimed for modern American cruise missiles. Because of their cost they are primarily intended for use as theatre nuclear weapons (see Chapter 3), but their accuracy makes them very useful for precise delivery of conventional, improved conventional or fuel air explosive (see below) warheads. Cruise missiles could deliver a crippling blow to headquarters and other high-value targets deep in the enemy rear. Although some might be shot down by low-level air defence, it is likely that with their 2400 kilometre range, a good many American Tomahawks could circumvent and elude enemy defences and perhaps hit a Soviet front or theatre headquarters. If the target were important enough there is no logical reason why a costly cruise missile should not be used to hit it: its conventional, improved or fuel-air warhead would be doing just the same job as a nuclear warhead. The problem is that the recipient, detecting a cruise missile on its way, would not know that it was non-nuclear, and might respond with apocalyptic consequences. The same argument goes for tactical ballistic missiles, and is one of the knottiest problems with the doctrine of conventional deep attack. Articles published in 1984 suggested that the Soviets were investigating sub-munition warheads for their own use. Such warheads, they said, achieved a more equable distribution over the target area, and were suitable for destruction of personnel, tanks, APCs and anti-aircraft sites, and for remote mining. Particular attention was devoted to the Lance sub-munition warhead.[6] A sub-munition or improved conventional warhead would be very suitable for the SS-21 *tochka* missile being deployed in Europe at the time of writing. Instant mine-fields from BM-27 would be very useful in, for example, sealing the flanks of an OMG penetration preventing counter-penetration or counterstroke (see Chapter 4) by NATO manoeuvre forces. However, Soviet requirements are somewhat different from NATO's and maybe for this reason the Soviets have shown more interest in a potentially more revolutionary new munition.

FUEL AIR EXPLOSIVES (FAE)

The United States used FAE in Vietnam and the Russians have apparently used them in Afghanistan. Although until now delivered in aerial bombs, there is scope for delivering FAE in large tactical missile warheads and their use, however delivered, will profoundly influence the land battle. The basic principle is to create an aerosol cloud of fuel-air mixture which is then detonated to achieve an explosive effect like that which drives the pistons of a car engine. The advantage is that whereas the blast of a conventional explosion tails off very rapidly, and is thus inefficiently distributed, the fuel-air mixture can be spread over a wide area and then detonated to achieve an even pulse with a force adequate for a given job. It is thus a technological expression of the military principle of economy of force. The main problems are achieving consistency in the size and mixture of the aerosol and precise control of detonation.

The peak over-pressure (that is, over and above normal atmospheric pressure) of a 500 kilogram methane-based FAE aerosol detonation attains 0.9 kiloponds per square centimetre (12.8 pounds force per square inch) at distances up to 100-130 metres beyond the outer boundary of the aerosol cloud itself. A kilopond (kp) is a kilogram force. This can be converted to pounds force per square inch by multiplying by 14.22. In imperial units, the term 'pounds per square inch' (psi) is often used to indicate overpressures. In fact, psi strictly speaking is an absolute pressure; overpressure should be measured in terms of force (pounds force per square inch). Psig is sometimes used to denote that it is a measure of force. At distances up to 170-190 metres beyond the aerosol cloud overpressures of 0.42 kp/cm^2 (6 psig) may be encountered. In the context of a nuclear explosion, overpressures of 0.366 (5.2 psig) are considered 'severe blast' and 0.19 kp/cm^2 (2.7 psig) 'moderate blast' (see Chapter 3). The blast effects of FAE are comparable with those of small nuclear weapons. FAE research has centred on the use of gaseous carbohydrates which decompose explosively igniting spontaneously in contact with damp air or certain materials, and which do not need oxygen for combustion. The explosion can develop with such intensity that ignition is propagated at supersonic speed, forcing the pressure wave ahead of the flame front. Until the mid-1980s, ethylene oxide was favoured for gas detonations, which made it possible to create explosions with 2.7 to five times the destructive power per unit area of a TNT warhead of the same weight. It is possible that overpressures could be obtained giving ten times the destructive power of conventional explosives. Thus the 1 tonne warhead of a tactical missile could give a yield equivalent to a 10 tonne conventional warhead.

Because of the way the shock wave is propagated, FAE may be particularly useful against bunkers and fox-holes. They may also help restore mobility as they are particularly good for clearing mines. In the late 1970s the Americans developed the FAESHED (FAE helicopter delivered) which was tested against over 4000 different mines. It produced a 100 per cent kill rate within an 8.8 metre radius for pressure-fuzed mines and within 25.9 metres for tripwire mines. FAE also work against seismic, infrared, electronic and magnetic influence-detonated mines.[7] They will also be exceptionally effective against remote sensors, or any type of delicate equipment. Once initial problems are overcome, FAE should be available fairly cheaply, and are likely to replace conventional explosives and maybe submunition warheads in many roles. They are one of the most significant and challenging developments in weaponry at the time of writing, and could dramatically affect future land warfare. In negating many of the effects of rapid or remote mining, they may be another example of the age-old pendulum of offence against defence, mobility against counter-mobility, as well as lethality against dispersion.

EXTENDED RANGE ARTILLERY

With the need to strike deeply into the enemy's follow-on echelons, and the increasing vulnerability and expense of manned aircraft, more emphasis needs to be placed on conventional artillery systems as well as MLRS. Rocket-assisted projectiles were used by the Syrians in the 1973 Middle East war, fired from Soviet M-46 guns. Development of rocket-assisted projectiles, which may extend the range of conventional guns by 50 to 100 per cent, continues in the West. The US Divisional Support Weapons System (DSWS) aims to produce a 155 mm howitzer able to fire rocket or rocket-ramjet propelled projectiles known collectively as the Advanced Indirect Fire System (AIFS). These would have a maximum range of about 70 kilometres. However, AIFS is designed primarily as an anti-armour weapon, as only the engagement of high-value targets would justify the high cost of rocket-assisted shells, and the DSWS, if it ever sees the light of day, will not do so until the 1990s.

In the interim, and for use against softer targets, an elegantly simple solution to the problem of increasing artillery's range has emerged in the shape of Extended Range Sub Calibre (ERSC) and Full Bore (ERFB) ammunition. An ERSC round fired from a 155 mm M-109 howitzer had a range of over 22 kilometres, as opposed to the howitzer's normal range of 14.6; a 50 per cent improvement. However it is obviously wasteful to have a projectile so much thinner than the barrel and because of their shape ERSC rounds are unsuitable for conventional high-explosive (HE) shells. ERFB shells fired from the Anglo-German-Italian FH-70 155 mm howitzer have increased its range by about 8 kilometres.

The most interesting ERFB development concerns so-called 'base-bleed' technology which was invented in Sweden. This consists of a container attached to the base of the shell, which is filled with a combustible material which burns to generate fuel-rich and oxygen deficient gases. This material does *not* provide extra thrust, but it does increase the pressure in the base area of the shell, reducing the base drag action by 80 per cent. Three types of drag act on a shell in flight: body drag, caused by rotation and friction; wave drag, caused by the shape of the shell's forebody; and base drag, which results from the partial vacuum formed at the base of the shell in flight, pulling it back.

ERSB and ERFB projectiles aim to reduce wave drag: base bleed reduces base drag, allowing the shell to decelerate more slowly and thus travel further. Base bleed can increase the range of a shell by 13 to 30 per cent compared with non-base bleed ERFB, and correspondingly more of an increase over conventional ammunition. Unlike the rocket-assisted projectile it provides a solution which is simple and relatively cheap.

Base bleed has been applied to the Austrian GHN-45 (Gun Howitzer Nonicum with a barrel length of 45 calibres). This howitzer fires standard NATO 155mm ammunition, and can fire a non-base-bleed ERFB shell to a range of 30 kilometres. Under the same conditions, it will fire a base-bleed ERFB shell to 39 kilometres. In the Middle East, it was able to attain ranges of 32 and 43 kilometres with ERFB and ERFB base-bleed shells, respectively, without appreciable loss of accuracy.

Is there a limit to how far tube artillery's range can be stretched? Earlier this century artillery of calibre comparable to modern 152 and 155mm pieces had a maximum range of perhaps 10 kilometres; now it is reaching four times as far, without involving other technologies such as rocket assistance. It may be that ERFB and ERFB base-bleed represent the maximum that tube artillery can be stretched; for longer ranges it may be necessary, and more likely, more cost effective, to employ other weapons, particularly rockets. In the last century the Russian rocket pioneer Konstantinov predicted that the problem of throwing a very large projectile with a very high velocity would be overcome by rockets, and would thus have predicted that the first man would reach the Moon in a rocket and not, as Jules Verne believed, fired from a gun. At shorter ranges guns are more economical and more reliable; as Tizard predicted in 1945, 'we cannot imagine rockets largely replacing guns for short range fire — say up to five miles [eight kilometres], although their present rather tentative use is likely to increase'.[8] There is, however, an area where both systems overlap, and where the choice depends on the nature of their action rather than their range. Even here, the distinction is not clear cut.

BURST FIRE AND AUTOMATED ARTILLERY

A number of salvoes delivered in rapid succession can be much more effective than a constant regular pounding. The rate demanded for a burst of fire is three rounds in eight to twelve seconds. This can only be achieved with 155 mm guns if mechanical assistance is given. Mechanical rammers are used, and are particularly important in self-propelled ordnance where conditions are cramped. Modern towed guns such as the Anglo-German-Italian FH 70 or the Swedish FH 77 have small engines for auxiliary propulsion and these can also be used to power a mechanical loader and rammer, as on the Swedish example. Future ordnance is likely to have a burst fire capability for a small number of rounds; beyond this, it perhaps becomes more cost effective to use multiple rocket launchers to achieve the sudden impact effect.

Automation has other advantages apart from facilitating burst fire. It enables the crew size to be reduced (especially important in the light of demographic problems in the more developed countries and training problems in those less so — see Chapter 2). It permits intermittent attendance at the gun and 24 hour operation, thus reducing crew fatigue. Finally it permits control from a remote position, greatly assisting the survival of the men. The United States Field Artillery have endeavoured to reduce the burden on artillery crews and execute routine decisions and calculations automatically. In 1982, Howitzer Test Bed (HTB) III was tested at Fort Sill. A self-propelled howitzer could receive a fire mission while on the march, pull into the side of the road and loose off the first round in 30 seconds. The only action required of the crew was to monitor the system and load the ammunition. The Americans are now working on a more advanced robot gun. A computer-controlled robotic arm will select the required round and charge and place them in the loading tray. The robot's software will be integrated with the fire control computer, allowing it to adjust the type of round, charge, timing of detonation and so on. The forward observer will remain the crucial element: the gun crew may only act as supervisors.[9] The trend towards making do with fewer men and enabling them to carry out supervisory functions, freed from basic donkey work, is clearly one which will continue in all aspects of military endeavour, but it must not be assumed that warfare will become anything other than an exhausting, terrifying, bloody business, even so. Equipment can go wrong, and the enemy is likely to have similar equipment.

FILLING THE GAP

We are presented with the picture of a battlefield where things are constantly stretching. Weapons fire at greater ranges, and therefore retreat beyond visual range, as artillery did at the turn of the last century. The proliferation of armoured targets has induced the major land powers to standardise on the 152 or 155 mm calibre. Anything smaller is relatively ineffective against armour except in the direct fire role. The increase in the weight and range of artillery has left the forward elements without very close and agile support. The popular 105 mm calibre is likely to be confined to operations in distant theatres where strategic mobility is crucial, or in difficult terrain, and this is reflected in the countries which continue to manufacture such weapons. The British light gun which proved so effective in the Falklands is a response to Britain's own unique requirements and her strong export market. Other nations still making 105 s are India, with her rugged mountain borders, and South Korea. The 105 is however disappearing from major continental theatres. This has left a gap, and just as a host of weapons evolved to fill the gap which opened when artillery first moved back behind the front line at the turn of the last century — machine guns, mortars, light 'infantry guns' — so a similar development is taking place today. Is there any weapon which has the traditional qualities of artillery: simplicity and resilience (without the complexity of a guided missile), regularity (not a one-shot weapon, like a missile, again), and versatility, able to fire high angle and indirect, but also to fire armour-piercing ammunition at a tank? The gun mortar, a recent development, has all these qualities, and mounted in a mobile armoured chassis, utilising the mortar's rate of fire and the compactness of its ammunition, it may fill the gap. In the West a number of gun mortars have been manufactured by the French firm Thomson Brandt. Although they are of small calibre (up to 81 mm) and short range, they illustrate the potential of the idea, and the Soviets have gone further with their ingenious 120 mm 'combination gun'. The first combination guns have been mounted on BMD air-droppable chassis, and the gun mortar's lightness combined with rate of fire and potency would be of particular value to airborne or airmobile units. However, there is no reason why these weapons should not supplant traditional light artillery in heavy ground units also.[10]

191

TANK DESIGN

The tank remains the epitome of modern large-scale land warfare. When space precludes a fuller analysis, tanks and aircraft are the two types of technology chosen by many commentators to illustrate opposite sides' relative strength. This is an oversimplification; tanks need infantry to screen them in towns or close country, and in the open they need mechanised infantry to clear and hold ground. They need artillery to beat down anti-tank weapons, perhaps more so now than ever before. But the tank is king of the land battle, embodying the three interacting qualities of firepower, mobility and protection in almost perfect equilibrium, and is the most expensive and sophisticated piece of land ordnance to procure. Yet tanks have changed surprisingly little since the 1920s and 30s, when the familiar turreted configuration appeared. When the Soviets demonstrated the advantages of sloped armour with the T-34, other nations soon followed suit and the box-like vehicles which opened World War II became the sleek Leviathans of today. After the Yom Kippur War some thought the tank had become too expensive and vulnerable for its own good, but that was over-hasty. The tank remains the only vehicle able to fight and move under artillery fire, and will remain a crucial component of major land warfare certainly for the next quarter century.

Designers differ as to the relative weight to be attached to each element of the firepower-mobility-protection triangle. The British and Americans emphasise firepower and protection, with the Chieftain at 55 tonnes mounting a 120 mm and on later versions carrying special armour (see below). The Germans place more emphasis on mobility, thus achieving protection by moving from one piece of cover to another, a view perhaps partly conditioned by experience in Russia. Their Leopard, like its name, is at 40 tonnes a smaller and more agile member of the big cat family. The Israelis, who have more recent experience of real large-scale armoured fighting than anyone else, have designed their *Merkava* ('chariot') to meet very special requirements, discussed below. The Russians, who have a tradition of excellence in tank design, manage to combine firepower mobility and protection while keeping the weight down to an extent impossible in the West by sacrificing crew comfort, selecting small crewmen, and other typically Russian expedients.

The constraints on tank design are remarkably consistent. Tizard's comments in 1945 are equally valid today:

The part that tanks will play in future battles depends greatly on the outcome of the continuous competition between the gun and armour. On the whole, scientific advances are likely to benefit the gun more than the protective armour. Not only will the power of penetration of projectiles improve but also and even more important, the chance of hitting a moving vehicle will increase considerably. Very large tanks, which are certainly technically feasible, are unlikely to gain an advantage from their ability to carry a heavy gun unless their vulnerability in all respects were very low. In tank warfare numbers are likely to remain more important than absolute size, although much is to be gained by increasing the power-weight ratio. Tanks that wade, float or travel under water have been already developed, and improvements are possible in the normal process of development, if they are considered to have a useful role in the future.[11]

Tanks have tended towards what Tizard would have called 'very large', until they have reached the feasible limit for a battlefield vehicle. One factor is that tanks have to get over or under bridges, and to be carried on rail flats. Continental railways are designed around wagons up to 4.4 metres high and 3.55 wide, and tanks have to fit those dimensions. The railway remains capable of carrying more ton-miles than any other form of land or air transport, and is likely to remain the principal means of strategic mobility over land in Europe, India and the Far East. Tanks much over 55 tonnes in weight will also place unacceptable strains on roads and bridges, especially when it is remembered that a tank and transporter together may weigh up to 80 tonnes. The Israelis, with their small country and wide expanses of desert, do not face quite the same constraints.

Conventional tanks have their turret in the centre, with the driver in front and the engine behind. This configuration gives rise to another classic trade-off: giving a tank a lower silhouette reduces its vulnerability in some ways but also limits the degree to which its big main gun can be depressed. This is important in enabling tanks to fire from a 'hull down position' — the tank perched on the back of a hill with its gun sticking over the top. A widespread view is that the Soviets have tended to go for absolute lowness, influenced no doubt by their flat terrain, whereas Western nations place more emphasis on use of the sinuosities of the ground and like to have more depression at the expense of greater height. This is an oversimplification. Firstly, the Russians have plenty of mountains, and conducted extensive operations in mountains in World War II (the Balkans, Manchuria). Secondly, it is the shape of the tanks and turrets which makes them blend in with the terrain — the curves meld perfectly with the slope of the hills — and not the height in absolute terms. Captured Soviet tanks have a log stowed at the back, above the tracks. Drop the log on to the ground, back onto it, and you have another few degrees depression.

As tanks became bigger, the power to weight ratio became a problem, and the British Chieftain was notoriously underpowered. The power to weight ratio of the Chieftain Mark V was 11.6 kilowatts per kilonewton (kW/kN), or 15.5 brake horse power per ton (BHP/t). The American M60's was 11.8 kW/kN (15.8 BHP/t), reflecting both countries' emphasis on protection at the expense of agility. However, there has recently been a revolution in tank power with the introduction of turbocharged diesel engines employed, for example, on the Challenger and Leopard II, and gas turbines as in the American XM1. These permit ratios of 19-22 kW/kN (25-30 BHP/t), which will greatly improve battlefield agility. A gas turbine engine produces greater power for a given size than a diesel, but uses more fuel, which means that larger fuel tanks are required. In the next quarter century it may be possible to reduce gas turbine fuel consumption, making them more attractive as tank power plants.

Anti-tank rounds defeat armour in three main ways. Solid shot and armour piercing discarding sabot (APDS) smash their way through using kinetic energy; high explosive squash head (HESH) also known as high explosive plastic (HEP), sends a shock wave through a steel plate to knock a scab off the inner face of the armour and the shaped charge warhead blasts a narrow but deep hole using a concentrated jet of gas generated by a conical cavity within the explosive charge. The latter requires less explosive than squash head and does not need the enormous velocity of solid shot and APDS. It is therefore ideal for light weight and infantry portable anti-tank weapons. Sloping and sculpting armour helps a lot; armour at 60 degrees to the vertical presents twice the effective thickness to a round travelling horizontally, and some rounds may glance off. By 1945, however, work was already underway on various 'compound' armours. By the 1980s these had reached a high stage of development, most widely publicised in the British Chobham armour. Details of these compound or 'special' armours are a closely kept secret, but essentially they comprise a sandwich of layers of steel, ceramic material and plastic containing mineral salts. The plastic absorbs the heat from shaped charges, the ceramic offers high resistance to kinetic energy attack while the steel holds it all together and adds its own strength. The discontinuity of the sandwich also defeats the squash head which requires a continuous medium to transmit its shock wave. Special armour is fitted to the front of the British Challenger and American Abrams tanks, and has given rise to a distinctive slab-like shape.[12] Special armours are extremely heavy, and this limits their application all over the vehicle, further increasing the attractiveness of top attack for future anti-tank weapons. The Soviets have introduced some sort of special armour on improved variants of the T-72 tank, but this has not caused the Soviets to forsake the traditional smooth rounded turret and probably comprises ceramic inserts in cavities in the turret armour. It is debatable how worthwhile special armour is; designed to resist ingenious shaped charge warheads, it would be little use against a very simple high-velocity kinetic energy missile (see below).

The turreted leviathan will remain the backbone of heavy armoured forces for the next ten years or so, but beyond that may be facing a crisis. Although the new generation of turreted tanks represents a quantum improvement in power to weight ratio and thus to tactical mobility, the sheer size of the vehicles may limit operational and strategic mobility and the unit cost is likely to soar through the level of the assault helicopter (see below). The weight of armour required to keep out specialised anti-tank projectiles is roughly 12 times that required to give immunity to bullets and shell splinters. Traditionally, this heavier armour has been concentrated against specialised attack from the front within a horizontal arc of 60 to 70 degrees and a vertical one of ten (from −5, that is, lower ground, to +5, slightly higher ground). This frontal arc remains valid for the primary kinetic energy attack delivered by the gun of an opposing tank. However, there is now a range of other threats. Between 5 and 15 degrees vertically there is the risk of direct fire munitions from fixed and rotary wing aircraft and ATGMs, especially given the propensity of modern helicopters to use 'nap of the earth' tactics. Between 15 and 50 degrees there is the closer threat from helicopters using a range of chain guns or cannon, and from 50 degrees across the top of the tank there is the threat of top attack, primarily from aircraft or indirect fire weapons (see above). The tank's roof is twice the area of its frontal aspect, and this may negate the value of its heavy frontal armour in future conflict. The turreted heavy tank may therefore be facing a crisis. In the words of the armoured warfare expert, Brigadier Richard Simpkin, it is 'over-evolved', and a fundamental change in tank design, perhaps in the position of the tank in the overall mix of armoured forces, is on the horizon.[13] There are two examples of tanks in service which may indicate the way ahead, after which prospects for the late 1990s and beyond can be examined.

Merkava

The *Merkava* represents perhaps a limited and traditional response to problems of tank design and to very specific lessons. The brainchild of General Tal, the Israeli 'chariot' recalls the battle of Armageddon at which its ancient namesake played a similar role: shock weapon, missile platform and carrier of troops. The Israelis began with a blank sheet of paper, and put preserving the lives of tank crewmen first. They are extremely proud of the result. The engine is therefore at the front, behind a well sloped glacis plate comprising, it is believed, several varied layers of armour and the fuel tanks and engine are incorporated into this protection scheme. The turret is small and well shaped, designed to minimise exposure to enemy fire when in a hull down position. Around the bottom of the turret there is an ingeniously simple chain mail arrangement consisting of heavy steel balls on chains to curtain the turret ring and pre-detonate shaped charge warheads striking that vulnerable line. The Israelis have successfully minimised damage should a *Merkava* be hit. In fighting against Syrian forces in 1982, several *Merkavas* were knocked out but the crews escaped unhurt and the tanks were got back into service with little difficulty. One *Merkava* was apparently hit by a HOT anti-tank missile which penetrated its front, destroying the engine, but did not penetrate the crew compartment. The tank is also fitted with the Spectronix fire control system which comprises a number of sensors attached to cylinders of inert Halon gas which is injected into crew and engine compartments the moment fire is detected. The gas is then immediately evacuated, before it has a chance to choke the crew. The whole process takes about a tenth of a second. The system costs about 1/200 the cost of the tank, and is thus a very worthwhile investment. Israeli tank crewmen also wear suits of fire-retardant cloth, which meant they suffered many fewer burn casualties in 1982 than in 1973.

The configuration of the *Merkava* allows a large compartment at the back, enabling entry to be gained to the hull through a rear door. Besides making it able to carry an infantry section or evacuate casualties, the rear door would if adapted also enable palletised ammunition and other stores to be loaded. This would be particularly valuable for tanks facing the enemy in hull down positions. All in all, the layout of the *Merkava* makes a great deal of sense.

The Merkava's 105 mm main gun is smaller than the 120 mm and 125 mm on British/American and Soviet tanks, respectively, but the Israelis have found no problem with it. Israeli tanks accounted for about 60 per cent of Syrian tanks killed in operation Peace for Galilee, and the 105 mm gun will remain effective at least to the end of the 1980s. The Israelis used the standard technique of improving the ammunition, in this case the M-111 'Arrow' armour-piercing fin stabilised discarding sabot (APFSDS) round. One Israeli officer asserted that the M-111 was 'the main technological advantage we had while entering the war'.[14] Syrian T-72s were reportedly engaged at ranges up to 3,500 metres, successfully, suggesting that some NATO estimates that T-72s are immune to 105 mm rounds are wrong. This example underscores an important factor in weapons procurement: it is often almost as good and certainly more cost effective to improve an old gun with new ammunition than to get a new gun. If the Israelis had found that the 105 mm was unable to dismantle T-72s, they would have been forced to fit a 120 mm gun to the *Merkava*, which is possible, but to replace all their other tanks. 3,000 new tanks with 120 mm guns, like Challenger, Abrams or Leopard 2, would cost about 7,000 million dollars at 1984 prices (coming up for half of Britain's entire defence budget).

Another example of the value of new equipment on old platforms was the digital fire control system. Tank battles are won by the side which fires the first accurate shot. Whereas conventional estimation techniques mean that four or five rounds may be needed even by a well trained gunner to destroy a tank at 2,000-3,000 metre range, digital fire control enables a less skilled gunner to do it with one or two. The system was first introduced on the *Merkava* in 1979.[15] These systems will become widespread in the future, but slowly, as they are very expensive.

The Turretless Tank

There are two main types of turretless tank: casemate-type vehicles, like the Swedish S-tank, with a gun mounted inside the hull of the vehicle, and external gun tanks. Simpkin has labelled both as 'topless' tanks but there are different design issues to be considered with each. Both have the following advantages to some extent:

— They make it possible to give the sides and top of the crew and engine compartments balanced protection against flank and top attack.
— They reduce the target area in the horizontal plane by some 40 to 50 per cent compared with a more conventional turreted design.
— They allow the big tank gun to be mounted on a vehicle of about two-thirds the weight of the equivalent turreted tank (35 to 40 tonnes as opposed to 50 or 60). This helps make the tank amphibious and reduces the associated engineer effort by some 70 per cent. One cannot look at a given piece of military technology in isolation.
— There is no reason why, with the optronics technology likely to be available in the 1990s, that there should be any loss of visual command of the battlefield, theoretically, at least.

The only turretless tank in general service at the time of writing is the Swedish S-tank (Strv 103B). By having the gun pivoted at the front they are able to achieve the desired 10 degrees depression, but at the same time the vehicle is very low, leading to a reduction in the amount of frontal armour and thus of the weight, down to a mere 38 tonnes. The gun has an automatic loader and a three-man crew. The gun is layed horizontally and vertically by moving the entire tank on its tracks. This necessitates a very fine hydropneumatic suspension system. Produced between 1966 and 1971, the S-tank was modified in the mid-1980s including a laser rangefinder and computer.

The Swedes are developing a new main battle tank which will probably be of the other turretless type, an external gun tank, like the Utveckling UDES XX 20 articulated tank destroyer. This might come into service around 1995. The external gun combines the advantages of the casemate type tank — a more compact and thus more easily protected crew and engine compartment, reducing weight and vulnerability by eliminating the high and heavy turret, with the turreted tank's ability to move the gun independently of the chassis, thus obviating the complex and delicate suspension system such as that used in the S-tank. Disadvantages are that the gun still has some of the height of the former turret, and that being stuck out (or up) on something of a limb it is vulnerable to fire. Although external guns usually have an armoured capsule or cassette around the breech mechanism, they must be more vulnerable to dislocation than when located in a turret or the hull. The statistical probability of a hit on the small upper surface of an externally mounted gun from a top attack weapon might be less than that of a hit on a large turret, but in terms of the tank's overall ability to fight this can hardly be seen as an advantage. Simplicity of sighting and laying will, in the author's view, tend to give the external gun an advantage over the casemate tank, but it is a finely balanced judgment.

The position of the gun, assuming that some sort of heavy gun remains a prerequisite for a tank-type vehicle, is less crucial than the position of the tank commander. Although theoretically a commander can acquire all the visual data he or she needs from optical instruments, there are psychological reasons why he or she needs to stay on top. There are clear advantages in having the rest of the crew inside a compact armoured carapace, but the commander will need to see out. The most obvious way would be to give him a transparent canopy or bubble to see out of. This would be gas and long-term radiation proof, and resistant to splinters and even small arms fire, but would need a stronger armoured cover to protect it from heavy attack. The hostility of the entire battlefield environment and threats from anti-optical weapons like lasers (see Chapter 6) may force tank commanders to work from inside their vehicles and the need to give maximum protection from heavy fire will further force them inside the hull.

Certain developments also suggest that the distinction between the tank and the armoured personnel carrier may become blurred. The *Merkava* carrying infantry and the Israelis' adaptation of old tanks to make ultra-heavy APCs are one example: the Federal German Army also believes that the infantry fighting vehicle (IFV) may become the pivot of the armoured force mix. IFVs like Bradley and Warrior are approaching the cost of main battle tanks, and Rheinmetall of West Germany have developed a plan to fit a low-velocity 105 mm gun to the top of the US Bradley.[16] The combination gun or gun mortar (see above) also provides an opportunity to give APCs or IFVs firepower approximating to that of a small tank or self-propelled gun.

From about 1995, therefore, the patent advantages of the topless or 'crew in hull' layout in terms of firepower, mobility and protection may prevail over tradition in the design of new tanks. Firepower, because a big gun can be carried with less associated weight; tactical mobility, because the overall weight is substantially reduced and the silhouette is lower; protection, because the crew is safely buried in the hull and armour can be more equitably distributed overall. There are penalties: the traditional grip of the tank and armoured unit commander on the pulse of the battle may be lost, but he will probably prefer that to losing his head. Crew in hull tanks would presumably be more vulnerable to mining, and the increasing importance of mine warfare is thus further emphasised. Older tanks will remain in service for many years, with improved ammunition, sights, rangefinders and other additions such as reactive armour, applied by the Israelis to their M-60 and Centurion tanks in 1982. The latter consists of boxes bolted on to the tank armour, each comprising explosive moulded between sheets of metal. When a shaped charge round strikes, the explosive goes off, disrupting the shaped charge jet.[17]

NEW THREATS TO TANKS AND ACTIVE PROTECTION FOR THEM

The greatest threat to tanks in the 1990s and beyond is likely to come from guided, primarily indirect fire, anti-armour weapons. It may not be feasible to give tanks heavy, special armour all over, as we have seen, and this, combined with their spiralling cost (over a million dollars for a relatively cheap new one at the time of writing) makes more radical forms of protection attractive. A tank defence system might comprise a quick reaction, vertically-launched missile with vectored thrust control to home in on attacking sub-munitions. Because of the cost and limited space on individual tanks, such anti-projectile missiles could well be mounted on special vehicles to move with tank platoons. The British are investigating the feasibility of such a system, provisionally called Porcupine because it shoots its defensive quills at the attacker. The system offers a real chance to mitigate the effect of large numbers of indirect fire top attack munitions (see above) falling on tanks well behind the FLOT. Although such a system may appear excessively elaborate and costly (one Porcupine would cost at least as much as a self-propelled air defence vehicle — probably more), that is not excessive given the cost and complexity of modern main battle tanks, and without it the tank as we know it has a distinctly questionable future. If such anti-missile missiles are deployed on or with tanks, it will be a further manifestation of the tendency of land warfare systems to acquire the characteristics of those at sea, like the Seawolf system deployed to protect major warships against sea-skimming missiles. As the numbers of these missiles and launch vehicles would be limited, the vehicles might be deployed only with major tank formations known to be particularly vulnerable — a NATO counterstroke force, or Soviet OMG, perhaps?

The other major threat to tanks in the medium term is a variant of the oldest one of all: the kinetic energy projectile. If it goes fast enough, a 5 kilogram metal rod can penetrate any thickness of tank armour, and clever or special armours are no more use against it than ordinary armour. Kinetic energy warheads obviate the need for expensive fuzing and explosives technology and are less vulnerable to electronic counter measures, bearing out the military truism that the simplest thing is usually the best. Proposals for hypervelocity KE projectiles flying at over Mach 5 (five times the speed of sound) are feasible, and such weapons may be deployed in the 1990s. The most promising method of launch would be direct fire from aircraft. Such arrows would be hard to stop. Ideally they would be terminally guided, but could be switched off in the final stages of flight to reduce vulnerability to active armour defence measures. If a lump of extremely dense metal were to hit a tank at over 3,000 miles per hour, however, no amount of ingenious armour would save it.[18]

Conclusion

The distinction between tank, APC, IFV, assault gun and self-propelled gun may become less clear in the next quarter century. It may even be possible to devise a single basic platform capable of mounting a variety of weapons including guns approaching tank gun size. Modern IFVs like the Bradley and MCV-80 (Warrior) present the opportunity to mount guns of 105 mm. calibre, making the distinction from the tank appear rather academic. It is the author's guess, however, that a distinct heavy main battle tank will continue to co-exist with such a family of vehicles (see also below).

HELICOPTERS

The advantages and potential of helicopters are already apparent from the examples of their use in recent wars in Chapter 1. As the battlefield becomes more dangerous for expensive fixed-wing aircraft, helicopters will take over even more of their fire support roles, as well as carrying troops and supplies swiftly and independent of terrain obstacles. Every recent conflict has seen helicopters used to a greater extent than in the last, although there are no examples of their being used in really high-intensity mechanised war. They are considered by some to be excessively vulnerable, complicated and expensive. However, if skilfully flown, helicopters are very difficult to see and to hit. Helicopters can hide on the ground or in a low hover, behind trees or buildings. Helicopters are also being designed with increasing emphasis on survival. The Soviet Mi-24 Hind has armour around the cockpit area, underfloor fuel tanks and ammunition storage areas, probably using titanium which is astonishingly strong and light and of which the Soviet Union has more resources than anyone else. It is also possible to pressurise fuel tanks with inert gases or fill them with a plastic honeycomb to quench fire when hit. Modern attack helicopters like the US AH1 Cobra are designed with flat canopy surfaces to reduce the glint, further reducing their prominence. The helicopter rotor is particularly visible and vulnerable. Duplicating control systems will reduce the danger of a chance round knocking out the rotor, with almost inevitably fatal consequences, and observation devices can be fitted to the top of the rotor, enabling the entire helicopter body to hide behind cover.

Helicopters move forward by tilting their rotors slightly to the front. This produces an up and forward motion but if the amount of lift is adjusted to the weight of the helicopter then the only movement will be forward. The main development at the time of writing is to have two contra-rotating rotors. These give more lift and or speed and, because the lateral movement of one cancels out that of the other, no tail rotor is needed to stop the helicopter itself spinning round. The latest Soviet battle helicopter, known as Hokum, has such counter rotating rotors, and is estimated to have a maximum speed of 350 km/h and a radius of action of 250 kilometres. Not having a tail rotor reduces its vulnerability to enemy fire and also means that rockets mounted on little stubby wings on either side of the fuselage will not damage anything with their exhaust. There has been considerable speculation as to whether this is the first purpose-built anti-helicopter helicopter. It may be, in which case its position as a component of the integrated AirLand Battle is an interesting one (see below).

Helicopters cannot carry enough ordnance to enable them to completely substitute for artillery's massed fire, nor are they sufficiently invulnerable to survive in close tactical contact like tanks. Experience in Vietnam and subsequent trials do however indicate that the helicopter has an important role to play in defeating enemy tanks, each helicopter able to destroy several tanks before being destroyed itself. The helicopter would not itself break through enemy defences, but might be critical in moving swiftly to counter an enemy breakthrough. For this reason, armoured formations are equipped with radar-controlled anti-tank guns such as the West German Gepard or the Russian ZSU-23-4. Helicopters will have to engage these as well as tanks themselves, and carry a mixture of weapons to do so. For example, the American AH-64 Apache carries eight Hellfire missiles (anti-tank) with a range of about 5 kilometres, two pods with 19 unguided rockets in each and a 30mm chain gun. In order not to be outgunned, it is likely that Soviet self propelled air-defence guns will be upped correspondingly.[19]

The successor to the Apache and other American helicopters will be the result of the LHX (Light Helicopter Experimental) programme, undergoing research and development at the time of writing and expected to be fielded from the late 1990s. It is the largest peacetime helicopter programme ever embarked on, with a requirement for 4,000 to 5,000 machines in the 2,700-3,600 kilogramme weight class. LHX envisages two variants of the same family: a light transport version (LHX-U, U for utility) and a scout or light attack version (LHX-SCAT). This would help reduce the large number of different helicopter types currently in service. The US Army wants a helicopter which is more reliable, easier to maintain and more likely to survive on the battlefield than present types. It also specifies suitability for desert operations ('hot and high'), and NBC protection. The choice of weapons for the SCAT version is uncertain but will probably use existing weapons types. Two strong contenders were a single seat contra-rotating rotor design using the advancing blade concept, or one with two tilt rotors (like aircraft engines at the end of little wings), which looks more like a fixed wing aircraft. The latter has now been eliminated. The first production LHXs would be delivered in the early 1990s with production continuing well into the next century.[20]

Helicopters will play a major role in inserting troops and weapons deep in the enemy deployment, or moving them swiftly to counter enemy penetrations. The helicopter will usurp the role which many in the 1930s envisaged for light tanks, striking deep and precisely at enemy command and control and other operational objectives. Another classic role for the helicopter is pursuit, traditionally one of the most demanding and neglected phases of war. The Soviets, with their age-old emphasis on pursuit, clearly have this in mind. Major land powers, certainly in Europe, may in future have enough helicopters to insert large, perhaps formation sized, forces in the enemy rear, escorted by attack helicopters. The enemy would have to use his attack helicopters to oppose them with the required speed, and we might therefore see battles between large helicopter-borne forces or the helicopters themselves in rear areas, while the contact battle between heavier armoured forces rages between them. Helicopter landing sites will be very vulnerable, and the search for increased range no doubt partly reflects the need for helicopters to operate from a safer distance back. The overall effect will be stretch: to stretch the contact area (which may become no-man's land) to the full range of helicopters, perhaps 200 kilometres. A very large part of the future of land warfare lies in the air up to about a hundred feet above the ground, an area where helicopters can fly or use their astonishing agility to rest or shelter on the ground, where although severed from the clogging terrain the helicopter can still use the ground's shelter, dodging behind its folds and emerging briefly to fire. It is an unfamiliar and exciting prospect. The merging of ground and air will become even more pronounced if a way is found to make a flying vehicle which is cheaper and simpler than present helicopters, and has more of the tank's resilience.

Such a machine has been advocated by the German General Dr Ferdinand von Senger und Etterlin, beginning with a lecture at the RUSI in February 1983 which centred on the Main Battle Air Vehicle (MBAV) concept. It was also taken up by the military theorist of the 1980s Richard Simpkin. An attack helicopter carrying no infantry like the AH-64 Apache, was seen as the flying equivalent of a light tank; the Mi-24 Hind, with its ability to carry troops, as a flying IFV (see above). Von Senger und Etterlin thought in terms of an air-mechanised division, whose prime role would be as an army group (operational level — see Chapter 4) reserve. The MBAV could compensate for its relatively weak protection by its mobility: it would be vulnerable to roughly the same spectrum of threats as the MBT/IFV, but its speed would reduce the vulnerability of its underbelly to chance machine gun or cannon fire. The American AARV (flying tank) proved able to withstand 0.5 inch (12.7 mm) machine gun rounds. There is a lot of sense in the MBAV idea. Having a resilient air vehicle able to engage in close combat effectively replaces two major systems: lift helicopters carrying ground-based AFVs, for one; furthermore, in order to defend against enemy helicopters, armies may be obliged to go for expensive tracked armoured vehicles with radar controlled guns like the German Gepard or the Soviet ZSU-23-4: an armed helicopter able to engage other helicopters would fulfil this role plus strike attack: two birds with one stone, again. Reservations have been expressed about the quality of crewmen (or women) required to fight a MBAV, but if the system is well armoured and simpler to operate, which should be possible using modern technology, the crew will need no more skill than those of the present very expensive tanks. Taken all together, the cost and manning requirements of MBAVs against those of assault helicopters *plus* transport helicopters carrying or resupplying light armoured vehicles *plus* increasingly expensive and vulnerable MBTs *plus* tracked anti-aircraft vehicles indicates that a homogeneous fleet based on MBAVs may be a very attractive option.[21]

The ideas of von Senger and Simpkin give substance to the thoughts expressed by the Israeli General Tal, that a flying tank is a real option, but whereas Tal does not believe that the helicopter can ever fully replace the tank, the German and the Briton think that it just might. In the major American and European armies, that is a possibility in the next quarter or half century; for other major land powers, other less radical options may be more realistic.

LIGHTER ARMOURED VEHICLES

The fact that main battle tanks and the new NATO IFVs are tracked should not distract us from the potential of wheeled vehicles. On flat and firm terrain wheels are more efficient than tracks, and it is much easier to change a wheel than replace a thrown track. Away from clay soil and peat bogs, the advantages are all with wheels. They move faster on roads, their fuel consumption is lower, and they are quieter and less fatiguing to drive. Brigadier Effendi of the Pakistan Army has advocated widespread deployment of wheeled vehicles by Third World countries which, he believes, can be given firepower approaching that of a tank. The advantages he quotes are that:

— The problem of moving tanks by rail or on transporters within a theatre is precluded. Lighter armoured vehicles can move swiftly along roads, combining strategic mobility with operational.
— Maintenance is cheaper and simpler.
— Third World countries can produce their own wheeled vehicles if they have a basic automotive industry. This reduces their dependence on more industrially developed countries for spares and maintenance, especially important in wartime
— The potency of the vehicle on the battlefield need not neces-

sarily suffer. A 90 mm gun firing APFSDS ammunition may be just as good as a bigger one, given that it is a sub-calibre penetrator which does all the damage. Guided missiles and gun mortars may also be fitted to lighter chassis.

— Light armoured vehicles are also quite capable of mounting rapid fire chain guns of around 30 mm calibre, ideal for dealing with the helicopter threat.[22]

GUIDED AND UNGUIDED ANTI-TANK WEAPONS

Some guided weapons have already been examined in the sections on artillery and missiles. Guided weapons have had a more pronounced effect on the battlefield than any other over the last quarter century; it remains to be seen whether they will do so over the next. They have provided infantry with the opportunity to engage armour, and for armour to be attacked at ranges exceeding those of tank guns themselves. They had a particular impact in the 1973 Yom Kippur War, but changes in tactics and improvements in armour protection may prove that to have been an isolated occurrence. Anti-tank weapons range from the light hand-held Soviet RPG-7 and the bigger British LAW 80 up to vehicle-mounted long-range anti-tank guided weapons (LRATGW). The former are usually unguided, and the need to make them man-portable limits their effectiveness against modern special armours. As a general rule, hand-held anti-tank weapons are unlikely to be effective against the front armour of tanks, but will pierce tanks' side armour from an enfilade position. Although the shaped charge warhead provides the most effective anti-armour capability for its size, limitations on what a man can carry are likely to preclude much further development in this field. There need not be any limit on the size of vehicle-mounted LRATGW. Most LRATGW use command to line of sight guidance. This means that the missile is flown along the line of sight from operator to target, being brought back on line if it wanders off. Later systems, such as the American TOW, have semi-automatic command line of sight guidance (SACLOS). Here the operator only has to keep his sight on the target, so the missile can be launched from a remote position. A particular problem with all these missiles is the need for the operator to keep the sight steady when he or she is cold, hungry, frightened and may be under attack. The

207

faster the missile goes, the less time the operator has to keep his or her nerve, but that requires a larger propellant charge which puts up the missile weight. The ideal system would be a 'fire and forget' missile which would home on to enemy armour. The problem there is that, unlike sea and air warfare, the land battlefield is a very crowded place, probably littered with burning vehicles and false heat sources. A fire and forget missile would almost certainly have to be heat seeking, and would be easily distracted. A radar homing system would also be distracted by background clutter. It may be possible to design a missile which would recognise the shape of an enemy tank, although that lies some time in the future. An easier solution would be to have a semi-active homing device, homing on reflected laser light from a target. The operator would fire the missile from a remote location and then lase the target from a line of sight position, in the same way as with copperhead (see above).

LRATGW can begin to destroy enemy armour at about 4 kilometres range, or indeed, as far as the visible horizon. At about 3 kilometres tank and anti-tank guns become effective and at 2 kilometres, man-portable anti-tank weapons. Light anti-tank weapons are used in close combat, ambushes, and when the defensive positions are actually overrun. Given the emphasis on the deep battlefield and the need to hit the enemy much further back, it is clear that an indirect fire self-homing anti-armour system, able to strike beyond visual range, is a pressing necessity.[23]

ENGINEER AND EARTH-MOVING EQUIPMENT

Throughout this book, the importance of terrain itself has been stressed, and armies' ability to negotiate terrain has always depended on engineers and in particular their ability to cross dry or wet gaps. The commander of NORTHAG, flying over the battlefield during exercise Lionheart in 1984, was struck by the number of fascines (rolled up palings) and bridges used to negotiate a fairly normal piece of country. Ninety per cent of gaps in Western Europe are less than 15 metres wide, so a simple bundle of sticks can make all the difference. For larger gaps the most developed armies have bridges launched from adapted tank chassis. Sixty metres of the British class 60 bridge can be constructed in 30 minutes. Military engineers will always devise ways of dealing with unforeseen circumstances, but the development of engineer equipment does not seem to be given as much attention as it deserves. Tizard's report noted the same thing,

> The bulldozer has proved of the greatest value in this war. It was produced originally for civilian purposes and is a simple invention which relies on the brute force of lavish power. We consider that the problem of shifting earth and rock either on or below the surface has never really received the scientific attention its importance in war would warrant ... we regard the investigation of the physical principles underlying soil movements of every kind as an example of the type of long term research which we would say would almost certainly yield results of importance for army operations. Our ignorance of the fundamentals in this field prevents us even from appreciating the possibilities of applying modern engineering technique and mechanical power to burrowing, or the feasibility of breaking through the soft top crust and carrying loads on the firmer subsoil.[24]

Underground warfare has taken place for thousands of years, particularly in sieges, and also characterised some operations in the Great War as both sides sapped towards the enemy lines and planted giant mines, like that detonated at Vimy Ridge. If, as is possible, future land combat in Europe takes on a positional nature, at least temporarily, or individual objectives are strongly contested, the use of modern technology to burrow through the earth faster than has ever been possible before could benefit the side which has paid most attention to it.

SMALL ARMS

It will be clear by now that major land combat depends very much on the long-range heavy weapons. The increasing use of the term 'personal weapon' underlines the fact that it is a man's or woman's private protection, a last resort. All the developed nations are now moving towards smaller calibres (5.56mm in place of the former 7.62) and shorter weapons which are more suitable for troops jumping out of or into armoured vehicles. The smaller calibre has many advantages. First, more ammunition can be carried, or alternatively the load and thus fatigue on the soldier is reduced. Because the muzzle energy of the round is less, the weight of the rifle can be less, too, which again reduces load and fatigue, and is also quicker into the aim with less recoil when fired. A 5.56mm weapon has less range and penetrating power than a 7.62, but in view of the changed role of small arms this clearly does not matter very much. Both the Soviets and the British have adopted new families of light weapons comprising an individual weapon and a light support weapon or machine gun. The latter (SA80) family, comprising the Engager individual weapon and the light support weapon (LSW), has begun to be introduced into the British forces at the time of writing. If heavier fire is required than the LSW can deliver, one would expect it to be provided by armoured vehicles.

The differing requirements of infantry and vehicle-mounted weapons can be illustrated by British experience. The old Bren gun was extremely popular as a section weapon, but in the 1970s was replaced by the General Purpose Machine Gun (GPMG) which, as its name implied, was designed both as an infantry weapon and a vehicle-mounted one. It was really too heavy for the former, and its belt feed picked up every piece of dirt available. As a vehicle weapon, it would probably not have been much use against enemy IFVs. At the time of writing, therefore, we see a bifurcation: lighter personal weapons and section weapons, while specialised weapons are being developed for vehicles, in the form of 20mm cannon and upwards.[25] This trend is likely to continue although heavier machine guns like the GPMG may be required in circumstances where lavish armoured support for infantry is not available, like the Falklands. The new light weapons also replace many of the sub-machine guns and smaller weapons issued to armoured vehicle crews, artillerymen and other specialists, thus further reducing the number of different weapons and ammunition in service, further contributing to standardisation and economy.

A most important requirement of small arms is that they should be simple. They get wet, covered in sand, and have to be taken apart, cleaned and reassembled in pitch darkness and a howling gale. The Soviet Kalashnikov AK series is an excellent example. A brilliant design, the AK-47 and AKM have a breech assembly which falls together like a Chinese puzzle with very few parts. Kalashnikovs were greatly prized by the

Americans in Vietnam, many of whom used captured specimens in preference to their issue M16s.

BODY ARMOUR

Reducing the weight of the soldier's armament and load may be very fortuitous, as it permits him or her to wear armour. Personal armour has never entirely disappeared from the battlefield; just as the last cuirassed cavalry were swept off the battlefield, armies began reintroducing steel helmets. During World War II air crews began to be issued with jackets containing metal plates to mitigate the effects of anti-aircraft fire which penetrated the aircraft, often causing hideous casualties. For this reason they became known as 'flak jackets'. These were suitable for aircrew sitting still, but were too heavy for active combat. During the Korean War the Americans began experiments with heavy gauge nylon cord woven into thick fabric, as well as other types of body armour. In the savage fighting in Korea, with much clearing of fox-holes and close combat, the value of body armour was proven and eventually a new fabric called Kevlar, a type of nylon, was developed which when tightly woven gave good resistance to missile attack. Kevlar cloth is now widely used to make body armour, and also has other applications. It normally comprises 12 to 30 layers. To protect against military rifles and machine guns, steel, titanium or ceramic plates have to be combined with Kevlar.

As noted in Chapter 2, man (and woman) power is a problem for developed nations, especially given the high degree of training necessary to operate modern weaponry. Anything to preserve the soldier's combat effectiveness is of great interest. The West German Army recently indicated that it wished to purchase several thousand protective jackets for its troops, and others may follow suit.[26] Body armour will be important both for the infantryman operating in the open and for armoured vehicle crews. It may have to be worn in combination with NBC protection as well. The reappearance of body armour on combat soldiers will probably be one of the most distinctive changes in the appearance of land warfare the next decade or so.

MORE DISTANT PROSPECTS FOR MOVEMENT OVER LAND

In the more distant future there are other possibilities for moving men and weapons mechanically over land. The first was advocated by Tizard in 1945, and has had recurring popularity in future war literature since. Tizard noted that some animals were speedier across certain types of terrain than any mechanical vehicle, despite a lower power-weight ratio and a higher ground pressure per unit area. This radically different system of applying power in animals necessitates an automatic self balancing mechanism which, he believed, 'it should not be beyond the power of engineers to imitate'.[27] In other words, a mechanical walking device. This would necessitate a higher centre of gravity, creating a high silhouette. In the 1960s the US Army envisaged using such mechanical mammoths to carry men and material across remote, marshy-forested areas.[28] Such terrain might be encountered in Alaska, Manchuria or the Soviet *taiga*. Unlike aircraft, such machines would not require landing sites or strips, and would be harder to destroy if seen. The fact that they have not been adopted enthusiastically suggests that the cost and complexity of such devices outweigh their advantages in what must be fairly special circumstances and terrain. Having said that, the spectacle of great armoured machines striding across lakes and marshes and endowed with a full suite of armaments could have a devastating effect on enemy morale if used with surprise. The Falklands conflict is one where such machines could have been used to advantage. Such a picture may seem far fetched, but it is not an impossibility.

The second main group of platforms are air cushion vehicles or hovercraft. The hovercraft was invented by the British and adopted with enthusiasm for military purposes by the Russians. It is very much a part of modern amphibious warfare. Hovercraft can traverse sea, ice, marsh or ground with equal facility, and are thus ideal for fighting in circumstances where action may switch rapidly from one to the other, or where ground and water are intermixed. The Iranian attacks on Iraqi positions in the Hawizah marshes (see Chapter 1) are an example of a situation where large, armoured and armed hovercraft could have been useful. On *terra firma*, the size of the hovercraft, its expense and vulnerability do not make it more attractive than other means of transport. The Soviets might use hovercraft in

assault crossings of very large rivers or lakes, but such operations can be considered as examples of amphibious warfare to
all intents and purposes.

The latest development is the so-called wing in ground
(WIG) craft. This combines the shape of a conventional aircraft
with a cushion of air generated by its proximity to the ground,
rather than simply using the wing to provide lift. The most
advanced exponents of this type of craft are the Russians, who
call them *ekranoplany* (*ekran*, a screen or curtain, and *plan*, the
lifting surface of an aircraft wing). An *ekranoplan* operates on
the principle that, at a height equal to half its wingspan or less, a
cushion of air is trapped between the underside of the wings and
the supporting surface (sea, ice, ground) below. WIG inhibits
the downwash generated by wing lift, reducing drag by about 70
per cent. This in turn reduces fuel consumption and allows the
payload or range to be increased. Whereas a conventional aircraft carries about 4 kilograms per horse-power of engine output, when operating within the Wing in Ground Effect the
payload can be increased by 500 per cent. WIG aircraft could
thus carry substantial force to locations, unperturbed by sea,
swamp or level ground conditions, and minefields. *Ekranoplans*
can also manoeuvre in the air like aircraft, although once they
leave the ground effect cushion (say 50-70 metres up for a 100-
140 metre wingspan craft) they lose the economies of WIG
effect versus a conventional aircraft. It should, however, be
possible to give them short bursts of intense power to overcome
this, thus making them more flexible and less vulnerable than
hovercraft. They could fly across shorelines and river banks,
marshes, into harbours and clear archipelagos, marshes, deltas
and lake areas. They may therefore be suitable for assault in
areas where land and water meet, over arctic ice or for
extremely efficient intra-theatre or strategic transport, perhaps
from the 1990s. They offer strategic flexibility for land-air operations without the technological complexities of landwalkers or
the vulnerability and limitations of hovercraft, and could be particularly useful in operations on the edges of major land theatres
or outside them.[29] It seems unlikely, however, that even these
will dent the dominance of the railway in large-scale movements
of heavy equipment and stores over land.

CONCLUSIONS

The trend, certainly in developed countries, will be to exploit technology to multiply the capabilities of human beings and save manpower. Artificial intelligence, particularly robotics, will be used to fulfil mechanical or arithmetical functions (artillery). More emphasis will be placed than previously on preserving the combat effectiveness of troops (reducing fatigue, body armour). Turning to specific technologies, tanks introduced in the 1990s may be radically different from traditional designs, but those introduced in the mid and late 1980s will be very similar to their predecessors and they will certainly be employed in very much the same way. Special armour has challenged the once prevalent view that the anti-tank guided weapon had spelled the end of the tank's primacy. The battle between the tank and the ATGW seems about evenly balanced, and artillery may be the deciding factor one way or the other. The fact that the most potent anti-tank systems — tank guns and ATGW — are effectively limited to a 4 kilometre-wide strip of action corresponding to visual range is a major discontinuity between technology and doctrine, and some sort of indirect fire anti-armour weapon must logically appear. In the 1990s it will, and may be the most revolutionary change in the conduct of land warfare since the helicopter. The world's infantries are being equipped with small arms that fire smaller calibre ammunition, and will engage the enemy at ranges considerably less than the 900 yards at which the British Expeditionary Force engaged the Germans in 1914. Troops wearing NBC protection plus body armour, face-masks merging into close-fitting, possibly Kevlar helmets, and carrying the new stubby small arms with optical sights, will look very much like apparitions from Star Wars. Yet, paradoxically, their role and employment will have changed less than any other arm. Conversely, artillery, which offers the most potential for change, will at first sight retain its classic shape and characteristics. Artillery is getting bigger and pulling back and the resulting gap is being filled by rapid-firing cannons and gun mortars. The emphasis placed by NATO and the Warsaw Pact on deep attack has placed and will continue to place even more emphasis on indirect fire weapons: conventional and extended range artillery, MLRS, and large tactical ballistic and possibly cruise missiles. Improved munitions, including 'smart' shells, will enable more and more of the tasks now performed by direct fire weapons to be undertaken by indirect, at much greater ranges. Inevitably, this places more emphasis on air and space systems for target acquisition.

The relative importance of surface to surface weapons systems and conventional air power will be a key issue. It is arguable that the greater vulnerability and expense of the manned aircraft and accuracy of surface to surface missiles will lead to the latter encroaching on the role of conventional air power to some extent. In the opening phases of a conflict, certainly, surface to surface missiles and artillery will play a key role in establishing where clear areas for aircraft to pass lie, and where they do not. However, for delivering a large concentration of conventional firepower, or improved conventional munitions such as fuel air explosives, especially for putting a number of such large munitions on a target with near pinpoint accuracy, it is difficult to replace conventional air power. Once a target is designated with a laser, it is easier and far cheaper to slide a number of aerial bombs down the beam that to fire several surface to surface guided missiles at it from a distance. Aircraft equipped with inertial navigation systems can laser designate a target and then keep the beam on it for the necessary time more easily than an exhausted, frightened soldier on the ground, and certainly much further in the enemy depth. The ingenious and considered interaction of air and ground systems will characterise the warfare of the future, but the latter are unlikely to supplant the former.

Returning to the contact battle on the ground, the helicopter will play an unprecedented role. At the moment it cannot replace heavy ground vehicles like tanks in the contact battle, but for striking deep, pursuit and operational level manoeuvre, whether by attacking forces or in order to counter penetrations, it will lift the bounds of land warfare into the lower atmosphere. At the same time, ground itself will remain cardinal, and engineer equipment will retain all its significance.

NOTES

1. Details from *Jane's Weapon Systems*, 1984-5.
2. Pierre Touzin, 'MLRS with USAREUR', *Armed Forces*, March 1984, p. 87.
3. LARS: *Armies and Weapons*, No. 41, February-March 1978, p. 39; MARS/MLRS: Ron Sherman, 'MLRS: the Soldier's System',

Military Technology, 28 November 1981, pp. 33-40; Wolfgang Flume, 'Artillerieraketensystem MARS/MLRS', *Wehrtechnik*, 11/1983, pp. 18-33; Charles J. Dick, 'MLRS: Firepower for the 1990s', *RUSI Journal*, December 1983, pp. 17-22; BM-27: author's *Red God of War* (Brassey's Oxford, 1986), pp. 149-51.

4. General SADARM concept in R.G. Lee, *Introduction to Battlefield Weapons Systems and Technology*, 2nd edition (Brassey's Battlefield Weapons Systems and Technology Series, Brassey's, Oxford, 1985), p. 48; MLRS phase three: Brian Wanstall, 'Sharper Surveillance and sensing submunitions spell tough times for tanks', *Interavia*, 8/1985, p. 863; Merlin: 'Merlin homes in', *Flight International*, 3 August 1985, p. 11. The 300 m² footprint is very small (equivalent to a circle 19.5 metres in diameter, at first sight not much bigger than a tank itself!). However, it effectively ensures that a near miss now becomes a kill.

5. ATACMS: details from Vought advertisement, various periodicals, late 1985. 'Army Tactical Missile System Contract Awarded', *Aviation Week and Space Technology*, 31 March 1986, p. 29. The report in Wanstall's article in *Interavia*, 8/1985, p. 863, that the US Army and Air Force had decided on a division of responsibility at the 70 kilometre line is incorrect.

6. Colonel L. Zabudkin, '*Kassetnye snaryady*', *Tekhnika i vooruzheniya* (*TiV*, 1/1984, pp. 36-7; Colonel V. Rokhkachev, '*Kassetnye boyevye chasti raket*', *TiV*, 2/1984, pp. 8-9. Whereas Zabudkin's article appeared in the 'In capitalist armies' section, Rokhkachev's appeared in the 'problems and perspectives' column, suggesting that the Soviets may be more interested in sub-munition warheads for their large tactical missiles than for smaller artillery shells.

7. FAE from *Jane's Weapon Systems*, 1980-1, pp. 405-6. Nuclear weapons from Reinhardt and Kintner, *Atomic Weapons*, pp. 171-2.

8. Extended-range artillery: R.D.M. Furlong, 'Extended Range Full Bore and Base Bleed 155 mm Ammunition' and 'The GHN-45: a new long range towed howitzer from Austria', *IDR* 6/1982, pp. 755-68; Tizard Report, *DEFE 2/1252*, p. 31, para 75.

9. R.G. Lee, *Introduction to Battlefield Weapons Systems*, pp. 44-6; R.I. Wrenn's letter 'Redleg circa 2050', *Field Artillery Journal*, September-October 1985, pp. 2-3.

10. See the author's 'Light Support — A New Solution', *Combat Weapons*, Winter 1985, pp. 68-73, and *Red God of War*.

11. Quote from Tizard, *DEFE 2/1252*, p. 31, para 73; tank design: Lee, *Battlefield Weapons Systems*, pp. 1-5.

12. Ibid., pp. 5-14; Douglas Hill, 'Protecting the Soldier', *Jane's Military Review*, 1985, pp. 161-3.

13. Brigadier Richard Simpkin, 'Closed Down for Combat?', *NATO's Sixteen Nations*, June/July 1985, p. 71.

14. Carus, *Lessons of the 1982 Syria-Israel Conflict*, pp. 22-31, quote on p. 23; also personal observation.

15. Carus, *Lessons*, p. 24.

16. Simpkin, 'Closed Down for Combat'.

17. Carus, *Lessons*, p. 29.

18. Brian Wanstall, 'Kinetic energy to take out tanks', Interavia,

3/1986, pp. 279-80.

19. Lee, *Battlefield Weapons Systems*, pp. 16-18, 212-28; Mark Lambert, 'Close air support comes down to earth', *Interavia*, 6/1985, editorial, p. 567; also Mark Lambert, 'First Havoc, now Hokum: What role for the new Soviet helicopter?' *Interavia*, 7/1985, pp. 798-99.

20. Ramon Lopez, 'LHX: helicopter program of the century', *IDR*, 5/1984, pp. 585-8; Mark Lambert, 'LHX — not just another helicopter, *Interavia*, 5/1985, pp. 488-50; conventional helicopter preferred: ibid., 'Is the 680 rotor Bell's LHX candidate?', *Interavia*, 9/1985, pp. 981-2.

21. Brigadier Richard E. Simpkin, 'Flying Tanks? — a tactical technical analysis of the "main battle air vehicle" concept', *Military Technology (MILTECH)*, 8/1984, pp. 62-80, and *Race to the Swift*, pp. 117-32, in particular pp. 121-7.

22. Colonel (now Brigadier) Mohammed Yahya Effendi, 'Armour: Firepower on Wheels: Third World Countries' Option', *PAJ*, September 1982, pp. 6-17.

23. Details are given in Lee, *Battlefield Weapons Systems*, pp. 155-64.

24. Tizard, *DEFE 2/1252*, p. 31, para 72: abundance of fascines, etc.: General Farndale's talk, *Counterstroke: Future Requirements*, RUSI, 15 October 1985, see also Chapter 4.

25. Lee *Battlefield Weapons Systems*, pp. 93-112, plus personal experience of small arms. British small arms: 'SA 80 is handed over to British Army', *Defence Material*, November-December 1985, p. 198.

26. Hill, 'Protecting the Soldier', pp. 163-6; Coates, *Wound Ballistics and Body Armour*, pp. 684, 765-6. According to Coates' exhaustive examination, the 'lesson of body armor was not learned until late in World War II and it was not until the Korean war that the numerous sceptics were convinced and body armor was accepted wholeheartedly'. In Korea body armour produced a decrease in the number of soldiers killed and wounded in action, a decrease in the severity of wounds and of loading on medical facilities, plus an increase in morale.

27. Tizard, *DEFE 2/1252*, p. 30, para. 71.

28. I.F. Clarke, *Voices Prophesying War*, (OUP, 1966) p. 194. In the mid-1960s the US Army had a test programme for 'landwalkers' which they envisaged being used 'for transport of personnel and cargo in areas where terrain or deep debris would make other means impracticable or where weather conditions or hostile air activity would preclude the use of aircraft.' Movement of the vehicle's arms and legs would correspond to the arm and leg movements of the driver. *Army mobility looks to the future* exhibition, New York World's Fair, 1964-5. Another device was the use of cargo rockets to deliver supplies to forces operating in remote areas (Clarke, p. 195).

29. Roy McLeavy, 'Soviet Navy develops WIG SS-N-22 missile craft', *Jane's Defence Weekly (JDW)*, Vol. 2, No. 2, 21 July 1984, p. 59. The Soviet Navy's WIG craft has a wingspan of 30.5 metres, giving WIG effect up to about 15 metres height, but bigger wingspans are presumably feasible.

6

Electronic Warfare (EW) and Directed Energy Weapons (DEW)

The next major war will be won by the side which best uses the electromagnetic spectrum. As we have seen, developments in weapons platforms and protection occur gradually and slowly, and the external appearance of the battlefield of the year 2000 or even 2010 is largely decided already. Electronic warfare on the other hand, is a field where changes are occurring rapidly, where nobody really knows what will happen 'on the day', a subject which all the major powers shroud in shadow, an area as dark and secret as it is vast and diffuse. This may in fact inhibit armies' ability to fight the electronic battle and must change.

The term Electronic Warfare (EW) embraces every aspect of war involving the electromagnetic spectrum. This is shown in Figure 6.1.

The main descriptive bands of the radar and radar frequencies in the electromagnetic spectrum — VHF, UHF and so on — are paralleled by lettered bands which are used to refer to military radio and radar systems. The system used by the US and NATO at the time of writing is shown in Figure 6.2, together with the old system which may still be encountered in literature on the subject. This should be borne in mind: Soviet counterbattery radars, for example, operate in the I and J bands, which clearly refers to the new US/NATO system, but not all references are so unambiguous. It can be seen that the commonly used millimetre wave frequences range from 26.5 GHz (just above a centimetre wavelength) down to 170 GHz (1.76 mm).

Although communications equipments are said to be tuned to a given frequency, a communications channel in fact embraces a band of frequencies. A broad band increases the

Figure 6.1: The electromagnetic spectrum

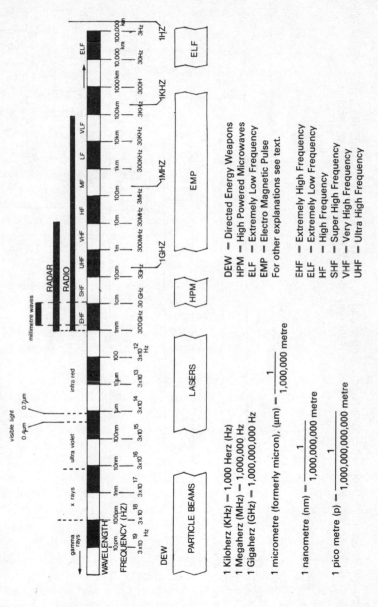

1 Kiloherz (KHz) = 1,000 Herz (Hz)
1 Megaherz (MHz) = 1,000,000 Hz
1 Gigaherz (GHz) = 1,000,000,000 Hz

1 micrometre (formerly micron), (μm) = $\dfrac{1}{1,000,000}$ metre

1 nanometre (nm) = $\dfrac{1}{1,000,000,000}$ metre

1 pico metre (p) = $\dfrac{1}{1,000,000,000,000}$ metre

DEW = Directed Energy Weapons
HPM = High Powered Microwaves
ELF = Extremely Low Frequency
EMP = Electro Magnetic Pulse
For other explanations see text.

EHF = Extremely High Frequency
ELF = Extremely Low Frequency
HF = High Frequency
SHF = Super High Frequency
VHF = Very High Frequency
UHF = Ultra High Frequency

219

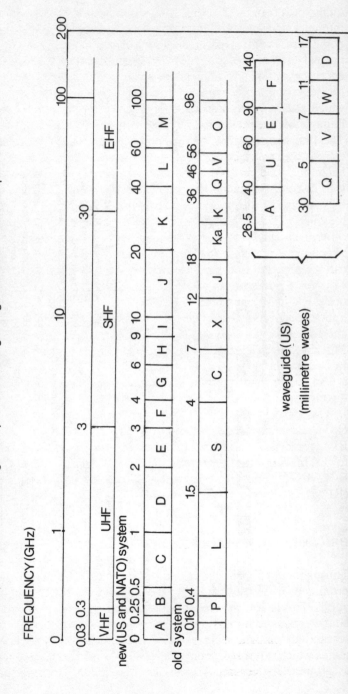

Figure 6.2: Standard frequency bands, showing broad descriptive bands (VHF, UHF, etc.), new US/NATO band system, old system, and US waveguide system for designating millimetre wave frequencies

220

quality of communications, but is correspondingly easier to intercept and/or jam. For this reason, narrow bandwidths are being increasingly used in the EW environment. Alongside the normal uses of the spectrum for communications, lie directed energy weapons and nuclear electromagnetic pulse. It is therefore appropriate to consider these in the same chapter as EW, which usually refers to combat involving all aspects of the communications frequencies. The latter consists of three main areas. The first is finding out about enemy electronic and communications equipment, called Electronic Support Measures (ESM). Secondly, based on the information acquired by ESM, the aim is to discomfit the enemy's electronic equipment and operations by jamming or deception, which is called Electronic Countermeasures (ECM). Thirdly, each side will endeavour to stop the other from employing ECM or reduce its effectiveness, whether by physical protection or design of systems, or by communications security and more deception. This is called Electronic Counter Countermeasures (ECCM).[1] There are also Electro-optical Countermeasures (EOCM) and EOCCM. Electro-optics covers the area of image intensifiers, low light television (LLTV) (TV and image intensifiers), and lasers, EOCM/EOCCM degrades/preserves the performance of these systems. In English the term Radio Electronic Combat Support (RECS) is also used to refer to military electronic warfare activity against the enemy.

The Soviets use much the same classifications. Radio-electronic combat (*radioelektronnaya bor'ba (REB)*) equates to EW, comprises radioelectronic suppression (REP), equivalent to ECM, and radioelectronic defence (REZ), equating to ECCM. The Russians also refer to radioelectronic deception (REM).[2]

ORIGINS AND DEVELOPMENT OF ELECTRONIC WARFARE

Throughout its surprisingly long history EW has been more prominent in the sea and air environments than in land operations. This is not surprising: aside from the general tendency of land weapons technology to be less sophisticated than sea or air, sea and air platforms present clearly identifiable targets in elements which do not stop electromagnetic waves in the same way as ground. Armies are also far less dependent on radar than navies and air forces, and their vulnerability to ECM is correspondingly less. There are nonetheless early examples of electronic warfare on land. By 1916, techniques had been evolved to intercept telephone messages propagated from telephone wires through the ground, and prior to the battle of the Somme the British issued orders prohibiting speech in clear on the telephone within 3 kilometres of the enemy lines. Communications discipline was lax, however, and the Germans learned of the impending assault. When the codeword for the troops to go over the top was given, the Germans, who had been sheltering from the artillery bombardment in deep dugouts, knew that the moment had come to return to the surface. This contributed to the excessive losses suffered by the British on 1 July.[3]

The widespread use of EW in the tactical land-air battle began in Vietnam, and this illustrates the way in which the pendulum of advantage swings from electronic weapon to ECM to ECCM and back again.[4] Although the main examples concern aircraft and air defence, there will in future be parallels for ground-based and tactical systems. One of the earliest examples of a systematic and co-ordinated EW attack as part of a major conventional offensive was the Russian invasion of Czechoslovakia in 1968. A powerful jamming barrage and huge clouds of radar-reflective chaff completely disrupted Czech warning and communications systems.

The Israelis have more recent experience of electronic warfare in a major land-air theatre than anyone else (the other recent example is the Falklands conflict, but EW was dominant in the politico-strategic, air and sea environments rather than in the land battle). The Arab countries have also made extensive use of Soviet weaponry and electronic equipment, which makes their experience particularly relevant to assessing how Soviet EW would operate in a future European war. Arab and Israeli experience once again highlights the total interdependence of air and land. Arab EW techniques included intelligence monitoring of Israeli broadcasts in clear, direction finding (DF) of Israeli transmissions in order to target them, barrage jamming to disrupt command channels and intrusions to give false orders. EW was particularly important for the Arab air defence effort, which negated much of the value of Israeli air power, and they employed extensive ECCM. In order to prevent the Israelis acquiring the locations and number of air defence radars by electronic intelligence (ELINT), the radars deployed forward to cover the initial assault over the Suez Canal were kept silent until the assault began. Each of the various air defence systems operated within a separate frequency band so that no one Israeli jamming system could blind them all. The Arabs also changed frequencies often, and used multiple and interchangeable guidance systems. Some worked on pulsed radar, others on continuous wave. Some of the radar tracking systems also had the ability to track optically so that operations could continue even in a high ECM environment. Others used infrared homing. Finally, the tactical mobility of the air defence radars was also an asset in the EW battle, enabling rapid changes of position after firing or being detected by Israeli ELINT.

The Israeli offensive into Lebanon in 1982 also demonstrated the importance of electronic warfare as an integral part of the modern battlefield, especially in the detection and destruction of anti-aircraft missile radars by aircraft and RPVs (see Chapter 1). Whereas in benign environments 'smart' weapons like surface to air missiles can be extremely lethal, ECM can make them totally ineffective. Electronic warfare equipment has therefore become as important as weaponry. Computerised determination of target co-ordinates, navigation systems, laser rangefinders, and laser target designators all exemplified the integral part that EW plays in the conduct of modern war. The introduction of systems which depend even more on electronics for their action, like millimetre wave seekers and other indirect fire anti-armour weapons, will further increase the direct involvement of EW in the ground, as well as the air-ground battle. Flares and other heat sources can be used to decoy and confuse 'smart' anti-tank projectiles as they have been for many years to confuse anti-aircraft missiles. The increasing role of the helicopter and the likelihood of helicopter to helicopter combat will enhance the importance of EW systems traditionally thought of as part of the air battle. At the same time, the need to manipulate EW systems well forward, as well as in the more remote battle against enemy air, air defence and operational command, will create a requirement for more educated personnel right in the thick of the fighting. The Israelis see that this could pose personnel problems, but not half as much as for their potential opponents, over whom they have a pronounced electronic and educational edge.[5]

BATTLEFIELD ELECTRONIC WARFARE

Electronic Support Measures (ESM)

The first ESM task is search and intercept. This involves scanning a part of the electromagnetic spectrum to classify all transmissions occurring in it, and can be done manually although Automatic Data Processing (ADP) can substantially speed up this lengthy and painstaking process. Enemy transmissions will come from many different locations and distances at different strengths, and will be intermittent. Modern digital equipment with panoramic displays enable the operator to see which frequencies are active and log even short transmissions automatically, which substantially reduces the workload. The next phase is monitoring, which involves continuously listening in to communications to provide further information for analysis. Direct intelligence information can be gained in the unlikely event of clear speech being used or, more likely, if encrypted traffic can be deciphered. Another very important part of EW is direction finding (DF). This uses the simple principle of triangulation, several DF receivers (at least three), to take bearings on the target transmitter. There are problems: obstructions like electric pylons, fences or terrain obstacles may act as second transmitters. Ideally a DF site should be well forward and in the open, but this counteracts the tactical need for concealment. In practice, there is a margin of error of two degrees or more in DF bearings, which means that electromagnetic DF needs to be corroborated by other means. This brings us to the final stage, analysis. An intelligent map study can often pinpoint an emitter known to lie within a triangle identified by DF. The rapid growth of ADP systems helps in this process. To be fully exploited, ESM equipment must be linked to a secure communications system (see Chapter 7). ESM mainly involves communications systems plus radar: ECM and ECCM cover a much wider range of electronic systems.

Electronic Counter Measures (ECM)

ECM comprises two main elements: jamming and deception. Jamming blinds and deafens the enemy's communications, but can be counterproductive. It draws attention to itself and its uncontrolled use is likely to conflict with ESM activity. A jammer has to have substantially more power than the system to be jammed, which makes it especially vulnerable to enemy EW. A common way of getting round the problems is to have two jammers which operate alternately from different places, reducing the chance of intercept ('jam and scram'). The three most common types of communications jamming are spot, barrage and swept jamming. Spot jamming of a specific channel or frequency is most common because it causes least interruption to friendly signals or ESM. Barrage jamming is the simultaneous jamming of a wide band of the frequency spectrum. It is less efficient than spot jamming as the available power is more widely distributed. As its name implies, swept jamming sweeps a signal rapidly up and down a frequency spectrum. It is important to monitor enemy frequencies while they are being jammed, to check that that jamming is effective or that the frequency has not been changed (called a 'look through capability').[6]

Electro-optical Counter Measures (EOCM) will become increasingly important in future. The most prominent area will involve lasers: as dependence on lasers to establish ranges, guide projectiles on to targets and destroy targets themselves increases, so will the need to counter them. A laser beam is highly directional and is thus difficult to intercept. On the other hand, it can be deceived very easily as it only operates within very limited frequency bands. Laser light cannot normally be seen, unless passing through a polluted atmosphere, and so it is important to devise a way of letting a target know when it is being lased. Fitting a laser receiver, equivalent to a RWR, is a first step but cannot in itself prevent a target being hit by other projectiles. Deceptive techniques are being developed which measure the laser's wavelength and pulse repetition frequency and then set up a similar but more powerful laser which can be used to illuminate a false decoy target, attracting any laser-seeking projectile towards the latter. This is particularly appropriate for static installations but would be more difficult to apply to moving targets such as tanks to counter a copperhead-type projectile. For the latter an even simpler device might be very useful: a powerful laser which will be directed against the source of any incoming laser automatically. The defensive laser would either destroy the observer's eye retina or craze the optics being used (see below), causing any laser-guided projectile to wander off the target. Passive EOCMs include smoke, aerosols or chemicals which will absorb or disperse a laser's energy. A simple mirror could be very effective against lasers, but other tactical considerations limit its application in battlefield situations. Dazzling the observer also works with other electro-optical systems such as Low Light television (LLTV), and optical chaff, comprising thousands of shiny sequins or tinsel-like strips can also delude or jam these extremely sensitive search systems.[7]

The other major form of ECM is deception. One can break in on enemy nets to waste time or gather information, or to encourage replies so facilitating DF. Alternatively, false information can be transmitted. The most famous example of this was used in the build up to the Normandy invasions in 1944, when radio networks were set up on the Kent coast to make the Germans think that the invasion was to be mounted in the Pas de Calais area, and phantom armies were created in locations where no troops were in fact massing for the attack. The real invasion army was concentrating much further west. In a future major European war such measures would be critical in hiding planned attacks, responses and reserves.[8]

Non-communications ECM takes many forms. The classic example is the launch of a flare to confuse the guidance system of a heat seeking missile. More complex is a technique developed by the Israelis using two aircraft, one of which would do a loop crossing back over its own flight path creating an area of intense heat, while another would fly on launching anti-infrared flares. An anti-radiation missile, designed to home on an enemy radar, is also a form of ECM. There is passive ECM, using techniques such as 'stealth' technology, reducing a machine's signature, its heat output and so on. Finally, radar can be jammed, but whereas in the case of aircraft and air combat it is sufficient to do this for a very short time, while the aircraft is moving rapidly, battlefield conditions are rather different. A battlefield jammer could easily be located and thus destroyed. There is, however, considerable potential for expendable or remote jammers.[9]

Electronic Counter Counter Measures (ECCM)

The most effective form of ECCM is not to put out radioelectronic emissions at all. The Soviets, with their emphasis on written orders, general instructions to be at a certain place at a certain time (a technique which owes something to the Mongols) and use of land-line systems are probably better equipped in this regard than their potential opponents. However, without radio communications modern armies could not function and measures have to be taken to minimise the likelihood of the enemy intercepting friendly transmission successfully. Another point is that total radio silence will create an 'electronic black hole', which in an area packed with military formations like West or East Germany will create suspicion that something important is in fact hiding there. The optimum solution is to use false signals to convince the enemy that something is there, but that it is not important or different from what it really is. Thus deception plays as important a role in ECCM as in ECM.

The key phrases in communications ECCM are Low Probability of Intercept (LPI) and Emission Control (EMCON). LPI depends to a large extent on training and discipline, including the use of impersonal terms and procedures to minimise the chance of the enemy successfully breaking in on the net. With the increased use of integrated cryptographic equipment and the growth of real time C^3I, the chances of the enemy decoding messages or at any rate doing so in time to be of any use is reduced. Nevertheless, the sheer volume of traffic can enable a major headquarters to be identified or the imminence of a major offensive or operation predicted. Technological ECCM measures in addition to automatic encryption are Frequency Hoppping (FH), Direct Sequence Spread Spectrum, Null Steering antennas, burst transmission and single-frequency rebroadcast. Frequency hopping to avoid interception and jamming is a well established ECCM tactic. The enemy's task searching for the signal is made more difficult and the power required increases with the number of channels he has to scan. In FH systems, sequence generators change the frequency in a random fashion determined by an electronically generated pseudo random code. VHF radios hopping at a rate of hundreds of hops per second are now in service, and most emphasis is being placed on VHF and UHF sets hopping at about this speed. Spread spectrum spreads the signal energy over a very wide bandwidth before modulating to a radio frequency and is thus difficult to intercept and jam as the whole very wide bandwidth must be covered. Also, because the energy density is very low, it is difficult to distinguish the signal from background noise. Null steering uses a null or cusp in the area covered by an aerial's signal, so that its coverage looks like a kidney. The cusp is pointed towards the enemy jammer to which the antenna is immune, enabling it to communicate with friendly aerials from other quarters. More than one null steering aerial, as they are called, can be used in concert with a friendly jammer to blind an enemy jammer while communicating with each other. Burst transmission is unsuitable for speech, but uses either a very narrow band for a long time or a wide band for a short time to fire off a very short signal. One of the oldest and most flexible examples of this is morse code, which is still used, for example, by special forces units operating in stay behind positions. More modern systems like the MEROD (Message Entry and Read Out Device) allow a coded message to be keyed in, recorded in its memory, checked and then broadcast in a short burst. The overcrowding of the electromagnetic spectrum, the increasing intensity and sophistication of ECM, will probably make burst transmission much more attractive in future and we may see a move away from voice radio back to modern equivalents of morse. Finally, single frequency rebroadcast extends the area coverage of radios and presents the enemy with a false picture of where the transmitter is.[10]

An example of ECCM in non-communications systems is frequency agility, which enables a radar to change frequency automatically when it is jammed. In missile guidance systems, a Home on Jam (HOJ) facility will cause the missile to home on the source of jamming automatically if jamming is attempted. The presence of two types of seeker, millimetre wave and IR, in the 203 mm SADARM is arguably a form of ECCM. Generally speaking, the cost of building ECCM protection into a system is about a fifth of that to the enemy of overcoming it.

EW UNITS AS A COMBAT ARM

It is only recently that EW has been recognised as being as much a part of front line combat as the armoured battle, the artillery battle and so on. The Soviets have made EW very much a part of their operations. They place relatively less stress on equipment sophistication than their main potential rivals, the

Americans, and more on ruggedness and strict communications and operational security (COMSEC and OPSEC). Whereas the US makes extensive use of ECCM circuitry, the Russians place the onus on the individual operator or officer to the extent that officers are often named in the military press if they transgress communications security rules. Radioelectronic combat units, to use the Soviet term, are organic to most operational formations, and at the tactical level their employment is most closely tied in with that of the artillery. Soviet radio intercept and DF units have broadband ESM support and ELINT assets but do not appear to have jammers. A DF platoon has a minimum of three DF stations while an intercept sub-unit might have five intercept positions operating on VHF channels. The divisional reconnaissance battalion also apparently has the ability to DF and intercept. A similar organisation exists at army level but still does not appear to be able to jam. Jammers will probably be deployed down to army level for specific operations, and would be able to jam any enemy radio link in, say, a corps area, successfully. It is likely that jammers would be used in conjunction with artillery in order to dislocate specific parts of the enemy C^3I structure at critical moments in the battle. In this respect, EW would be used like a 'fire strike', not the only parallel with artillery practice. There would be close co-operation between reconnaissance troops with their EW intercept capability, artillery and ECM troops. The artillery and EW plans are closely co-ordinated, with ESM units also acting as target acquisition systems. Besides the natural connexion between EW and artillery support, the particular dominance of artillery precedent in the evolution of Soviet military thinking and attitudes must have had a distinctive effect. The emphasis on relatively simple but rugged systems, the electronic barrage and the great power of Soviet transmitters all recall Soviet artillery philosophy.

Soviet open source writings indicate that radioelectronic combat involves, in particular, jamming in support of air defence operations, suppressing radar bomb sights, radio navigation equipment, and radio control links, as well as jamming in support of ground operations, suppressing radars, command posts, communications centres and nuclear delivery systems. The main technological aspects discussed are radar jamming systems using wide barrage and narrow band spot noise, pulse, chaff and decoys. They also stress pulse and simulation techniques for jamming enemy command guidance systems and procedures for noise jamming of amplitude modulation (AM) and frequency modulation (FM) signals. Like other armies, the Soviets realise that electronic DF is not sufficiently accurate of itself to locate targets for artillery but may be so for multiple rocket launchers. They also realise that enemy jammers are particularly easy to locate because of their peculiar signal and power output.[11] Reznichenko's *Tactics* places radioelectronic combat (Russian REB) as one of the essential aspects of modern combat after fire and manoeuvre. EW is a critical part of the battle at the tactical as well as the operational-strategic level:

> In the tactical zone of military action a distinctive radio-electronic battle will take place. The commander must take timely measures to successfully suppress the enemy's radio-electronic assets (ECM) and defend his own (ECCM) against enemy suppression. The effectiveness of weapons systems and the success of friendly forces in the battle as a whole will, in large measure, depend on the outcome of this (electronic) battle.[12]

The US Army began to develop combat EW units as a result of lessons of the 1973 Yom Kippur War. In late 1974, the Intelligence Organization and Stationing Study (IOSS) was ordered to plan the integration of intelligence and EW assets within corps and divisions. The new units — battalions for each division and groups for each corps — were caled Combat Electronic Warfare and Intelligence (CEWI) units. This soon came to be pronounced 'seewee', which one astute commentator has pointed out sounded more like a shoe polish than a potentially battle-winning military arm. On the other hand, the need for CEWI units to stress their importance and the contribution they could make rather than rest on as yet unearned laurels was a powerful incentive to excel.

CEWI units were not just intelligence organisations but combat units and their designations as battalions or groups reflected this. At the same time, the interlinked roles of EW and intelligence are self evident, and it is entirely appropriate for EW and intelligence personnel to form part of the same battalion. CEWI battalions formed an integral part of the divisions as part of which they would operate in war and trained to do just that. To this end, it was stressed that CEWI personnel were not just technicians but combat soldiers in every sense, and had to be able to survive in the thick of the fighting. The CEWI battalion commander was made a supporting arm commander, like a gunner or a sapper, and not just a staff officer. Finally, the presence of the CEWI battalion as an integral part of the division gave personnel of other arms in the division the opportunity to learn and assimilate the cardinal role of EW in modern warfare. Established military ideas militated against the CEWI concept: it was held that EW and intelligence functions were more effectively performed at higher levels, back from the heat of the fighting, and that it was impossible to have first-rate technicians who were also first-rate combat soldiers. As we have seen, the Israelis have also had problems with the latter, but it is a problem that must be solved. Lastly, it can be argued that concentration of EW and intelligence assets at a low level may interfere with the separation of tactical and operational intelligence, and in fact delay the exploitation of the latter. However, the inexorable tendency for different combat arms to be progressively integrated at lower and lower levels makes it almost certain that EW units will follow the same path.

Like the Russians, the Americans see EW as complementary to fire support. With ammunition so scarce, it is only natural that the US Army should find EW jamming an attractive alternative to physical destruction of enemy command and control. To do this effectively will require thousands of emitter signals, enemy and friendly, to be filtered to determine when to listen, when and what to jam. US thinking recognises that crude barrage jamming makes one's own side vulnerable to detection and destruction, and that because both sides use similar frequencies (particularly VHF for communications), may inhibit one's own command and control. Instead, US Army jamming must be 'like an electronic piranha, short and vicious; it attacks the guts of the message. It is the electronic key that can unlock communications security'.[13] In this sense, good EW must share the characteristics of any successful military action. Such an approach is more vital to a technologically superior army which relies on electronics to co-ordinate technologically sophisticated weapons; barrage jamming of the entire spectrum or large chunks of it will be more to the advantage of the less electronically sophisticated, especially if he has trained extensively to do without radio communications.

One of the most important EW exercises of recent times was

conducted by the US Army in March 1977. The US 1 Cavalry Division played the part of an enemy force equipped with EW assets normally assigned to three or four divisions, while 2 Armoured Division with its new CEWI battalion tested their own ability to fight on an intensive EW battlefield. The conclusions were surprising and point the way to the future of EW on the battlefield:

— Jamming in fact improved the enemy's signals intelligence because most operators were not trained to recognise jamming and usually just turned off their speech security (ECCM) equipment, in which case jamming was stopped. They often concluded, erroneously, that the speech security equipment had been to blame for poor communications;
— Jamming seriously disrupted artillery fire missions by cutting forward observers off from command posts and higher command posts from gun positions;
— Jamming equipment needs to be rugged and as mobile and protected as any other in the force it supports. The US Army accordingly put more stress on tracked and armoured vehicles and rapid deployment of EW antennas;
— Because of the variety of frequencies which had to be jammed, a CEWI vehicle had to contain a large number of different types of equipment.
— CEWI units were more effective when handled and treated as combat units, not as a valuable basket of fragile egg-heads.[14]

At the time of writing the US Army is allocating EW a share of resources but, as always, resources are limited. EW's unfamiliar and elusive nature makes it a less obvious priority than more conventional weapons systems, but priority it is. The British Army has also recognised the importance of EW. The first British tactical EW unit was formed in 1977. The first aim of EW is ESM: identifying enemy locations, orders of battle (OOBs) and formation boundaries, identifying the principal command posts, artillery and air command and liaison points, which can usually be done by logging the density and location of emitters. Next comes target acquisition (see also Chapter 7), perhaps cueing more precise target acquisition systems such as drones. Finally comes the active EW battle — ECM. In order to carry this out the British Army has deployed DF and jammer squadrons, controlled by a control centre collocated with Corps

HQ. The heart of the EW battle is called the intercept complex, which controls and tasks the DF detachments, analyses the results and passes them to battle group commanders. Liaison with the other arms is carried out, as with any other combat arm, by EW officers at formation (brigade and divisional) HQs. The importance of such units within army organisation will undoubtedly increase.[15]

NEW AND FUTURE EW DEVELOPMENTS

The increasing role of EW has many implications for platforms and delivery systems as well. EW assets will have to be given armoured vehicles to provide a measure of protection, with tracks to enable them to get to any suitable sites — it will be remembered that siting EW equipment is particularly difficult. The process of search — intercept — direction finding — analysis must be expedited and interlinked as far as possible by automated means. ECCM measures such as spread spectrum and frequency agility must be built in to the EW system to permit secure propagation and analysis of the information. All land systems face an inherent weakness in reaching far beyond the FLOT, and this is one reason why EW has for so long been far more prominent a part of the air battle. Terrain, obstacles and screening all limit the depth to which EW systems located with friendly forces can see and blind the enemy. For this reason, remotely delivered jammers and sensors for delivery by MLRS warheads are an attractive option. Jammers can be automatically triggered by friendly transmissions. Although it is often difficult to get a conventional high-power jammer close to the target, small jammers fired from guns or rocket launchers can be delivered sufficiently close to the objective to compensate for their lack of power. The main weakness with these remote jammers is that their power supply has to be small and thus they have a limited life. Closer to one's own units or formations, decoys could be planted or again delivered by artillery or rockets to confuse enemy smart munitions; one might expect the Soviet artillery to be interested in a powerful decoy which could carpet the area through which tanks were advancing, thus drawing SADARM projectiles away from tanks, or perhaps the tanks themselves might carry them.

In purely technological terms there are two particularly

promising developments at the time of writing. The first is millimetre waves. These give good performance at lower elevations, and are thus suitable for sea skimming or low-flying RPVs, and the narrow beam operates to the disadvantage of systems trying to jam them (ECCM). They are particularly suitable for the seekers of 'smart' munitions, as they can cut through night, fog or other particles in the atmosphere. On the other hand, a millimetre wave seeker cannot tell the difference between a live tank and a dead one: a heat seeking, infrared device can. The second, which is just coming into focus, is a means of generating Electro Magnetic Pulse (see Chapter 3) using a chemical trigger, which can be delivered using artillery shells. This could have devastating effects on the recipient's C³I and tactical communications.[16]

'HARD KILL' EW — DIRECTED ENERGY WEAPONS

Directed Energy Weapons (DEW), the 'death ray' which has for so long featured in science fiction, are now being developed for strategic and battlefield use. In addition to being a radically new type of weaponry in their own right, they interact closely with other forms of EW, because electronic and electro-optical systems form particularly soft targets for them.

DEW are a family of weapons: lasers, radio frequency weapons (high powered microwaves — HPM) and particle beams. Directed energy is an aimed beam of electromagnetic energy or subatomic particles concentrated into a highly directional beam and deposited on the target. The main advantage of such weapons is that the beam travels at the speed of light and virtually straight. The speed of light is over 350,000 times faster than the average rifle bullet. A DEW will thus destroy a target virtually instantly, without the agonising wait while, for example, an artillery shell or a LRATGW plummets towards its target. Equally important, it is not necessary to aim off to hit a moving target, such as an aircraft. During the time it takes a DEW beam to travel 1 kilometre to a target, an aircraft at that range travelling at the speed of sound will have travelled about 1 millimetre. The very complex computer systems which have been evolved to overcome the tracking problem for anti-aircraft guns or missiles, or, indeed tank guns, would no longer be required. The instantaneous effect of DEW also means that the person firing the DEW can immediately assess the effect of the weapon and pull the trigger again if necessary. Furthermore, the enemy does not have time to manoeuvre, take evasive action or countermeasures. The narrowness and swiftness of the beam also prevents the enemy acquiring the system as a target. Against this there are two disadvantages. The first is that a DEW must be a line of sight weapon: it cannot arc over terrain cover like an artillery shell. Secondly, and this has been the main problem until now, enormous power is required to create a beam strong enough to do significant damage, which is expensive and difficult to generate in vehicles of battlefield size.[17]

Lasers

The power output of a high-energy laser exceeds 20 kilowatts; that required for a laser weapon would be several hundred to several thousand kilowatts. Targets engaged by a high-energy laser become thermally overloaded, that is, they weaken structurally, burn or melt. Although high-energy lasers have burned holes through metal structures, the most promising battlefield application so far is against optics. Laser light hitting a tank's vision block will craze it, like marble, blinding the tank. This effect can be achieved at ranges greater than those of conventional tank gun engagements, in a split second. Even low-energy lasers are effective against many of the optical systems on which modern soldiers rely: image intensifiers, television cameras or infrared sensors. This is because all these optical and electro-optical sensors are designed to detect very small amounts of a given type of radiation and magnify them, and are thus extremely sensitive. The most obvious example is that consumate optical device, the human eye. Blinding, whether temporary or permanent, could result from a laser striking a gunsight, periscope or binoculars. This could have a major effect on morale and readiness as troops would be unwilling to scan the battlefield for long periods. It seems that laser weapons have sufficient potential to justify their development and low-powered laser weapons may be fielded in the next 10 to 20 years. The high power needed to create lasers capable of piercing armour would tend to limit their role to damaging optics and electronics, but they could still be very effective against armoured vehicles and helicopters.[18]

As we have seen, lasers have a variety of uses in battle: finding the range to a target, marking and illuminating the target for a guided conventional shell or bomb to home in on, or actually destroying or incapacitating the target itself. There is no reason why a future laser weapon should not combine all three functions in one, with different power settings depending on the use to be made of it. On low power, it could determine whether a target was in range for laser damage, and perhaps determine something about the nature of the target. Depending on that, the second or third mode could be selected. Such a laser would be a very versatile and therefore cost effective piece of equipment.

Radio Frequency Weapons

Radio frequency weapons cause damage by surrounding a potential target with an intense radiation field that can induce lethal voltages and currents into sensitive electrical and electronic circuits. As most military systems being fielded today rely heavily on these, radiation weapons could be devastatingly effective and, indeed, cancel out many of the advances in weapons technology. Particularly promising are high-power microwaves (HPM), which can render weapon fuzes in missile warheads inert or else detonate them. They could presumably also set off ammunition in tanks.

Mention must also be made of the potential of Very and Extremely Low Frequency (VLF and ELF) weapons. Very low frequencies of about 8 Hz can be transmitted through the earth and it has been suggested that the Soviets used such a transmission to provoke the 1977 Peking earthquake. If such techniques could be perfected they could substitute for subterranean nuclear bursts, reflecting Tizard's view that the properties and mechanics of earth and soil movement could and should be studied more zealously. On the other hand, such uses of VLF would probably have somewhat unpredictable results which would, as always limit their value as instruments of operations and tactics. Extremely low frequencies (ELF) have less effect on the earth's structure but more on animals and people. Many atmospheric disturbances, which can affect people psychologically occur within this frequency band, and ELFs are similar to biological rhythms. The human brain's frequency is about

8Hz. Frequencies of 1.75 to 5 Hz have caused reduced activity in birds, and such ELF vibrations could be turned into a weapon which, given its low frequency, would be very difficult to detect and counter.[19]

Particle Beam Weapons

Particle beams are not part of the electromagnetic spectrum proper, but damage the target by straightforward kinetic energy, like a bullet or solid shot. Although the particles are very small, they are travelling at the speed of light and, since the energy of a moving object equals mass times the square of velocity, they can hit very hard indeed. A charged particle beam (CPB) weapon comprises an accelerator plant, a power generator, particle injectors and extremely high capacity condensers capable of storing very high power levels. Such machinery is generally very large. If a CPB weapon were used against a land target such as a tank, it could produce an appalling effect on the inside of the armour, like a HESH round (see Chapter 5). It could also generate lethal secondary emissions (X- and gamma rays) from the beam particles' interaction with the particles of the material struck. However, the shorter the beam's wavelength, the less easily it is propagated through the atmosphere, and in this respect particle beams share the characteristics of X- and gamma rays. On the ground, even the most powerful CPB would have a maximum range of only 5 to 10 kilometres. In space, on the other hand, there is no atmosphere and CPB may be ideal as space weapons. On the battlefield, however, covered in mud, fog and smoke, the energy needed to propagate a CPB any distance would seem to be out of all proportion to its advantages. It might nevertheless be possible to clear a path for a particule beam using a high-powered laser or HPM, further adding to the attractiveness of having different sorts of DEW operating from the same power source or platform.

CPB weapons would also create residual radiation like the radiation arms which the D-Day planners feared (see Chapter 3). A report by Chinese authorities after the 1979 war with Vietnam indicated that large numbers of Chinese soldiers had been hospitalised for eye and brain injuries, which some have inferred to indicate that the Vietnamese were party to Soviet tests of radiation weapons. All the indications are, however, that

237

CPB and related weapons are most likely to be of use in space and not in the thick, muffling atmosphere close to mother earth.[20]

Battlefield DEW

One of the major advantages of DEW on the battlefield taken as a whole is that they do not require bulky ammunition, and thus resupply. The 'ammunition' is electromagnetic energy or subatomic particles. DEW require fuel to generate the energy, but when balanced against the enormous weight and bulk of conventional ammunition, plus the problems of storing and protecting it, the fuel requirements become less onerous. DEW must be particularly attractive in an environment where armoured forces are seeking to move fast and without encumbrance, where they may penetrate deep into the enemy rear and be cut off from resupply. Obviating the need to account for, store and transport much ammunition would free personnel to play a direct role in the battle.[21]

DEW are therefore likely to begin to complement conventional weapons in the near future. Many conventional weapons have minimum engagement ranges: LRATGW, for example. DEW would fill this gap. Artillery, with its ability to fire indirect, would engage distant targets with improved conventional munitions, fuel air explosives and smart submunitions, as we have seen in Chapter 5. DEW would, however, replace the shorter range direct fire weapons: the same weapon could be used against helicopters or tanks and IFVs. Ground formations so equipped would be freed from cumbrous logistic chains to some extent, although they would no doubt carry some conventional ordnance as a back-up and for special requirements. There would be more emphasis on 'soft kill' optics and sensors, since battlefield mobile DEW would be unlikely to dismantle armour, at least in the near future. But DEW's instant effects would knock out or blind a proportion of an enemy's forces, forcing troops to dismount if they wanted to carry on the fight, and making it quickly obvious which vehicles were still coming on; these could then be engaged with more conventional ordnance. Very powerful lasers, HPMs or particle beams are unlikely to be deployed forward, but could be harnessed to powerful static generators to provide point defence of static installations, particularly against air attack. Again, this interacts with theatre land warfare as rear areas are likely to be under attack from operational-tactical surface to surface missiles. DEW would form a good defence against these, and with their speed of engagement could be used for rapid sequential attack of, say, a massed helicopter *desant.*

In the author's view, employment of DEW will be on a relatively limited scale in the next quarter century. They are probably only a feasible option for the superpowers, and even their resources are limited. DEW have relatively more potential for space applications, and investment in battlefield DEW is likely to be correspondingly limited. Like many new forms of military technology, they might be employed at first in limited numbers for special purposes (to free a Soviet OMG or US deep attack force from conventional ammunition constraints, perhaps?). In that case, as always when new technology is employed in limited numbers, their initial impact on the battlefield is unlikely to be decisive. In a large-scale battle their ability to kill targets instantly at long ranges could have a dramatic effect. Furthermore, if one side were to have them and another not, the psychological impact could be much greater than their real military worth, as with the initial use of gas or the tank.

CONCLUSION

The importance of electronic warfare cannot be overestimated. The world's greatest armies are of one accord on that. The Soviets are probably the most advanced in the application of brute electronic force in the land battle, and their approach mirrors their artillery tradition. As early as 1905, the Imperial Russian Navy disposed of the cruiser *Ural* with a radio transmitter of staggering power for its day; now, the Soviet Army outnumbers its potential NATO adversaries 13 to 1 in ground-based jammers.[22] Radioelectronic combat (EW) comes after fire and manoeuvre in the Soviets' latest tactical bible, Reznichenko, reflecting the Soviet Army's appreciation of its importance. The most technologically developed exponents of EW are the Americans and the Israelis, the latter with a conspicuously successful record of its practical employment. NATO's joint *ATP-35(A)* makes passing reference to EW and considers it as one of the 'general tasks in battle', but could give it more emphasis as a decisive form of combat. The 1982 American *FM100-5* stresses EW rather more, giving it priority treatment after nuclear and chemical weapons in Chapter 4, and puts *integrated* EW between fire support and engineer support in Chapter 7 on the conduct of operations.[23] Yet, as General dePuy observed, even the US Army

> is not yet comfortable with Electronic Warfare. The senior leaders have little firsthand experience and thus little confidence or skill in its use and tend to leave it, unintegrated, in the hands of specialists. The specialists, in turn, are faced with a tradition and structure of secrecy and compartmentalization — a hangover in part from the days of ULTRA.[24]

DePuy became commander of TRADOC in 1973, and was instrumental in shaping the 1976 edition of *FM100-5*. This in turn set in hand a lively debate which would consume much of General Starry's attention when he took over from dePuy in 1977 (see Chapter 4). DePuy was one of the formative influences on modern American operational thinking and his views on EW were and are highly significant.[25]

As often happens, the vocabulary of EW is inadequate to project its importance. 'Electronic warfare' suggests a series of random and unconnected aspects of military operations rather than a powerful, potentially devastating force like 'firepower superiority'. EW units, especially 'seewees', still lack the panache of paras, commandos and armour, although their contribution in a future major war will be as or more decisive, and the demands placed on them greater. The use of the electromagnetic spectrum is a vast and wide-ranging challenge; electronic warfare is like firepower, a concept capable of infinite variety and limitless application. The similarities with artillery are striking; like artillery, electronic assets are not prominent in peacetime, manifesting themselves only in war. Then their domination of the ether and crushing effect on enemy command, control, communications, intelligence and morale parallels that of fire, while their ability to deceive and surprise exceeds it. In our search for a more evocative name for the units which will dominate the outcome of future wars, we might draw the artillery parallel, as the Russians do when they talk about electronic suppression. Electronic warfare assets are the artillery of the ether, electronic firepower. As with all new aspects of military art, EW began attached to strategic aims and objectives, and has rapidly become integrated at lower and lower levels. EW units are now part of forward divisions and below, and like artillery, again, have had to become tracked and armoured like the formations of which they are a critical part. These trends will continue. As always in the development of military art, the greatest uncertainty and the potential for decisive use of the new arm lies in the extent to which it has been and will be assimilated into the structure and methods of armed forces. EW technology will undoubtedly advance, and so will its platforms and protection, but the greatest change could be one of psychology and attitude.

NOTES

1. Electromagnetic spectrum: R.G. Lee, *Introduction to Battlefield Weapons Systems and Technology*, 2nd edition (Brassey's Battlefield Weapons Systems and Technology Series, Brassey's, Oxford, 1985), p. 118; Mario de Arcangelis, *Electronic Warfare: from the Battle of Tsushima to the Falklands and Lebanon Conflicts* (Blandford Poole, 1985), p. 209; Igor D. Gerhardt and Colonel Peter Heimdahl, 'Star Wars Weapons on the Battlefield', *Army*, July 1985, p. 24; ESM, ECM, etc.: pp. 129-33; A.M. Willcox, M.G. Slade and P.A. Ramsdale, *Command, Control and Communications (C³)* (Brassey's Battlefield Weapons Systems and Technology Series, Vol. VI, Brassey's, Oxford, 1983), pp. 4-5, 79-105. Mario de Arcangelis' 'Electronic Warfare and Land Battles', parts 1 to 3, *Armies and Weapons*, Nos. 39-41, 1977-78, pp. 59-62, 53-6, 63-6, is in fact mainly about air and sea, although studies of EW in any medium are relevant.
2. EOCM, EOCCM: de Arcangelis, *Electronic Warfare*, pp. 218-19; John Marriott, compiler, *RUSI and Brassey's Weapons Technology*, 2nd ed. (Brassey's, Oxford, 1978), p. 144; Soviet terminology: *SVE*, Vol. 7 (Voyenizdat, Moscow, 1979), pp. 29-31, particularly *radioelectronnaya bor'ba (REB)*.
3. Russo-Japanese War from de Arcangelis, *Electronic Warfare*, p. 12; Somme, *Electronic Warfare: the New Operational Environment*, a seminar at the Royal United Services' Institution (RUSI), 9 May 1985, 'Possible EW Operational framework'. The proceedings were written up in David Bolton (ed.), *The Challenge of Electronic Warfare* (Whitehall paper No. 1, Royal United Services Institute for Defence Studies, 1986).
4. de Arcangelis, *Electronic Warfare*, pp. 160-73.
5. Invasion of Czechoslovakia: Gerald Green, 'Soviet Electronic warfare: *Maskirovka* and REC', *National Defense*, April 1985, p. 34; 1973, ibid., pp. 38-9; 1982, Carus, p. 45, and interviews with Israeli officers.

6. Scope of EW: *RUSI, Electronic Warfare, Lessons of the 1982 Syria-Israel Conflict.* 'Possible EW Framework' and 'EW on Land'; Willcox, Slade and Ramsdale, *Command, Control and Communications*, pp. 79-93.

7. de Arcangelis, *Electronic Warfare*, pp. 218-9.

8. Marriott, *Weapons Technology*, pp. 147-8.

9. de Arcangelis, *Electronic Warfare*, pp. 194-5.

10. Willcox, Slade and Ramsdale, *Command, Control and Communications*, pp. 93-105.

11. Green, 'Soviet Electronic Warfare', pp. 35-8, mainly citing Department of the Army, US Army Intelligence and Security Command, *Soviet Army Operations, IAQ-13-U-78*, pp. 4-79, 581-2.

12. Reznichenko, *Taktika*, p. 41 (bold type in Soviet edition).

13. Don E. Gordon, *Electronic Warfare: Element of Strategy and Multiplier of Combat Power* (Pergamon, New York, 1981), pp. 69-71, quotation on p. 71.

14. Ibid., p. 72.

15. RUSI, *Electronic Warfare*, 'EW on Land'.

16. RUSI, *Electronic Warfare*, 'Future Developments in EW'.

17. Gerhardt and Heimdahl, 'Star Wars', pp. 21-2.

18. Ibid., p. 22.

19. Radio frequency weapons in Gerhardt and Heimdahl, 'Star Wars', pp. 23-4; VLF and ELF weapons in de Arcangelis, *Electronic Warfare*, pp. 221-3; Tizard, *DEFE 2/1252*, p. 31, para. 72.

20. CPB weapons: de Arcangelis, *Electronic Warfare*, pp. 299-300, Gerhardt and Heimdahl, 'Star Wars', pp. 23-4; clearing a path for CPB with HPM, ibid., p. 24; injuries to Chinese: de Arcangelis, pp. 300-1.

21. Economising on ammunition, Gerhardt and Heimdahl, 'Star Wars', pp. 24-5.

22. Outnumbering NATO in jammers: Green, 'Soviet EW', p. 42.

23. *Ural*, de Arcangelis, *Electronic Warfare*, p. 14. *ATP-35(A)*, second draft January 1984 (see Chapter 4). 'General tasks in Battle' comprises Intelligence, Mission and Planning, C³I, Combat Support, Security and Protection, NBC Defence, Road Movement in the Combat Zone, EW, Combat Service Support and Psychological operations in that order. *FM 100-5 Operations*, 20 August 1982; EW in battlefield environments: chapter 4 (pp. 4-4 to 4-5) after Nuclear and Chemical, and in chapter 7, pp. 7-18 to 7-19.

24. General Starry's Introduction to Gordon, *Electronic Warfare*, p. vii.

25. General de Puy's career and importance: John L. Romjue, 'The Evolution of the AirLand Battle Concept', *Air University Review*, May-June 1984, pp. 5-6.

7

Command, Control, Communications and Intelligence (C³I)

The characters C³I should be pronounced 'C *cubed* I'. This encapsulates the mutually supportive and exponential value of a superiority in all these areas or, conversely, the spiralling penalties of a deficiency. They are also completely interlinked. A classic example of how not to do it is the charge of the British Light Brigade in the Crimean War, when a force of light cavalry, ideal for patrolling or pursuit, was launched against the wrong objective, because of ambiguous orders and inadequate surveillance of the battlefield. The objective — Russian artillery in position — was quite the worst possible one for such a force to attack, and the error was compounded by the nature of the ground. Disaster resulted. As battles extended over an area way beyond the compass of visual range and couriers could no longer convey messages sufficiently rapidly, the scope for snarl-ups became even greater and the electrical and electronic means of communication which had to be used introduced the new electronic warfare element. The evolution of C³I is closely intertwined with that of EW, but it also involves the vast and unquantifiable area of human intellect, instinct and judgement. The evolution and future of C³I cannot be separated from personal command, generalship and the art of war itself. Command is a dynamic process, involving the interaction of personalities with events as they unfold, and is therefore in itself the least susceptible to automation. Control is the supervision of subordinate command. Within broad directives, subordinate commanders should be free to run the battle as they think fit with a minimum of interference. The senior commander can intervene if necessary, a good example being the relief of General Ritchie by Auchinleck during the Gazala battles in May 1942. Ritchie had been free to fight his own battles but when it became obvious that Ritchie had failed, Auchinleck was able to step in. Communications are utterly indispensable to the whole process, and are most directly dependent on technical developments. For that reason, they are considered first. Intelligence is not just gathering information but also processing it, collating it and distributing it. Modern ADP systems should be able to make the task of sifting information and getting it to the right people easier, but there are problems. As one Israeli general put it, the problem is not so much providing information in 'real time', but of 'getting the real information in time', a subtle but crucial distinction.

BASIC COMMUNICATIONS

Communication on the battlefield or between it and rear areas is either by radio or line, the former offering freedom of movement but, as we have seen in Chapter 6, increasingly vulnerable to interception or jamming. Futuristic impressions of warfare often envisage other media of communication being used, such as television, but more complex methods require much broader bandwidths, thus limiting the number of channels and increasing vulnerability. A television channel would take up the same space as 250 VHF to EHF voice channels, making it very extravagant for military communications and vulnerable to EW.

Radio

Radio waves are propagated by four main means, of which three can project them over the horizon:

— Space wave (line of sight). This is used for VHF and higher frequencies and comprises a direct wave and a ground-reflected wave. The direct wave passes through the troposphere and is bent slightly downwards by atmospheric refraction. If the aerials are close to the ground there will be a significant ground-reflected wave which can interfere with the space wave if the transmitter is badly sited.
— Surface wave. This is the first method of propagation over the horizon (OTH). Radio waves can follow the sinuosities of

the ground along the surface. A surface wave induces electric currents in the surface over which it passes, so that the wave becomes attenuated. Above a few Megaherz the attenuation is considerable and the surface wave becomes insignificant.
— Ionospheric reflection. Between 50 and 500 kilometres above the earth lie layers of air ionised by solar radiation. The exact distribution of these varies from day to night and between summer and winter. The upper layers (F Layers) reflect radio waves from about 3 to 30 MHz (HF). The lower (D and E) layers attenuate these waves. It is, however, possible to bounce radio waves off the upper layers, and at night, when the lower layers are weak, the signals can carry great distances. HF waves are very long and travel both by surface wave and ionospheric reflection. A HF wave will in fact bounce off the ionosphere, hit the earth and bounce back up again. This phenomenon is called skywave and enables HF sets to communicate round the world. It also causes the main drawback of HF communications, because stations from great distances can interfere with what is supposed to be a local network.
— Tropospheric scatter. The troposphere is the lowest part of the atmosphere, up to about 10 kilometres. Over the horizon propagation can be obtained by using highly directional antennas and directing both transmitter and receiver at the same area of atmosphere which is called the scatter volume. High power levels are necessary to achieve this effect, which is particularly useful for propagating UHF signals. The transmitters and receivers therefore have to be very large and emit considerable radiation. They are useful for high-capacity, static links and have been extensively deployed by Soviet forces in Afghanistan for long-range UHF communications. Line communications will also play an important part in future operations.

In addition to these scientific principles we must mention specifically:

— Satellite communications (Satcom). Increasing use is being made of communications satellites which are essentially microwave relay stations in the sky which can be used for over the horizon communications. The satellite receives signals in one wavelength and re-transmits in another, typically 8.5 GHz for the uplink and 6.5, say, for the downlink. An example is the British Skynet 4 communications system for all the UK services operating in the UHF, SHF and EHF bands. The first of the three satellites should be launched in mid-1986. In the next quarter century satellite and space technology in general, and the space shuttle in particular, will make it possible to put larger and larger satellites into orbit. This in turn permits greater power and wider bandwidths, which means that speech can be carried whereas once only telegraphy was possible, and the ground receiving terminals can be made smaller and more mobile. A typical satellite ground receiver can be carried on a man's back. The Soviet Union is placing increased emphasis on satellites alongside tropospheric scatter for long-range communications. Both provide secure, ECM-resistant dialogue at the strategic and operational levels, certainly down to army, although satellite terminals could be deployed further down the chain of command — as in the case of an OMG, for example?

Line

Although it is envisaged that most tactical communications, at least among Western forces, would be by radio, there will certainly be line links as part of trunk systems and back from higher tactical headquarters. The Soviets place more emphasis on line to provide a back-up to radio or to replace it altogether. If operations assume a positional character the importance of line systems is also likely to increase. Although line radiates, and can therefore be intercepted, as we saw happened on the Somme in 1916 (Chapter 6), it is still much harder to detect than a radio link. However, lines are vulnerable to sabotage and interception by enemy forces operating covertly, and therefore rear links have to be patrolled and protected. If cheap, lightweight cable is available, then it is possible to provide disposable line links, perhaps dropped by helicopter. This would be of particular use when faced with massive hostile EW, or if a forward or isolated unit was required to set up a more than transient defensive position. Likely defensive positions can also be wired in to a communications system before a conflict starts, which has obvious attractions on a battlefield where enemy thrust lines are fairly predictable, like West Germany (see also Chapter 8).

Advances in line types are making line communications increasingly attractive. Fibre optics will be of particular importance in the next few years. Light can be guided along small diameter optical fibres (2 to 200 micrometres) with low attenuation and a high bandwidth, which means that good quality communications can be achieved. Fibre optics offer a number of advantages for military communications. Fibre optic performance is continually improving and costs decreasing, while the cost of conventional copper cable is growing. Above all, fibre optic cables do not radiate, and are immune to radio frequency noise and therefore offer revolutionary resistance to ECM. The fibres can be made of glass or plastic. Plastic fibres are extremely tough but cause high attenuation which limits the range of such cables to a few tens of metres. For longer cables, high-quality glass is needed.[1] On the other hand, glass is discoloured by nuclear radiation, which means that in a nuclear environment fibre optics would lose many of their advantages. Research is being carried out to attempt to alleviate this, but at least fibre optics would be fairly secure against *chemically*-induced EMP (see also Chapter 3).

TACTICAL COMMUNICATIONS

Forward units and formations use the flexible system known as net radio, with stations able to keep in touch with each other while on the move. HF radio is very useful in urban, jungle or mountainous regions because its long wavelengths can to a certain extent bend round corners. The British Clansman manpack radio, the PRC-20, has a range of 50 kilometres by surface wave and up to 300 by skywave. On the other hand, as explained, HF is liable to interference, and the long HF wavelength demands a relatively long antenna. VHF waves are not so good at bending round obstacles and VHF communications have a much shorter inherent range than HF. However, they are far less prone to interference than HF and because more bandwidth is available Frequency Modulation (FM) is possible, as opposed to AM. This further enhances quality and enables FM sets to home in on the wanted signal while suppressing unwanted ones. The Clansman VHF manpack PRC-352 has a range of 16 kilometres and the vehicle-mounted PRC-353, 30 kilometres.

Military radios have to be extremely rugged and need a number of other qualities which mean that they appear to lag far behind civilian radio equipments in sophistication. They have to be simple to operate, and a number of different sets have to be able to operate from one vehicle and communicate with each other on the same net. Commercial radios are relatively cheap but have found favour only in internal security situations.[2] The characteristics of HF and VHF radio waves are well known and conform to fundamental laws of physics which cannot be changed. The main advances which may occur in tactical radios over the next quarter century are therefore likely to result from improvements in power sources: the ability to concentrate more power in a smaller space, rather than from any fundamental change in the types of frequency used.

TRUNK COMMUNICATIONS

Trunk communications provide the communications needed by formation commanders and staffs. They have provision for picture, data and telegraph transmission as well as voice traffic. Early military trunk systems paralleled the chain of command, so that each headquarters was a large communications exchange as well as fulfilling its function as the formation's brain. The sheer size of such a complex posed problems, and the ideal criteria for a communications site are not the same as those of a higher tactical or operational headquarters. A first step was to remove the communications nodes from the operational and tactical headquarters by a short distance so as to create a separate but parallel communications network. Headquarters needed relatively small radio sets with fairly weak emissions to communicate with the nodes of the trunk system, further reducing their vulnerability. An expanded system of this type was exemplified by the British Bruin system, which might operate as shown in Figure 7.1. Each of the corps and divisional headquarters shown in the diagram has two communications centres. A further advance is to provide a 'step-up', that is, a reserve headquarters which can move to exploit the communications links to the fullest extent and, as soon as it is in place, take over from the former headquarters. All these systems, however, rely on the chain of command pattern. Modern trunk communications use an entirely different concept: an area system, as shown in Figure 7.2. A network of centres are deployed throughout the theatre or area of operations, and headquarters on the move can plug in to any convenient centre.

Figure 7.1: Expanded chain of command system with step-up (step-ups or alternate HQs are shown as hollow squares), similar to British Bruin system

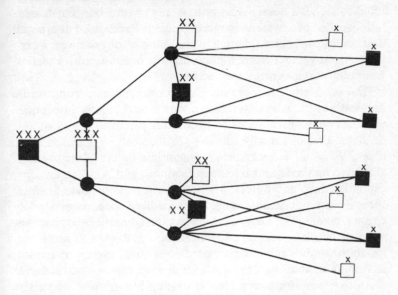

Figure 7.2: Area system, as exemplified by Ptarmigan. Explosions indicate communications nodes destroyed by enemy action

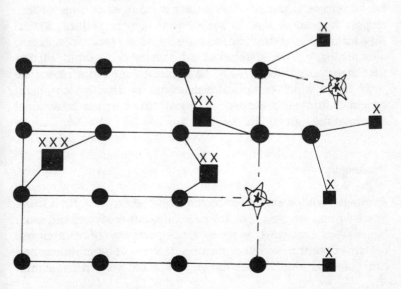

It can be likened to a chess board with movements of signals possible vertically, diagonally, or in any combination of these. Along this grid orders and messages flash forward and back. Unlike a chess board, the grid is not static, but constantly redrawn. A grid system is more resilient because of the large number of alternative routes available, and offers more flexibility of movement both for the tactical headquarters and the communications centres themselves.

The main mode of communication over modern trunk communications networks is voice, which is particularly important when a commander needs to impart his personality and mood or divine that of his subordinates (Raful's call to Avigdor, 'try, please, *hold on!*') at a critical moment in a battle. Most systems also have facsimile and telegraph facilities, and ADP communication between computers. The latter can transmit data at slow speed over a telegraph channel and medium speed over a television channel. The network connects the computers so that the same database is held at each location. ADP systems are ideal for statistics and standardformat data such as orders of battle, ammunition holding, casualty lists and so on. All staffs have access to the information, vastly cutting the amount of paper that has to be dealt with and giving an instant picture of cold statistics which make up much of the matter of war.

Modern trunk systems use digital techniques, which operate by converting the smooth flow of a signal to a series of pulses. If the waveform is sampled more than twice in each cycle of the highest frequency, that is sufficient to give a picture of the waveform. Digital transmission offers substantial advantages over analog, but the system has to be digital throughout, otherwise digital signals have to be converted to and from analog at some point, which complicates matters. The British Ptarmigan system is the most developed digital trunk communications system at the time of writing.

Ptarmigan

Ptarmigan will be employed by the British Army and Royal Air Force in part of the ultimate potential theatre of land-air war: North-West Europe. It is a true area system (see above) covering the entire theatre into which headquarters and mobile users can connect. Digital techniques and computerised switching permit the users, each of whom has a unique number which can be worked out from their appointment, to be contacted automatically when dialled. A new feature is single-channel radio access (SCRA), which enables mobile units to key into the trunk communications system.

The communications nodes (previously called communications centres — Comcens) are usually deployed not more than 25 kilometres apart. These must be stationary to operate but must move frequently to keep pace with the ebb and flow of battle and for survival. The corps headquarters is served by a major node with access for 150 users. Divisions and brigades are linked to the nearest node by radio relay, with access for up to 25 brigade users and rather more from each division. In addition to these static links, a mobile user is connected to the system by SCRA which semi-automatically reconnects it to successive points in the area system as it moves forwards ... or backwards. If one of the links between nodes is knocked out, a call is automatically re-routed. Ptarmigan is also designed to interconnect with systems used by neighbouring armies and meets the internationally agreed EUROCOM civilian communications standards. It can also interconnect with Bruin-equipped formations and with combat net radios used by units and sub-units. The latter is accomplished through the combat net radio interface (CNRI) using a single voice channel.[3]

Rita

The British hoped to sell Ptarmigan to the United States Army in competition with the French RITA (*Réseau Integré des Transmissions Automatiques*), part of a new approach to American defence procurement. The contractors submitted their final tenders in April 1985. In spite of political pressure from the British, RITA won, the decision being announced in November, 1985. The fact that it was $3.1 billion cheaper at current prices was one reason, but the Americans also felt that it was preferable because it had been in service with the French and Belgian armies for two years. Ptarmigan, on the other hand, had only gone to I British Corps in the spring.[4] This is a timely example of how important it is that equipment should be assimilated into armed forces. Such a system, even if technologically less advanced than its competitor, as RITA was less advanced

251

than Ptarmigan, is often preferable to a spanking new piece of kit as yet unassimilated, where bugs still have to be ironed out and soldiers and commanders educated in its use. The American decision to procure elements of the RITA system ended a long period of uncertainty about an American Mobile subscriber equipment (MSE), as the full package will be known. In the 1960s the US began developing an analog trunk system called Mallard, in co-operation with the United Kingdom and Canada. This went well from 1967 to 1969, when the Americans withdrew. The British then met the interim requirement for a battlefield trunk communications system with Bruin (see above), and in 1971 they began to develop Ptarmigan while the Americans started work on their own system called Tri-Tac in the same year. Tri-Tac was originally an analog system, but changes in electronics technology and the introduction of digital systems enabled mobile subscriber equipment (MSE) to be deployed further forward, leaving Tri-Tac further back. This in turn led to a greatly expanded MSE programme which by 1983 envisaged equipping 25 American divisions with MSE. In order to achieve this quickly, an off the shelf purchase was needed, and so Ptarmigan (around which the original MSE concept had been designed) and RITA were invited to bid.

A typical US Army corps level deployment of the RITA-based MSE would cover a 37,500 square kilometre area and involve some 8,100 subscribers of which about 6,200 would be static and 1,900 mobile. MSE is scheduled for full deployment by 1993, although some have warned that this does not allow enough time for full testing. Then it will equip five US corps and 25 divisions. According to the US Under-Secretary for the Army, this

> will be the first time in history of the army that all of its units, both active and reserve, will have fully interoperable encrypted, jam-resistant mobile tactical communications equipment.[5]

The original RITA system began development in 1974 and has been developed on an evolutionary basis to meet the requirements of tactical C^3I to the end of the century. Communications equipment at each node is entirely self contained and is installed in standard shelters. The normal distance between the nodes, shown in Figure 7.3, is 35 to 40 kilometres.

Figure 7.3: RITA system within a corps area

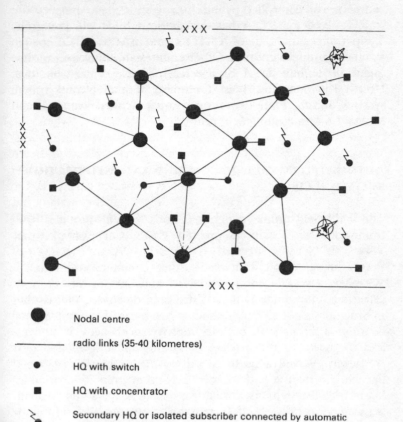

● Nodal centre

─────── radio links (35-40 kilometres)

● HQ with switch

■ HQ with concentrator

⌇● Secondary HQ or isolated subscriber connected by automatic radio integration

Source: *Jane's Military Communications*, 1985, p. 823.

Subscribers in the immediate area of a node are connected by cable or wire, but there is also a facility for a remote 'concentrator' — a centre which can provide access to the system for a group of users some distance from a node. The concentrator can be linked to the node either by cable or radio link. The main facility for transmission between nodes is provided by digital microwave radio (DMR). There is also a link with mobile radios, a teletype service and data processing. The network is controlled by a network command centre called the *Cecore*, which provides a real time display of traffic along each branch of the network and an immediate indication of faults and con-

253

gestion. This, the circuit switches and the message switching centres are all controlled by micro-programmed computers.[6]

RITA and the RITA based American MSE will therefore equip a substantial slice of NATO forces in Western Europe in a future European conflict. Other countries will not necessarily queue up to buy RITA as a result of the US decision; the United Kingdom and West Germany have their own trunk systems, and the Ptarmigan system might be attractive to richer Middle Eastern customers in future.

AUTOMATED COMMAND, CONTROL AND INFORMATION SYSTEMS (CCIS)

The battlefield trunk communications system provides the framework for a fully automated CCIS. For example, the Wavell CCIS being supplied to the British Army is based on Ptarmigan, although it involves other communications links. Wavell is a mobile computer-based network for storing and retrieving information with a 'distributed database', that is, the information is not all held in one or two parts of the system but distributed throughout, both to improve its chances of survival and to speed up the process of getting the information out (retrieval). Wavell aims to speed up the processing of intelligence information and to keep a constant, readily accessible log of friendly strengths, casualties, positions and so on. Wavell is based on so-called Staff Terminal Equipments (STEs) located in command vehicles (see Figure 7.4). The STEs can be consulted either using Ptarmigan or dedicated local connections. The Wavell system is compatible with the West German Heros and the United States Sigma systems, making cross-fertilisation of information possible within the army group and presumably even between army groups.[7]

Because all commanders have access to the same information, it is no longer necessary to assemble them at formal 'O' Groups: instead, the O Group takes place on the dashboard of each commander's vehicle. Wherever each commander is on the battlefield, within the Ptarmigan-like web, the system knows his or her location. The commander of Northern Army Group can have all four or five corps commanders on net within 45 seconds. It might seem that the ability to know the position of every major unit and formation commander could make them

Figure 7.4: The British Wavell System

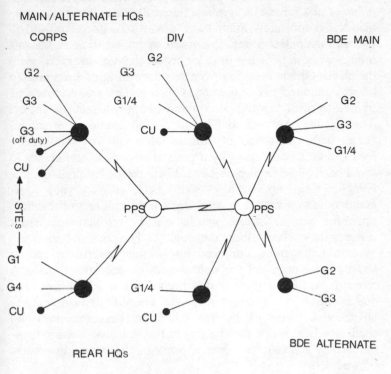

Wavell is based on a series of work stations (STEs) dedicated to particular users (G1, etc., the 'G' numbers being British Army staff appointments). There are additional STEs for common users (CU).
PPS — Primary packet switch
Dark circles are access nodes
(Source: *Defence Material,* September-October, 1985, p. 144)

vulnerable to identification by the enemy, but apparently the use of very narrow bandwidths makes it very difficult for unfriendly forces to find them. Problems could also arise if, for example, a German corps under Northern Army Group was required to fight in a different way from a German corps in Central Army Group, although the Germans would be used to doing things one way. As noted in Chapter 4, control involves giving broad objectives and aims, and should not involve too much peering over the subordinate commander's shoulder. The fact that different NATO corps might fight in a slightly different way need not necessarily matter. Furthermore, progress towards interoperability in NATO continues and this applies particularly to the use of automated C³I. A final problem is that the constant influx of new information in real time will tempt the senior commander to constantly amend and tinker with his plans, and to partially assimilate some new piece of information at the last minute without allowing time for orders to be issued right down the chain. Orders resulting from such new insights need time to be disseminated and executed. Commanders will have to be trained to resist this temptation and to apply a realistic cut-off date or time. Automated C³I will give the senior commander access to a vast range of information about his subordinate forces, and if badly used by a general who lacks the ability to stand back and delegate, this could be a recipe for disaster. The Genghis Khan approach — stand back and let your commanders get on with it — applying a little rudder to the whole operation here and there, will have to be instilled into senior commanders even more thoroughly. The risk of misusing modern C³I systems and, conversely, their enormous, as yet unfathomed, potential for deft control of operations, make it more imperative than ever that the system is fully assimilated and commanders practised in its use. The side deploying a less advanced C³I network but one which has been exercised and used may beat a side just finding out how to use a more technologically sophisticated one: another of the recurring verities of war.

SOVIET C³I

In some ways the traditional Soviet emphasis on centralised control combined with considerable latitude to subordinate commanders in the way they carry out a given task, not dissimilar to the Mongol system, is well suited to exploit modern C³I technology. It was Marshal Sokolovskiy who first drew attention to the need for automated command and control as long ago as 1962. Computers were needed not only to control the flight of ballistic missiles and aircraft but military operations in general, and without automation 'effective command and control of the armed forces in modern war cannot be assured'.[8] In 1972 a most important book appeared, Druzhinin's *Concept, Algorithm Decision — Decision making and Automation*. This is required reading for all Soviet officers and officer cadets.

Druzhinin's conclusions are broadly that in the uncertainty and fog of war the commander is constantly subject to stress and confusion and that he needs all the help he can get without letting the machine take over and swamping him with excessive information, and that by using automation to perform the simpler and more mundane if time-consuming calculations the commander is freer to exercise instinct and creative thought. Few would disagree with any of that. Since then, the automation of C^3I has been the theme of recurring Soviet books and periodicals. By the early 1980s the Soviets were employing a third generation of unified computers based on the Riad (Ryad) series developed in Eastern Europe and now deployed down to tactical (divisional) headquarters. A Soviet or NSWP divisional commander is therefore now able to use a data retrieval system situated at front or even theatre level, and this has become more effective with the introduction of the Riad-2 models with their larger memory, semiconductor primary memory, block-multiplexer channels and improved peripherals (the latter being a weakness in Soviet computers so far). This C^3 system seems to be chain of command rather than area in form but there are apparently alternative control centres which reduce vulnerability. Although Western computers and CCIS are undoubtedly more sophisticated than the Soviets', the Soviet systems have been operational since the mid-1970s whereas the NATO systems are only coming into service at the time of writing.[9]

Essentially, Soviet battlefield C^3I automation handles and sifts the information going into a headquarters; calculates simple problems like when a motor rifle regiment is likely to hit the enemy; presumably keeps a tally of ammunition, personnel, casualties, fuel and so on; and performs the calculation of 'norms' on which the Soviets rely to calculate for example the number of shells needed to suppress a target. If somewhat crude by Western standards, the Soviet equipment is probably much better integrated into the command and control structure generally. The Soviets are also showing marked interest in automated real time target acquisition and fire control, as we shall see.

INTELLIGENCE, TARGET ACQUISITION AND FIRE CONTROL

Wellington said that he had spent most of his life trying to guess what he might meet with on the other side of the hill or round the next corner, and this problem was exacerbated in this century by the need for artillery and, later, missiles, to fire indirect. Distant targets, especially enemy artillery, could only be located by sound ranging or aerial photography. Both of these took time and were not 100 per cent accurate. If a future war is characterised by high mobility, even if this is only on a small scale (see Chapter 8), these methods will not be suitable.

Satellites will clearly play a very significant part in targeting land ordnance in the future, and the outcome of war on land will depend very much on what happens in space or in the upper air. The United States certainly expect the bulk of their intelligence of enemy positions and force movements to come from satellite and airborne surveillance, but the interactive nature of war may force emphasis back to ground-based intelligence gathering and target acquisition. The American Joint Stand Off Target and Reconnaissance System (JSTARS) is due for airborne testing in late 1988. This is designed to detect slow moving and stationary targets on the ground and to direct weapons to attack them. It is based on the Boeing 707 aircraft and uses technology demonstrated as part of the USAF's Pave Mover programme in 1982, particularly the use of a sideways-looking airborne radar. This means that the aircraft can detect targets far behind the enemy FLOT without venturing there itself, for which it would surely be too vulnerable. The aircraft could direct strike aircraft, Air Launched Cruise Missiles (ALCMs), MLRS and ATACMs (see Chapter 5) on to enemy ground targets. Development and testing should be complete by 1991, when a final production decision could be taken.[10]

Technology is also being derived from the US Army's battlefield data system (BDS) and Stand Off Target Acquisition System (SOTAS). The latter is crucial to the operation of MLRS and ATACMS. It can operate at night and in adverse weather to give a moving picture of moving targets in real time far beyond the limits of a forward observer's vision. The information is provided with sufficient accuracy to allow target engagement by artillery and missiles. Acquisition is carried out by an airborne element in a Black Hawk helicopter while the processing takes place in a vehicle on the ground. Another important part of the patchwork of target acquisition is the high flying Lockheed TR-1 aircraft equipped with the Precision Locating/Strike System (PLSS).

PLSS is undergoing trials in the USA at the time of writing and is likely to be operational in Europe before long, perhaps 1990 or so. TR1 aircraft with PLSS would probably deploy in threes, executing three distinct tasks. One is the detection of enemy radar transmissions which can be precisely fixed in concert with ground surveillance; the second is monitoring the positions of friendly aircraft and missiles (duplicating to some extent what Wavell can do) and finally vectoring attacking aircraft and missiles on to selected targets.[11] Systems like this will inevitably be sold to other powers, especially in the Middle East and South Asia.

The vulnerability of large manned aircraft and the need for surveillance methods organic to ground forces has placed much emphasis on the use of unmanned drones or remotely piloted vehicles (RPVs), such as the US Army operated Aquila. Current drones lack the ability to report back in real time, but this should be remedied with the appearance of the British Phoenix battlefield surveillance RPV. Phoenix is equipped with an infrared sensor so it can see by night as well as by day. A production contract for Phoenix was imminent at the time of writing this book. It will fly just behind and perhaps 2,000 to 3,000 metres above the FLOT, relaying information to a central control point on the ground, well protected against attack. A sensitive thermal imager and possibly a laser rangefinder can be fitted into the small airframe thanks to the latest microelectronics. The image is enhanced in the control centre so that a clear steady picture is obtained by day and night. The Phoenix can roam for two to three hours out to a range of 70 kilometres from base and can conduct surveillance out to 40 or 50 kilometres beyond the FLOT. Although the aircraft is recoverable (hence its name), and relies on its small size, low noise and radar signature to minimise the possibility of detection, heavy casualties are still envisaged in the high-intensity European battle environment, and several hundred Phoenixes will be procured eventually. The British are also interested in a smaller drone called Raven and a higher flying manned surveillance system to give a broader picture called Corps Airborne Stand-Off Radar (CASTOR). As in tactics and operations, battlefield surveillance requires a number of interlinking and overlapping systems. Any interesting targets identified by CASTOR could be further investigated by Phoenix. Another area which will become very important in the future is that of Unattended Ground Sensors (UGS). UGS could be delivered by MLRS or ATACMs, firing cheap and disposable sources of intelligence deep into the enemy deployment. The information provided may be crude, but sufficiently detailed and accurate to enable Phoenix or similar drones to be dispatched to investigate further. Finally, in concert with these various remotely piloted vehicles and remote sensors, helicopters will continue to provide surveillance. In order to reduce their vulnerability a number of mast-mounted sensors are being developed, carried in a large ball or cylinder atop a helicopter's rotor blades so that it can see from behind cover. The distinctive ball arrangement may contain a variety of infrared, television, or laser apparatus.[12]

The Soviets call the process of detecting targets, then locating them precisely enough for targeting weapons, and then allocating targets and fire missions automatically, a reconnaissance destruction complex, a rather useful term. There are two types: a reconnaissance fire complex (ROK, in Russian), which is primarily designed to target artillery, and a reconnaissance strike complex (RUK), whose 'destructive element' comprises tactical or army air, tactical or operational missiles. Therefore a reconnaissance fire complex is primarily tactical and a reconnaissance strike complex more operational. Soviet open source analysis of the foreign military press describes both Assault Breaker and PLSS as reconnaissance strike complexes; SOTAS would be a reconnaissance fire complex. The Russians are clearly interested in developing such systems themselves, and have analysed American experience carefully. That of Vietnam, they say, has shown that the aircraft can no longer play the role of the 'unpunished killer' and this has heightened the requirement for a system like PLSS. With their huge artillery force, and the need to limit ammunition expenditure to retain mobility, the Russians can be expected to see an artillery reconnaissance fire-and/or-strike complex as a high priority.[13]

C³I ON THE FUTURE BATTLEFIELD

What difference, if any, will all this make on the future battlefield? The value of automated C³I is most closely connected with that most vital factor on the battlefield — time. In war, 'time is the most precious of all'. In the case of a major counterstroke by Northern Army Group operational level reserves in a European war (see Chapter 4), the potentially decisive value of automated C³I in determining the critical moment is obvious. Striking deep does not just mean striking deep in terms of space, but in time too — predicting what the enemy will do 24 hours ahead, by plotting, analysing and extrapolating from his movements. The flow of accurate up-to-date intelligence could enable a NATO commander to launch the counterstroke with deadly precision, driving straight for the jugular of the enemy penetration. Traditional intelligence gathering methods have been unable to obtain and interpret intelligence sufficiently quickly, let alone see into the future. The time taken for various sources based on experience in Vietnam is shown in Figure 7.5. Modern C³I and fire destruction complexes operating in real time should make information available instantly, but it still has to be thought about and acted on. The best way to see how it might work is to use historical examples and assess how different it would have been if modern C³I had been available. In Operation Peace for Galilee, for example, the Israelis had excellent technical means for gathering intelligence but were still apparently unable to locate all enemy formations. This allegedly prevented them thrusting for the Beirut-Damascus road, which was unprotected, although they did not know until too late. The classic example comes from 1973, during the initial unsuccessful Israeli counterattack in Sinai on 8 October. It was almost entirely a question of people being at fault.[14]

None of the major problems were due to any technological inadequacy. The Israelis had good airborne and ground surveillance equipment, yet it was a troop of reconnaissance vehicles from Sharon's division and not any technical means which identified the gap between the Egyptian 2 and 3 Armies which enabled the later, successful canal crossing to take place. The communications equipment was good, certainly better than in 1967, but communications were hampered by bad siting and sloppy procedures which also enabled Egyptians to hit Israeli targets with artillery. Yet modern C³I equipment could have reduced some of the problems, provided it worked reliably and without interference. Brigadier-General Gabi, motoring south

261

Figure 7.5: Timeliness of intelligence reports versus time

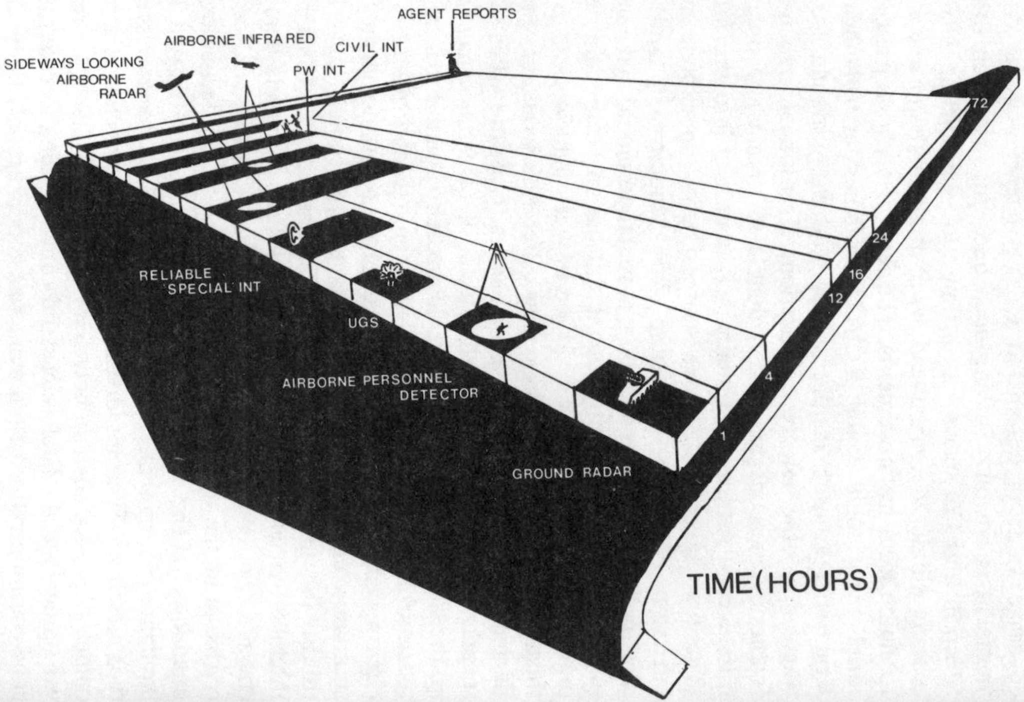

AGENT REPORTS

CIVIL INT

AIRBORNE INFRA RED

PW INT

SIDEWAYS LOOKING
AIRBORNE RADAR

RELIABLE
SPECIAL INT

UGS

AIRBORNE PERSONNEL
DETECTOR

GROUND RADAR

TIME (HOURS)

72

24

16

12

4

1

The average time elapsed from an event to the receipt of a report at headquarters, according to US experience in Vietnam. The fastest methods, such as ground surveillance radar, give reports almost instantaneously. Agent reports took on average three days, making them useless for battlefield operational purposes. The time taken is shown against the inexorable flow of time.
Source: Martin Van Creveld, *Command in War*, p. 248, remodelled by the author.

UGS — Unattended ground sensors; PW int — Prisoner of war interrogation
With ground sensors, the speed of intelligence from sideways-looking airborne radar should be greatly increased.

to roll the Egyptians up from the flank (itself perhaps a mistaken interpretation of the 'indirect' approach, given that the Egyptian position along the canal was much shallower than it was wide), was surprised to meet no resistance; in fact he was five miles from the canal, caused by a map reading error, had missed the Egyptians and was rolling southwards with his side towards them. A position Azimuth Determining System could have prevented that, although it could not have enabled him to carry out his instructions to 'destroy the Egyptians while staying out of range'(?). The constant monitoring of friendly forces' positions would have enabled Gonen and Adan to locate all their subordinate units at any time, thus removing any uncertainty as to who had crossed the canal and where. Various sensors, whether UGS, carried in helicopters or fixed wing air, and considerable use of drones, would have enabled the Israelis to locate the Egyptian positions which is so crucial for working one's way through a web of fire points. The Israelis showed a stunning lack of interest in precise location of targets (something on which the Soviets place much emphasis); it is as if they thought they would find them by instinct. Improved tactical communications might have made a difference in keeping unit commanders in touch with formations, and, more critically, good long-range satellite or tropospheric scatter systems would have made it easier for Tel Aviv to keep in touch with Gonen, thus enabling him to go further forward. The ability of a senior commander to turn a 'directed telescope' on to a key area, as van Creveld has called it, actively finding out what is really going on, would have helped dispel exaggerated reports of stunning Israeli successes in the first hours.[15] The main reasons for the Israeli failure could not have been solved by technological means, however: a lack of trust among senior commanders, a chain of command which failed to operate properly, and faulty perceptions attributing attitudes to the enemy which they did not have, which would have made any technical intelligence about their movements useless in predicting their future actions.

The Russians recognise the importance of continuity in putting new C³I systems into perspective, as well as the criticality of timing. In a milestone article in October 1985, Professor Major-General I. Vorob'ëv, a prominent Soviet authority, noted that reconnaissance strike complexes like Assault Breaker could reduce the time taken to engage targets by 10 to 15 times. Two aspects needed to be considered: the technical, connected with the widespread automation of control, and their operational tactical, or actual battlefield employment. The key elements in automation were microprocessors and computers. Vorob'ëv detailed the results of exercise Caucasus-85, which entailed the capture of a mountain pass by two opposed sides. The forward units of the two sides found themselves equidistant from it, with few obstacles on the route. The western side aimed to overcome a wide zone of fire obstacles in the valley in front of it. The eastern had to destroy the enemy's covering force and then move into the mountainous terrain, which was practically without roads. The outcome of the conflict would depend almost entirely upon the speed with which the two sides could react. The Russians also understand the importance of a 'deep knowledge of the enemy's tactics'. Given the NATO countries' current emphasis on the AirLand Battle, said Vorob'ëv, which aims to use surprise, the enemy's unpreparedness and fragmentation of the enemy's deployment, it is vital to maintain a solid defence and use time to the defender's advantage. The Russian general noted with concern foreign claims that Assault Breaker could destroy targets within 10 to 15 minutes of detection, but remarked that manoeuvre units would have to train to move within the same time either to avoid the strike or to minimise its effect by other means.[16]

UNCERTAINTY EVERYWHERE

This chapter has included a good deal on changes in C³I technology because that is what is going to be different in the future. The essence of command and the manipulation of forces will not change. The best solution will be, as Clausewitz intimated, to have a genius in charge. Clausewitz was also speaking for the future as for the present and his own time when he said that 'a great part of the information obtained in war is contradictory, a still greater part is false and by far the greatest part is of a doubtful character'.[17] Coming to terms with that requires instinct, genius, what Napoleon called 'a superior understanding'. One must agree with Martin van Creveld:

> Taken as a whole, military forces, for all the imposing array of electronic gadgetry at their disposal give no evidence whatsoever of being one whit more capable of dealing with the information needed for the command process than were their predecessors a century or even a millennium ago.[18]

As we have seen, modern C³I equipment can apparently remove some of the uncertainties, but technological advances are rarely confined to one side, and never for long. In a European war, take the example of a Russian general captured by the forces of some NATO formation far behind the NATO FLOT. Is he an OMG commander? Did his pilot make a map-reading error and fly off course before crashing? Or have one's own forces, whose positions are still, let us suppose, faithfully recorded on the screen of the Wavell type system, in fact over-run a category three Soviet division in defence? The answer can be found, but the general is not going to tell us immediately and it may take time to see how our own dispositions in fact relate to the enemy's. In any such example, from the interrogator getting the information out of the Russian general to the intelligence officer having to interpret it and our own general having to act on it in combination with inputs from other sources, it is ultimately a matter of human judgement and of instinctively knowing what is and is not important, and what makes sense.

There have been numerous — too many — attempts to impose order on the random, uncertain phenomenon of war. This is compounded by the obsessional propensity of many writing in the military sphere with technology. In the November 1981 edition of the US Military Review, eight articles were concerned purely with the technology of command while only one explained why this should not be so. There is no harm in trying to analyse the uncertainties of battle in a rational way and devising possible ways of overcoming them, provided this is kept in perspective. A number of possible measures are:

— Exercising commanders, staffs and units in conditions of minimum communication to get them used to the idea of thinking for themselves.

— Resting and rotating commanders and staffs to keep them alert and avoid saturation.

— Avoiding single options or obvious strategies (although the straightforward can sometimes be the right one, as perhaps with Gabi's brigade — see above).

— Using shadow staffs and commanders to feed major surprises into exercises, without regularity or warning.

— Removing key personnel from headquarters during exercises, to simulate the effects of accidents, delays and casualties.

— Preparation of 'fire brigade' teams to establish alternate headquarters or bolster them in case of trauma (a device used by both Israelis and Russians).

— Avoiding standard and predictable 'DS [Directing Staff] solutions' in training exercises.

— Training commanders and staffs to do other people's jobs if need be.

— Constantly reiterating that war is an uncertain business, that surety is unattainable and that the one thing that is certain is that things will go wrong and that the enemy will do other than the expected.[19]

These broad principles are good as guidelines for developing tutored instinct, but very little else. It is highly significant that the Germans, among the most efficient practitioners of military art in recent times and users of the most advanced technology of their day relatively recently, in 1939-45, were the most adamant retainers of the formal study of military history in their commanders' and staffs' curriculum. A treatise by a German general written as late as 1951, 'in the light of our time', reiterates the same points as Clausewitz, Schlieffen, Moltke and Freytag-Loringhoven. The genuine military leader knows that 'In war, chance — *sa majesté le hazard* — plays a great role. It is through prudence and foresight that he deprives chance of everything that can be torn away from it.'[20] 'An essential part of the training of leaders and general staff officers ought to be devoted to the behaviour of leaders whose plans are being destroyed by the influence of fate and who are menaced by failure and defeat.'[21] Like just about every great commentator on war he reiterated that military judgement and genius are instinctive but based on long experience and study of actual campaigns, in all their diversity. Generals must study how to react when faced with the unexpected and bad, like Pilsudski, faced with the breakthrough of Budënny's I Cavalry Army in 1920, an operation which has many lessons for the modern Soviet OMG concept and countermeasures. They must also know how to deal with unexpected good fortune; to notice an opportunity and grab it, to pursue relentlessly, to know when to throw caution to the winds.

There is no school, no doctrine, no book that can teach highest military leadership. If it is good the doctrine teaches the eternal value of simple principles and shows their application. The doctrine transmits to the student the technical conditions of the art of war too. They are constantly changing. The student must do the real work himself, erecting it on these foundations ... It is important to find out how the leading generals have been acting, whether and where they have been offending against the principles of military art, the reasons that brought about their successes and their failures.[22]

Whereas some have endeavoured to construct theoretical models for the study of command and control, and of military art in its entirety, this author believes that the subject is, like modern science, empirical. Military history is the record of the only valid experiments.

GENERALSHIP FOR THE TWENTY-FIRST CENTURY

It would be charitable to assume that the absence of any real higher military training for land forces commanders in NATO countries is a reflection of the belief in the impossibility of teaching higher military leadership. There has until recently been a good deal of prejudice against military history as the means of developing the higher commander's mind to deal with the unexpected, the irrational, the unknown effects of weapons on tactics and operations in future war. The Americans and Germans, have now attempted to remedy this by the use of historical example, as in *FM 100-5*, but there is a danger of letting a superficial acquaintance with a few examples pass for what is really needed. It is refreshing to note that historical examples are used in a novel and stimulating way in the new British *Army Field Manual,* 1985, Part One, *The Application of Force.* Although the Americans were the first to do this in recent years, the British have now put their very fine tradition of military history to practical use. It is to be hoped that British officers will read it for pleasure, and not only under duress.

How will C³I technology affect generalship on the future battlefield? It is not all negative. Personal leadership involves projecting the leader's personality, determination, charisma. Television would be one invaluable aid in that, although as we have seen it is far from ideal as a normal battlefield communications system. People also have to be trained to use it to come over well, but if well used it could help a commander galvanise widely separated formations and infuse an understanding and sense of purpose. The helicopter could be used to insert complete new command teams well forward. In an era of continuous, highly demanding operations, reserve command teams might infuse valuable fresh blood and clear thinking, and they would be essential if a complete command headquarters were annihilated. There are arguments against it; traditionally, the senior deputy or commander of a subordinate unit would take command, but if the senior deputy has gone up in smoke with the commander, and the commander of the subordinate unit is terribly tired or has not a grasp of the whole area of responsibility, transplanting a new command cell might be ideal. It could also add a new element of uncertainty for the enemy.

The future commander will, as we have seen, have access to information about the enemy's location, strength and weapons, but the enemy will know the same about him. Therefore, surprise and deception are as critical as ever, and feel for the battle — *fingerspitzengefühl* — is as critical as ever. To keep hold of the pulse of the battle the commander must be forward. On the modern battlefield, night will be as clear as day, and units, including senior commanders, will have to move and disperse more widely and frequently than before. The commander will have to share danger, stress and physical privation with his or her subordinates, and do so for an extended, unforeseeable period. Headquarters will be highly susceptible to deep attack and commanders will probably have to spend long periods in NBC kit (see Chapter 3). This will place demands on higher commanders' physical toughness and powers of personal leadership greater than in the recent past. The World War I general distractedly surveying the battlefield from the safety of a comfortable château may be a historical aberration, and it is probably no accident that this coincided with a hiatus in the art of war itself. The successful commander of the future may have more in common with Genghis Khan and his generals, owing as much to physical courage, prowess, and low cunning as to tutored intelligence.

Changes in weapons and platforms will also have a direct effect on generalship and the training of generals. Not only will they have to work with their equivalents in other services, given the way that air and sea power will also influence the hinterland battle; the air-land battle itself will have many of the characteristics associated with other forms of war. As the British General Wavell pointed out nearly half a century ago,

The commander with the imagination — the genius, in fact — to use the new forces may have his name written among the 'great captains'. But he will not win that title lightly or easily; consider for a moment the qualifications he will require. On the ground he will have to handle forces moving at a speed and ranging at a distance far exceeding that of the most mobile cavalry of the past; a study of naval strategy and tactics as well as those of cavalry [or tanks] will be essential to him. Some ideas on his position in battle and the speed at which he must make his decisions may be derived from the battle of Jutland; not much from Salisbury Plain or the Long Valley. Needless to say, he must be able to handle Air Forces with the same knowledge as forces on land.

It seems to me immaterial whether he is a soldier who has really studied the air or an airman who has really studied land forces. It is the combination of the two, never the action of one alone, that will bring success for a future war. Add to this that the commander's studies must have a background of common sense, and a knowledge of humanity, on whose peculiarities, and not those of machines, the whole practice of warfare is ultimately based.[23]

Wavell's thoughts are even more apposite to the 1980s, 90s and 2000s than they were to the 1940s. Highly expensive platforms, fixing their position by inertial navigation, firing from the move at other targets, also on the move, forces becoming interposed, will indeed have many of the characteristics of naval war, and the land commander will have very substantial air forces under his direct control. As we have seen in Chapter 4, this has already caused acrimony within the US armed forces, and may in the next 25 years raise major questions about traditional career patterns and the divisions between branches of the armed forces.

CONCLUSION

In the inevitably imperfect world, a military organisation either has to increase its ability to process information compared with its opponent or else be designed to work on less information. The former will lead to the multiplication of communications channels and staffs to process the information (as, apparently, in NATO at the moment). The latter may have two consequences; the first is the drastic simplification of the organisation, so it operates like clockwork (the Mongol battle drills, Frederick the Great's automatons). The second is the division of the task into parts, with each element able to cope with a whole range of possible challenges, if necessary, alone, as a microcosm of the whole. Examples are Napoleon's divisions, Moltke's Army Corps, German stormtrooper detachments in 1918, the Israeli *Ugdah* in 1967, and the general tendency, this century, to task organise the different arms at lower and lower level. This generally results in simpler, more compact and elusive command. Whereas American and British headquarters are gigantic, seeking to ensure their viability (in the correct sense of that word) by dispersing elements among armoured, isolated vehicles, duplicating information and possibly resulting in a bunch of lonely, frightened men exchanging useless information, the Israelis and the Soviets have their commanders collocated, the artillery and the air right up with the all-arms commander. Command is centralised, but it is centralised far forward. This interconnects with the principles of *Auftragstaktik*, or the mission-orientated system, where higher commanders set broad guidelines and minimum objectives, and let their commanders get on with it, keeping an eye on what is happening through the directed telescope and only interfering if absolutely necessary. The higher headquarters is a small and informal organisation to keep the various elements working towards the same objective. Van Creveld believes that the most successful armies have been those that did not attempt to turn their soldiers into automatons and did not try to command everything from the top. Examples of this devolution of command are Napoleon's marshals, the Russian Military District, Moltke's army commanders, the storm detachments in 1918, the Israeli army.[24]

None of the great land commanders of history enjoyed any technological advantage over their opponents in methods of C³I, or, indeed, anything else. Simplicity, flexibility and responsiveness was a function of organisation and training (the Mongols, Napoleon), and sometimes of discipline as well (Frederick). It is sensible to use modern technology to expedite the acquisition and processing of information, but organisation and training is even more important, and excessive concentration on technology at the expense of the former could be self destructive. The complexity of modern C³I equipment makes it necessary to devote much of the training effort to getting used to the equipment itself, even before it can be used creatively to simplify and lubricate the process of command. As with logistics (see Chapter 8), the multiplication of C³I systems has kept pace with, perhaps exceeded, the rate of improvements in mobility and communications themselves, and may actually be slowing things down — witness the increase in the size of command headquarters. This is apparent from all the empirical evidence — the study of the military past — and the solution lies there, too.

NOTES

1. Definitions of command, control, Ritchie, etc.: 'C³I — the evolution of a concept', *Defence Material,* September/October 1985, pp. 142-3; bandwidths, means of propagation, fibre optics: R.G. Lee, *Introduction to Battlefield Weapons Systems and Technology,* 2nd edition (Brassey's Battlefield Weapons Systems and Technology Series, Brassey's, Oxford, 1985), pp. 117-21; A.M. Willcox, M.G. Slade and P.A. Ramsdale, *Command, Control and Communications (C³)* (Brassey's Battlefield Weapons Systems and Technology Series, Vol. VI, Brassey's, Oxford, 1983), pp. 7-44, 114-7.
2. Lee, *Battlefield Weapons Systems,* pp. 122-4.
3. Willcox, Slade and Ramsdale, *Command, Control and Communications,* pp. 47-53, 69-76.
4. For a preview of the decision and argument about need for

COMMAND, CONTROL, COMMUNICATIONS AND INTELLIGENCE

trunk communications: 'Ptarmigan calling', *Times*, 19 September 1985, letters page; confirmation: 'Britain fails in bid for biggest US defence order', *Times*, 6 November 1985, p. 1; 'France wins £3 billion US order', *Daily Telegraph*, 6 November 1985, p. 1; Hugh Lucas, 'Ptarmigan, $3.1 billion more, loses to RITA', *Jane's Defence Weekly*, 16 November 1985, p. 1,066.

5. Quotation from Lucas in *Jane's*, p. 1,066; Bob Raggett, 'US Tri-Tac system set to get back on course', *Jane's*, p. 1,067. RITA system: *Jane's Military Communications*, 1985, pp. 822-7.

6. 'Wavell: Battlefield CCIS for the British Army', *Defence Material*, September-October, 1985, p. 144.

7. 'O' groups, etc.: General Farndale's talk at RUSI, 15 October 1985.

8. Quotation from Sokolovskiy, *Soviet Military Strategy* (first edition, 1962), p. 301, cited in John Hemsley, *Soviet Troop Control* (Brassey's, Oxford, 1982), p. 169.

9. Hemsley, *Soviet Troop Control*, pp. 169-82, 227-30; V.V. Druzhinin and D.S. Kontorov, *Ideya, algoritm, resheniye (prinyatiye, reshenii i avtomatizatsiya)* (Voyenizdat, Moscow, 1972), translated as *Decision Making and automation: Concept, Algorithm, Decision* (United States Air Force, US Government Printing Office, Washington, DC, 1978); Druzhinin's article *'Avtomatizirovannaya sistema upravleniya boyevymi sredstvami'* ('Automated system of directing military assets'), *SVE*, Vol. 1 (1976), pp. 77-81. For other literature see Hemsley's bibliography plus I.M. Golushko and N.V. Varlamov, *Osnovy modelirovaniya i avtomatizatsiyi upravleniya tylom (Principles of modelling and automating the rear services)* (Voyenizdat, Moscow, 1982).

10. Wellington, to J.W. Croker, 1845, cited in Heinl, p. 161 (there are many versions of the 'other side of the hill' quote, all different: Wellington may have repeated the same thought on several different occasions); JSTARS: 'Joint USAF/Army JSTARS System Set for Airborne Test in 1988', *Aviation Week and Space Technology*, 9 December 1985, pp. 91-9.

11. PLSS: Steve Broadbent, 'Bird's Eye View of the Battlefield', in Michael J.H. Taylor (ed.), *Jane's Aviation Review* (Jane's, London, 1985), pp. 59-64, esp. p. 64.

12. Phoenix, Raven and Castor in Broadbent, 'Bird's Eye View', pp. 59-63: An example of the mast-mounted sight is that on the OH-58D which houses an infrared thermal imaging sensor, laser rangefinder/designator, 12× magnification television camera; *Aviation Week*, 9 December 1985, p. 17.

13. Major-General M. Belov and Lieutenant-Colonel V. Shchukin, '*Razvedyvatel'no-porazhayushchiye kompleksy armii SShA*' (Reconnaissance-Destruction Complexes of the US Army), *VV* 1/1985, pp. 86-9. *ROK* stands for *Razvedyvatel'no-ognevoy kompleks*; *RUK* for *Razvedyvatel'no-udarny*. Assault breaker is depicted diagramatically on p. 87, PLSS on p. 88. See also the author's *Red God of War*.

14. Martin van Creveld's masterly *Command in War* (Harvard University Press, Cambridge, Mass., and London, 1985), pp. 203-31,

table from p. 248.
15. Van Creveld, *Command on War*, pp. 226-31. False reports of successes, pp. 220-1.
16. I Vorob'ëv, '*Vremya v boyu*' ('Time in combat'), *Krasnaya zvezda*, 9 October 1985, p. 2. An interesting study on timing is Lieutenant-Colonel Syed Fazal-ur-Rahman, 'Flow of Time and its Dimensions', *PAJ*, January 1977, pp. 1-18.
17. Clausewitz, *On War*, Book 1, chapter 6, 'Intelligence in War'.
18. Van Creveld, *Command in War*, p. 265.
19. Dr. Roger A. Beaumont, 'Certain Uncertainty: Inoculating for Surprise', *Air University Review*, July-August 1984, pp. 8-16. Eight articles and one: Van Creveld, *Command in War*, Chapter 4, note 1, p. 294.
20. General der Artillerie Friedrich von Boetticher, *The Art of War: Principles of the German General Staff in the light of our time. A Military Testament* (Bielefeld, May 1951), unpublished typescript, translated by the US Army Foreign Military Studies Branch, MS No. P-100, p. 15 of typescript.
21. Ibid., p. 17.
22. Ibid., pp. 19, 20-21.
23. General Sir Archibald Wavell, *Generals and Generalship: The Lees Knowles Lectures delivered at Trinity College, Cambridge in 1939* (Penguin, Harmondsworth, 1941), pp. 29-30. The choice of Wavell as the name for the new British CCIS was particularly appropriate. Long Valley is in Aldershot, now dear to the memory of those who have done parachute training.
24. The three methods of simplifying command and some of the examples are Van Creveld's. *Command in War*, pp. 264-75, quote on p. 269. On the Mongols see the author's 'Heirs of Genghis Khan', *RUSI*, March 1983; on military districts, D. Skalon (ed.), *Stoletiye voyennago ministerstva* (*A Hundred Years of the War Ministry*) (St Petersburg, 1902), Part III, *Otdel* VI, pp. 251-3, 493-4.

8

The Nature of Future Land Warfare

What, then, will future air-land warfare be like? In Europe, many would envisage a swift offensive by one side, characterised by high mobility. The defence, if anything even more flexible and agile, would use its probably superior technological means of command and control to move its limited forces, thus achieving temporary superiority at decisive points and moments. Soviet forces would endeavour to go round hard objectives, to outflank or simply ignore them. Or would they? Could they?

THE EMPTY BUT CROWDED BATTLEFIELD

From the viewpoint of the individual on it, the future battlefield will look very empty. Martin van Creveld painted a vivid picture of the empty battle area, here and there a target appearing, being engaged by an anti-tank missile, perhaps, or a laser designator, and then a flash far off and an explosion as an invisible artillery shell plummets precisely to its target.[1] In immediate terms the battlefield must be fairly empty, except for limited moments when forces concentrate for attack; the sudden irruption of a mass of tanks, preceded or accompanied by a dark curtain of choppers swooping and spitting fire. Artillery will certainly be widely dispersed, even the Russians considering splitting batteries into sections and NATO forces possibly deploying guns individually. The larger tactical missiles will be deployed in ones and twos, far apart and needing space to move. Helicopter landing sites will have to be some way back from the forward positions: we can and should dispense with the conventional term 'line'. Other units, like EW detachments, will need to be as far forward as more traditional combat units, further extending the requirements for space laterally as well as in depth. All this dispersion *takes up space*. The same was true of the Great European War of 1914-18; likewise, the impression of emptiness was superficial. To avoid presenting targets to enemy artillery, the forward edge of each side's deployment was held by dispersed outposts, often involved in vicious and aggressive combat action at the lower tactical level, holding positions in shell-holes. The dispersion gave rise to what John Terraine, describing a photograph of a typical Great War engagement, called the 'forlorn loneliness of the front line'.[2] Dispersion at the lower level, paradoxically, led to clogging of the battlefield at the higher. Both sides' deployments extended effortlessly from the Alps to the sea, and outflanking or manoeuvre became impossible. This is vividly shown in Figures 8.1 and 8.2. From their initial deployments in Figure 8.1, the opposed sides sought to outmanoeuvre each other. A Great War division could, according to various subsequent analyses, dominate, control and impede enemy movement over a 10 kilometre front. If we therefore allot each of the 88 German and 76 Anglo-French divisions involved a 10 kilometre square, and place them side by side, it is easy to see why they clogged up the entire breadth of front and prevented a decisive breakthrough or envelopment by either.[3]

From the data in Chapter 4, it is clear that a much more dispersed modern division, disposing of much greater firepower, would dominate and fix a 30 kilometre square area, at least (in fact, increases in the firepower and range of weapons suggest, logically, that it would be more). If we do the same for NATO and Warsaw Pact forces in Germany, or likely to be deployed in Germany in the opening days of a future European war as shown in Figure 8.2, we cannot escape the conclusion that the battlefield as a whole would be vastly more crowded than that of the Great War; that the complex of interconnecting fire positions and carefully sited long-range weapons would weave a stultifying, trapping web over a vast area. Finding a way round a flank, through a thinly held position or sliding down a formation boundary would seem to be far more of a problem than it was in the Great War. Even a huge superiority massed on a very narrow axis, as often happened in the Great War, would be no more likely now than then to punch a hole if the defence were

Figures 8.1 and 8.2: The
empty but crowded battlefield

8.1 shows initial deployments in 1914:
German and French armies and BEF
Sources: *Military Operations, France
and Belgium, 1914: History of the Great
War based on Official Documents
(Official History),* (Macmillan, London,
1937), map opposite p. 15. Figure 8.2:
1914, ibid., Appendices 1 (British), 3
(French), 6 (Germans). Belgian field
forces and their fortress garrisons,
with whom the Germans had to
contend before facing the British and
French, are not included. 1986-90:
*NATO and the Warsaw Pact: Force
Comparison* (NATO Information Office,
Brussels, 1984), p. 19. It is assumed
that a 1914 division could dominate
and impede enemy movement along a
10 kilometre front: a late 1980s one, 30
(see text).

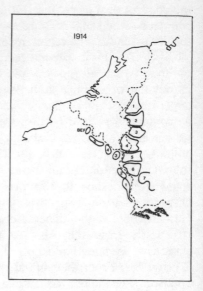

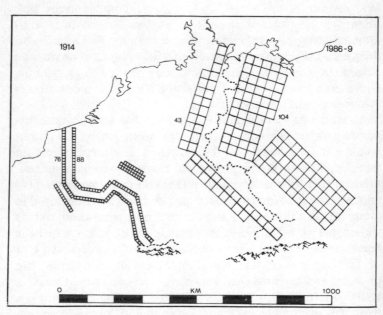

276

tied together by a responsive C³I system and rapidly mobile reserves. You can argue forever about how many divisions would be available on a particular day, at a particular moment, whether it is appropriate to take the division as the standard building block, or about disparities between the strength and endurance of NATO and Warsaw Pact divisions. It is the overall strength deployed within a limited area which counts. Units and formations are like atoms; seen close up, they comprise insubstantial particles whirling in space. Taken together, and seen from a short way off, they constitute solid matter, and that solid barrier could extend over all Germany. Whichever way you look at it, Europe is just not big enough to permit the deployment of all the forces scheduled to go in there in war, appropriately dispersed, and still permit unlimited manoeuvre.

RATES OF ADVANCE

Connected with space is the issue of pace. Armies have become more dependent on other supplies from home as their equipment becomes more and more complex and their soldiers more demanding. Although there are stories of trains of wagons laden with arrows being carried to the battle of Flodden in 1513, medieval armies could do without vast supplies of ammunition, and what ammunition was expended could be recovered and used again. This was not the case with the millions of shells which had to be available for any Great War offensive, and even less so with big and highly expensive items of modern ammunition such as guided missiles. Small armies could live off the land without stripping it bare (and as long as there was just enough food for their own purposes, it did not matter to them if they did). The vast armies which the demographic revolution of the eighteenth century brought about, and the even vaster ones resulting from the technological and organisational revolution of the nineteenth, could not do this and had to be supplied from the rear. Increased mobility has therefore been outweighed by the counter mobility resulting from larger armies, more complex weapons systems and, on the field of battle itself, weight of fire. The Israelis, who are the most enthusiastic apostles and practitioners of what is simplistically and elliptically called 'mobile warfare', are quite clear about that. As Figure 8.3 shows, nobody has ever attained the 27 kilometre per day norm

Figure 8.3: Rates of advance: fact and fiction?

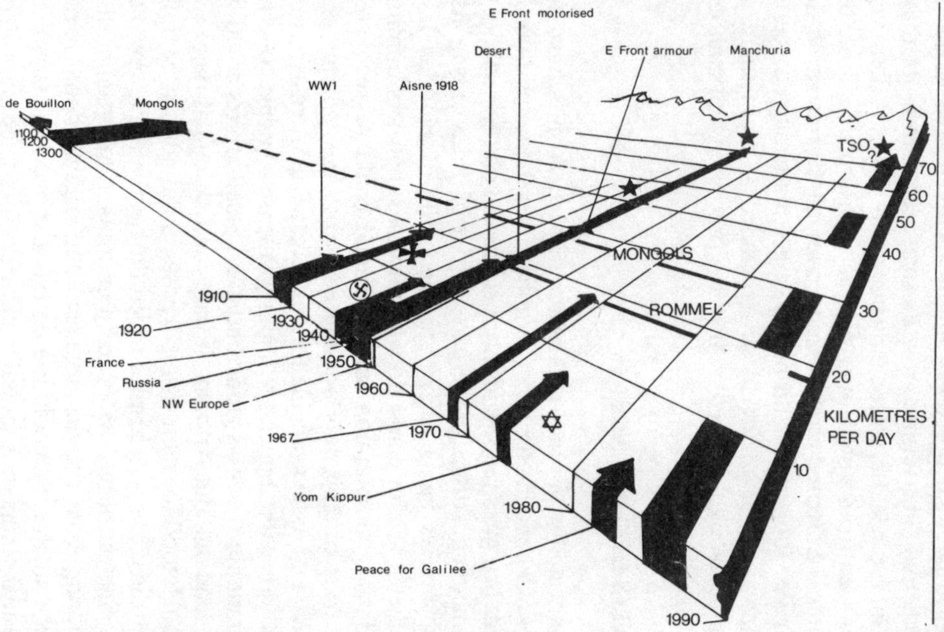

of the Mongols. In case it is alleged that these figures do not compare like with like, the Israeli source confirms that these comparisons were done on the basis of a common denominator in terms of the number of breakthrough battles, engagements and encounters along the way. Thus in the Israelis' own land Godfrey de Bouillon only managed 1.6 kilometres per day during the First Crusade of 1096-9. Napoleon managed 12 kilometres: The Germans in France in 1940 only managed 10 kilometres per day and in Russia in 1941, in spite of all that has been written about *Blitzkrieg*, 5 kilometres per day. The Americans and British managed about the same after the invasion of Europe in 1944. The average rate of advance of the Israeli ground forces in the Six Day War of 1967 was 60 kilometres per day but that was based on far fewer breakthrough battles and was untypical. According to Israel's greatest authority on mechanised combined arms warfare, under test conditions the Israelis would have managed about 17 kilometres per day, the same as Rommel in North Africa. Latest wars have confirmed the slowing up trend: the Yom Kippur War saw the Israelis advancing about 5.6 kilometres per day and Operation Peace for Galilee (again, exceptional circumstances), about one.[4]

The Soviet Colonel Sidorenko cited a different set of figures to illustrate that the tempo of operations had increased and would continue to do so. In the Great War the average rate of advance during major attacks did not exceed 4 to 6 kilometres a day; on the Aisne, in May 1918, the Germans attained the highest rate of the entire war, 18 kilometres. During the later stages of the Soviet offensive in the Great Patriotic War, in 1944-5, rates of advance reached 15 to 20 kilometres for rifle troops and 20 to 30 for tank and mechanised units, although in some individual sectors this went up to 70 or 80. In the Manchurian operation (see Chapter 4), the Transbaikal front attained 50 to 80 kilometres per day over a ten day period, and it is on this that the most favourable (to them) Soviet assumptions about rates of advance in a European Theatre Strategic Operation appear to be based.[5] However, we have no way of comparing these with the Israeli model and criteria, and the more rapid examples cited are those of formations which have broken through a major defensive belt and are exploiting fast and far into the enemy depth, with little opposition, rather than fighting a series of encounter and breakthrough battles throughout. If we take the entire distance covered by Soviet armies and fronts in Europe from the time they started winning (for the sake of argument, the counteroffensive at Stalingrad on 19 November 1942) to the fall of Berlin on 8 May 1945, we get about 2,000 kilometres in just over 900 days, or 2.2 kilometres per day. The Soviets were for much of the time battling against a deeply echeloned defence, subject to major strategic operations by the Germans against them (Kursk) and probably fought far more major breakthrough battles, meeting engagements, defensive battles and special operations (the relief of Leningrad) than the Israeli model provides for. Nevertheless, the final sweep to victory by a battle-seasoned Red Army against German and Japanese forces who had been substantially weakened, albeit indirectly, by other Allied action, cannot be taken as typical for a future major war. A total of 70 kilometres a day would seem a very optimistic target for Soviet forces to aim at; if they managed 20 they would be doing better than Rommel. NATO estimates which envisage Soviet forces reaching the Rhine by day five (see Chapter 4) seem a little pessimistic, if undoubtedly possible.

STASIS

There are serveral other reasons why stasis might occur:

Weight versus Mobility

As we have seen, modern industrial armies need massive logistic support. At the battle of the Somme in 1916, the shells required for the British offensive (107,000 tons) had to be carried to railheads by train, and then dumped. From there, there was very little possibility of moving them forwards or backwards, and so logistics dominated strategy and operations very directly. If a breakthrough did occur, supplies could not be moved up over the broken, cratered terrain, and the advance ground to a halt. One can imagine the same thing happening with the Soviets' emphasis on massive destruction by artillery to guarantee, expedite and protect the movement of mechanised forces. A Soviet battalion attack on a well-prepared position would, according to the textbooks, need about 2,000 rounds of artillery ammunition, and if this is multiplied by the number of engagements the ammunition requirements look phenomenal. Soviet experience suggests that the faster forces move, the less ammunition is required; it is only when they are stuck that heavy concentrations of fire are needed to clear the enemy out of the way, and in those circumstances supply is easier. Another relevant factor is the greatly increased number of precision-guided and other more efficient projectiles. With their usual remarkable perspicacity, Tizard's team predicted that:

> There is no indication that the actual weight of bombardment on an objective will need to be higher in a future war than it has been in this. The use of projectiles with a higher charge weight ratio, the better control of artillery fire, the more accurate and extended use of aircraft and medium range rockets in tactical bombardment are all likely moreover to lessen the total weight of equipment and ammunition necessary to achieve a given effect at the target. Thus the dead weight burden of material that has to be transported with an army will be reduced ... We expect the present scale of fire power with improvements in efficiency to be maintained. Moreover, mobility and flexibility of operations will increase. In sum, the change will be towards combining the mobility of the less encumbered forces of the past with the tremendous firepower of the present.[6]

In some ways, Tizard was quite right. The new Soviet 203 mm (eight inch) high-powered gun model 1975, for example, represents an improvement in mobility rather than firepower *per se*. On the other hand, Tizard does not seem to have taken into account the greater hardness of modern targets. Everything in the forward areas is under armour, and therefore the weight of fire has had to be increased to some extent. 155 mm and 152 mm has become the standard calibre for major land theatres, and in order to fix and immobilise a hostile target before it has time to move, more shells have to be fired at it in less time. Improvements in efficiency and lethality have perhaps controlled this tendency, and in the future smart munitions and more efficient area weapons (see Chapter 5) may do so some more. The fixed-wing aircraft is probably past its peak as a method of battlefield weapons delivery, but helicopters continue to fulfil Tizard's prophecy of the extended use of aircraft. However, it is hard to see resupply getting any easier. The new multiple-launch rocket systems, even if used sparingly and selectively, will require considerable numbers of replacement rockets, and it will be difficult to get large numbers of these (each 220-227 mm in calibre and 3 metres long) up to forward areas, always supposing they exist or replacements can be manufactured in time. The lessons of recent history indicate that ammunition requirements will be phenomenal, and we shall return to the implications of that later. On the basis of recent evidence, it is quite likely that modern weaponry and its support requirements,

> far from reducing the gap between the mobility of armies (as determined by the nature of their means of transport) and the ability of their supply apparatus to keep up, will widen this gap still further.[7]

General mud

A major factor inhibiting movement in the Great War was the effect of firepower and frenetic activity combined with the heavy, clayey soil and west European rainfall. The battlefield rapidly became a bog. The bombardments of World War II, particularly by the Soviets, were much more intense than those of the Great War but only went on for hours rather than days, thus preventing the elements getting inside the soil and turning it to the consistency of porridge to the same extent. Also, they were much more accurate, delivered at point targets and distributed throughout the enemy depth rather than all along a thin frontage. Finally, it was usually unnecessary to use artillery fire to cut wire, as in the Great War, more efficient means being preferred. It was therefore possible to go round areas which had been subject to particularly destructive shell fire. However, the effects of air and artillery bombardment on towns were particularly marked, rapidly turning them into rubble, which has proved an ideal landscape for defence. Photographs of Stalingrad and Cassino show this clearly. Wherever modern firepower has been concentrated for any length of time it has pulverised the landscape. During the American defence of Khe Sanh in 1967, air bombardment blasted the surrounding rolling woodland into a 'moonscape of craters, many of them as large as backyard swimming pools'.[8] It is improbable that air power would be brought to bear in the same way in a European conflict, but there are other factors. The first is that the weight of tanks has increased very considerably. Once these 60 ton monsters start leaping around the already tortured soil of Europe, they will cause it to disintegrate rapidly. In the British exercise Lionheart in late summer 1984, heavy rain fell in the area of lower Saxony where a ten-day simulated battle was scheduled to take place, 'turning large areas into quagmires'. This was not initially even attributable to armoured vehicle movements, but it soon became obvious that the £8 million which the British had earmarked for compensation to landowners out of a total of £31 million for the entire exercise was going to be needed.[9] The combination of large-scale armoured movements and rain in a future European conflict could have effects similar to the bombardments of the Great War, severely hampering the ground movements of follow-on echelons. Helicopters would help overcome zones of quagmire, but, as we have seen, they cannot substitute for ground movement in more than a small percentage of cases.

Urbanisation

The potential European theatre is heavily built-up. There is a village every few kilometres, in every direction, a large town every 20 kilometres or so. In Russia in 1941-2, the Germans generally tried to avoid villages, and the Red Army similarly tried to bypass built-up areas, at least with the forward echelons.[10] When armies got stuck into fighting in urban areas, it was time consuming and costly, and slowed down the pace of advance and tempo of operations. Stalingrad is the outstanding example, but the Soviet assaults on Königsberg and Berlin also deserve study. In a future European conflict it will be impossible to avoid built-up areas, some of them very large. The best way through a built-up area is along wide motorways and thoroughfares, and those are predictable. Bridges, main roads and other routes are clearly identified and will be turned into minefields, craters or traps at the very beginning of hostilities. There is also considerable scope for directing urban development with strategic aims in mind. Development can be used to channel enemy movements into suitable areas for killing zones, and combined with existing features such as railways and canals to create discreet modern versions of Vauban's ditches, bastions, scarps and covered ways. At Königsberg in 1945 the destruction of the forts and other permanent defences woven into the urban landscape took four days of shelling before the Russian assault troops went in. This was the first Soviet artillery preparation of the war of such duration.[11] To a Soviet general charged with reaching the Rhine in (say) five days, the pattern of West German terrain, especially its urbanisation, must look pretty frightening.

Counter-mobility

The importance of the combat engineer in land warfare has never been fully appreciated, and in the land-air battle of the future he or she will be even more important. The scatterable mine, able to be programmed to do a variety of jobs, could have more potential than anything else to negate current plans, either for a swift offensive or for the swift movement of reserves to counter it. According to the Israeli Brigadier-General Katz's assessment, the attacking (Warsaw Pact) forces in a fictitious European war use scatterable mines to create a defensive belt around them which cannot be crossed. NATO forces find air-dropped forces in their rear, surrounded by an impassable belt of mines. The enemy would be able to isolate the fighting area from the rear without any difficulty, in one night's fighting. Thus the considerable improvements in countermobility weapons will not only work to the advantage of the side on the strategic defensive. Intelligently utilised, they could prevent the latter manoeuvring, paralysing the defensive and protecting the corridors, breakthroughs and *desants* of the strategic attacker.

NATO's defensive posture is not ideally suited for manoeuvre above the tactical level

As we have seen in Chapter 4, it looks as if NATO would be prepared to accept limited Warsaw Pact penetrations in order to expose them to decisive counterstrokes. But NATO is hardly in a position to utilise the full depth of West Germany to lure the opponent to destruction, as it must defend that soil. Generally speaking, there is no point in withdrawal because in the absence of reserves it is useless to trade space for time to mount the counter-offensive. That may be changing, but NATO is under strong pressure to fight for every kilometre — or 30 kilometres — of ground. In the overall context, this must militate against large-scale manoeuvre.

Martin van Creveld argued on the basis of the Yom Kippur War that the Israeli *Blitzkrieg* of 1967 was old-fashioned, not only by the standards of its own time but 'even in terms of the latter years of World War Two'.[12] *Blitzkrieg* campaigns became increasingly rare, foundering on great fortified belts like that of Kursk. By the end of that war it was reckoned that an attacker needed a five to one superiority, at least, on a principal axis of advance to beat an enemy who was neither shattered nor incompetent. Van Creveld believes that this disparity is likely to grow rather than diminish. Whether or not that is true, there is a considerable body of evidence to suggest that a future major war in Europe would not be characterised by swift and dramatic movements but by a series of violent but ultimately indecisive actions.

DURATION

'The first thing to be borne in mind is that the next war will be a long war.'[13] Bloch was right about the World War I in this respect, as in many others. Most people imagined the war would be over 'in six weeks,' while some Russians predicted six months.[14] The effect of this belief in the 'impossibility' of a long war was that nations concentrated on stockpiling arms for a short war, rather than on developing the capability to produce armaments: armament in breadth, rather than in depth, as it were. NATO is in a similar position today. During the 1970s, NATO planning for a war on the European Central Front was based on the extraordinarily firmly held belief that 'it will be a short war'. If any other kind of war had occurred, NATO would have been in trouble. The precise assumptions by countries and alliances to calculate their war plans are highly classified, but from discussion in the open press it is clear that the incredible six-day war assumption has at least been ditched, and that the aim would be for European or European-based forces to conduct the war until transatlantic resupply can become effective.

285

This might be about three weeks. However, conflict would not necessarily end there. Is it really possible that after the international situation had deteriorated sufficiently for the two major world systems to risk the consequences of a world war, that they would resolve the issues in a few days or weeks? Only if one were to win a rapid victory, which, as we have seen, is far from certain. The precedents of recent wars do not suggest that they are becoming any shorter. This raises the question of the relationship between the overt use of conventional military force and other forms of struggle; Vietnam alternated between guerrilla, mid-intensity and full-scale war over a period of 30 years in which two major protagonists, both superior to the communists technologically but less committed as nations, were eventually beaten. It would be inaccurate to think of this as a 30-year conventional war. The final collapse of South Vietnam, at the stage when the North had begun to conduct more or less conventional operations using tanks and artillery, was so rapid as to surprise not only the South Vietnamese, but the North as well. The fate of South Vietnam was sealed in perhaps 20 days, from the attack on Ban me Thuot on 10 March to the fall of Da Nang on 29 March. The final conventional operations lasted from the fall of Phuoc Long on 6 January to Saigon's unconditional surrender on 30 April. But this happened to a state in a precarious geographical position, collapsing from within, and placed in a position where, if it did not of itself bring about victory for the North, its continuation by battle was sure to do so. The American withdrawal had left the South Vietnamese conditioned to rely on air and motor transport which became increasingly rare after 1972, and without a viable command structure (the Americans had dominated it). This was compounded by the greatly increased mobility and logistics of the North Vietnamese, enabling them to concentrate armour and artillery at will, and the lack of it on the South Vietnamese side caused by shortages of fuel and spares. Then there was the absence of a mobile South Vietnamese reserve to counter the North's various concentric attacks. Political organisation disintegrated, commanders preferred to return to their families rather than lead their troops. *And still it took 20 days.*[15] Seen in this way, there are clear parallels with a Europe where NATO has become fragmented, where left-wing governments apathetic if not sympathetic to the prospect of Warsaw Pact dominance have taken power in some states (West Germany, the

Netherlands, Denmark, Norway?), and where the link with the United States has been severed and US forces withdrawn or subject to hostility. In such a situation, the Warsaw Pact might deliver the military *coup de grace*, like the North Vietnamese. But is such a relatively swift and clean military campaign likely against a strong, united NATO with some US troops in place, even if partially surprised? The only way out is that one side or the other will decide the struggle is 'not worth the candle'. But this is unlikely: pride, self delusion, and the very real prospect of 'just one more short pull', all play their part. The classic example of a long and indecisive war is the Iran-Iraq conflict, which is examined in detail, along with its lessons for other theatres of war, in Chapter 1. Some will argue that it is untypical, and every war is indeed unique, but we neglect the lessons of wars in non-European theatres at our peril. The American Civil and Russo-Japanese wars with their duration and employment of field fortifications were accurate precursors of the Great European War, but were largely ignored, as we have seen.

Within the context of the war as a whole, individual actions are also likely to last a long time. The lessons of Yom Kippur suggest ferocious engagements lasting 120 hours without a lull.[16] Participants will inevitably collapse from physical, mental and logistic exhaustion and some suspension will ensue. The demands that these intensive actions will place on resupply and the very availability of ammunition, particularly high-technology arms, must cast doubt on their ability to influence the conduct of war for more than a short period. In the Yom Kippur War, the ratio of anti-aircraft missiles fired to aircraft destroyed was, according to one estimate, 80 to one. Cases were reported of Israeli tanks still driving around with up to 14 pairs of missile guidance wires draped round them. Israel lost more tanks than the United States produces in a year. To resupply them, the Americans had to scrape the bottom of even their mighty barrel. Arabs and Israelis were running out of ammunition after only a week of murderous fighting. In the conflict, 3,000 tanks were lost by both sides, about a third of NATO's present total. The need to get tanks back into action quickly, a prominent lesson of that war, is clearly recognised in the design of the *Merkava* (see Chapter 5), but even so the destruction of sophisticated equipment in any future major war will be colossal, imposing limitations on the intensity of subsequent fighting. Where will replacements be found when the exhausted survivors of the opening battles sink back into underground lairs to gather their strength for the next round? Guided missiles can only be produced slowly, as can other complicated munitions: terminally-guided MLRS warheads, for example. A few hundred or thousand a year is the maximum of which most NATO nations are capable without a major mobilisation of industry. After the initial exchanges, both sides would have to revert to a plainer diet of bombs and bullets. The conflict is likely to '... degenerate into slugging matches going on interminably until one side or the other gives way because of sheer exhaustion'.[17] Such battles would also acquire a more old-fashioned appearance, and the destruction and breakdown of communications all across the battlefield could quite possibly favour the side with the simpler and more plentiful equipment. If this is a problem for the industrialised arms-manufacturing nations, it is even more one for arms-importing countries. The indecisive nature of the Iran-Iraq war has undoubtedly been a result in part of the lack of spares and supplies for sophisticated weapons and platforms, particularly aircraft, for which both sides depend heavily on imports. In the Middle East, South Asia and the Far East particularly, the uncertainty of replenishment and resupply from allies in a fraught international situation will tend to favour the development of simpler, indigenous forms of weaponry, including the cruder chemical agents. India's manufacture of Soviet designed equipment under licence is an obvious example of a desire to minimise or reduce this problem.

In the event of a long war, therefore, NATO in particular faces a tragic irony. If attacking forces are held or substantially slowed, what does NATO do then? Surrender, or go nuclear, because it has shot its last precision-guided bolt? Or go on fighting a long war, reverting to simpler but more plentiful weaponry? A gruelling, old fashioned *materialschlacht*, like the Iran-Iraq war, a space age Verdun?

TURN YOU TO THE STRONGHOLD

Throughout military history, defenders have often turned their 'circumstances to advantage in advance'.[18] Field or permanent fortifications are of particular value to an antagonist whose key industrial or political assets lie close to the frontier, like France in 1940 or West Germany today. Although much maligned, what there was of the Maginot Line performed very well; it was simply not finished and the Germans went round it. Neither the Wehrmacht, the Soviets nor the Israelis have found any difficulty in reconciling a mobile doctrine with fortifications. The Soviets constructed formidable fortified regions before the Great Patriotic War, which the Germans considered to be more of an obstacle than the Maginot Line, and today have extensive fixed defences along the Chinese border. The Israeli Defence Force is still committed to the construction of massive defensive positions, 'complementing and commensurate with its mobility and demonstrating that the former need not inhibit the latter'.[19] Modern conditions are making the two-man slit trench look increasingly inadequate and the British are introducing new pre-formed elements to strengthen field fortifications. The application of modern materials to field fortifications may be an important trend in the next quarter century. Overhead protection is being stressed, in the face of the expected indirect fire artillery bombardment, but experience from the Falklands has shown that when trenches are built with open sides and a thick roof on the top the effect can be to funnel the blast from nearby explosions with lethal effect.[20] Future trenches may therefore be fully enclosed, with pre-formed embrasures. In order to retain wider arcs of fire, there might be a case for ready-made turrets or sponsons, leading in fact to a small fort. From here it is a short jump to permanent or pre-placed fortifications.

A number of writers have advocated extensive use of pre-placed, hardened fire positions. They would integrate well with the complex counterpane of West German terrain. If chemical warfare began, encumbering mobile forces with bulky and uncomfortable equipment, gas-tight underground installations might hold out against great odds. Given the high rate of ammunition expenditure envisaged in the opening phases of a European war, the ability of a fort to provide a safe haven for large stocks of ammunition could again give it an advantage. The defence of a fort requires a lower standard of training, so militia units could be used, freeing regulars and front line reserves for more demanding manoeuvre operations, expeditious in a time of manpower shortage. Shelters would not necessarily be permanently occupied, but units might leapfrog backwards and forwards, keying into a secure land-line communications systems which would fit well with pre-positioned defences.[21] The arguments for permanent or semi-permanent fortifications, in combination with powerful, mobile reserves, are persuasive for anybody needing to buy time from a numerically superior attacker. Modern technology could give fortification a new lease of life (see also Chapter 4).

Such a scheme could impose a different form on the fighting. As Soviet forces penetrated they might not act in the classic manner, sweeping round to a flank to envelop, with NATO forces countermanoeuvring and crashing into their rear like a giant revolving door, or cracking the defence in the middle and enveloping outwards, like an outward opening double door. Instead, as forces penetrated, the defence, tied together by a network of commands and signals, would close behind them; attacking forces would find the skin around the wound they had created healing. They would find themselves stuck in a web, engulfing them like quicksand or glue. There would be movement of defending forces, but over relatively small distances: a series of pawns on the chequer board, moving a single space to kill the trapped queens, bishops and rooks. Heliborne forces would be like knights, able to jump over defences, but with limited range and their landing sites particularly vulnerable to indirect fire. The attacker would be worn down by a process of attrition, constantly surprised by the force and form of the defender's attacks. This is not the image of future war which many have predicted: it is the Dragon Variation.[22]

FLESH AND BLOOD

The prospect of a long, static slogging match has profound implications for everyone: troops initially deployed, reserves and civilian populations. In the opening phases of a European war casualties would be enormous. In recent wars waged by developed countries, often against less developed opponents, it has been possible to reduce the risk of death faced by wounded soldiers dramatically by prompt evacuation. In Vietnam, the Americans used helicopters to get casualties away from the fighting with astonishing speed. The Israelis did the same in Lebanon, preventing deaths which would almost certainly have occurred in any previous war. There are stories like that of the young man whose head was nearly cloven in two by a fragment from a Soviet multiple rocket launcher, but was given prompt skilled surgical attention and saved. The brain damage that resulted later caused its own social and psychiatric problems, but wounds to other organs can be more completely healed. Mindful as ever of the need to minimise casualties and thus sustain civilian morale, the Israelis have a policy of sending fully trained doctors well forward. This has been the subject of much debate as they inevitably suffered casualties and doctors are rare and valuable commodities. The Americans preferred to rely on heliborne casevac to well equipped hospitals. In the Falklands, the British were in a different position, outnumbered and without the elaborate and plentiful logistic infrastructure employed in Lebanon and Vietnam. They placed reliance instead on prompt basic first aid, and a high level of training down to individual soldiers. The spectacle of ordinary British soldiers administering saline drips to casualties surprised many when viewed on television.

Modern techniques for treating and evacuating casualties have made a significant difference where a small proportion of a nation's resources are deployed in a relatively limited conflict. But what would happen in a major European war? Scarce and expensive helicopters cannot be spared to hoist every wounded soldier out of action immediately, and the sheer volume of casualties is likely to swamp available medical facilities. Based on historical data, such as the 100,000 men the Soviets lost in their final drive to Berlin, against an exhausted but fanatical enemy, and taking into account the lethality of modern weapons and the intensity with which they would be employed, what guesses can we make about the number of casualties in an all-out hot war in Europe? In the assault on Goose Green in the 1982 Falklands conflict, 2 Para lost about 11 per cent of its strength (17 killed and 35 wounded out of a strength of 450), during a 36-hour engagement (in fact most of the fighting took place during 24). That was considered a remarkably small toll for an action of that length and ferocity in conventional war.[23] On that basis alone we might reckon on at least 45 per cent casualties in four days of conventional war, 55 per cent in five, assuming continuous operations as discussed above. In the British Army of the Rhine alone there could be at least 18,000 casualties in the first three days but if caught by surprise and not fully deployed, and given the particular intensity of an initial Soviet attack, that could quite easily be doubled or even trebled. Assuming roughly a quarter of those were killed outright or died quickly, how would the British cope with, say, 40,000 casualties to be treated and evacuated in the first few days? The elaborate structure employed by the Americans and Israelis could not be emulated in a major European war: the British system of relying on the individual soldiers' training would be the main guarantee of survival. It would be necessary to allot priorities to casualties, and to adopt the Great War system of treating those with a good chance of survival, and abandoning those whose chances were slim. Evacuation would be hampered by deep penetration and desant operations, and by crowds of civilian refugees clogging the roads, many of whom would also undoubtedly become casualties. Geneva Convention I lays down that casualties received at a military dressing station or hospital should be treated in order of medical priority, whether one's own soldiers, enemy or civilian. One suspects, however, that under intolerable pressure surgeons and medics would have to take some very hard decisions based on other priorities.

Furthermore, this just assumes a conventional conflict using familiar weapons. What will be the effect of flechette rounds? Unlike a bullet, which can possibly be extracted, a flechette or two will be almost impossible to find and remove and may result in long-drawn-out agonising death. Modern science may have reduced some of the risk of gangrene (although even in the Falklands gangrene was an ever present danger), but it has created other lingering horrors. If chemical weapons were used on a wide scale — or at all — they would make large-scale medical treatment of casualties impossible. Every casualty has to be thoroughly decontaminated before a doctor or medic can get near him or her. The complete collapse of medical facilities under an all-out conventional and chemical onslaught is one reason why the ability of armies to fight cohesively has often been considered as limited to a few days. On the other hand, if chemical warfare resulted in a major slowing of the tempo of operations, as it probably would (see Chapter 3), that might balance out the additional load on medical services, and the chemical war could be waged at a fairly low level of intensity for a longer period.

What would the population of Western Europe and, for that matter, the increasingly quizzical population of the Warsaw Pact countries, enjoying an unprecedented standard of living, make of all this? Throughout history, people have always thought that they had become so smart and sophisticated that nasty old-fashioned things like war could not happen. That seems to have been very much the attitude in 1914, and exactly the same sense of amazement was felt by the British in 1982 when they watched a full-scale conventional operation getting underway. Are Western nations capable of facing up to the demands of a major war which would, as we have seen in Chapter 4, engulf the entire depth of Western Europe, especially a long war? The need to conscript men and women, to direct the economy ruthlessly, would cut across cherished ideas of individual liberty. Even before the Great War, people wondered,

> What is one characteristic of modern Europe? Is it not the growth of nervousness and lack of phlegmatic endurance, of stoical apathy? The modern European feels more keenly and is much more excitable and impressionable than his forefathers. Upon this highly excitable, sensitive population you are going to inflict the miseries of hunger and all the horrors of war.[24]

Once again, the Great War parallel is uncannily apt for today. Even professional soldiers find the unaccustomed barbarism of living in the field and fighting hard to take; no matter how modern the equipment, the whole business does not seem to belong to the twentieth century, or the twenty-first: 'Crawling out on wet nights, mewling in the bitter cold, You from your all electric cities . . .'[25]

THE MIDDLE EAST, SOUTH ASIA AND THE FAR EAST

Israel is the most developed major land power in any potential theatre of major land war outside Europe, and its situation is in some ways similar to that of European NATO. With no space to give up, and centres of population and industry close to the border, any future conflict involving Israel will almost certainly involve a spirited attrition battle on her borders: if the screen breaks, she is done for. Israel might carry out deep strikes into the rear of attacking forces, the revolving door, but the terrain makes this more feasible in Sinai than in the closer country to the north. As in NATO Europe, there are political problems in hitting deep at the enemy with ground forces, more so even than with air strikes like that against the PLO headquarters in Libya

293

in October 1985. Secondly, the Arabs have proved themselves very good at defence, and it is debatable whether Israeli penetrations into Arab territory would now enjoy the success they did in 1967. Airmobile operations might provide a way of distracting enemy attacks and tying up disproportionate forces but the Israelis themselves are remarkably cautious about such schemes; airmobile, including heliborne, forces are too lightly equipped and too vulnerable, in the Israeli view, and they know more about the reality of high-intensity war than anybody else. With the restoration of relations with Egypt, and Israel with-drawn from Lebanon, it is possible that there may at last be a prolonged period of freedom from conventional war in the area, but terrorism and guerrilla warfare will continue unabated. Further east, the Iran-Iraq conflict will continue in its present form until an accommodation is reached between the powers, perhaps with a change of government in either, or both. It is difficult to see how Iraq could occupy Iran to the extent necessary to force it to do their will, not least since there are three times as many Iranians as Iraqis (see Chapter 2). Similarly, it is unlikely that Russia would stand idly by if Iran threatened to occupy Baghdad. The Iraqis seem committed to holding the Iranians off in an attrition battle, and, as seen in Chapter 1, the defensive conducted with skill is proving very much the stronger form of war. The Russians are unlikely to consider an invasion of Iran a rational instrument of policy, given their experience with the Afghans, but they might consider an airborne or special forces operation against, say, Teheran, in pursuit of a specific political objective. If the Russians entered Iran, it is likely that the Americans would respond in some way, perhaps with their rapid deployment force, but once again their objective would be limited, probably confined to occupying and securing a particular area, like the Straits of Hormuz. It is unlikely that the Americans and Russians would decide to practise their respective variants of the AirLand Battle in the middle of Iran. A straightforward border confrontation between the USSR and Iran could, however, develop into a classic land battle, in which the Soviets would probably slice through Iranian forces with armour and comparative ease. Minor conflict is likely to continue in Afghanistan and in the area of the Afghan/Pakistan/India border. The Soviet operation in Afghanistan will continue to have the characteristics of a low- or mid-intensity war, with extensive use of helicopters and firebases. The most likely scene for major mechanised battles is an all-out Soviet/Pakistan or Pakistan/India conflict. As we have seen in Chapter 4, both India and Pakistan are studying AirLand Battle and envelopment techniques, and the terrain on the southern part of the India/Pakistan border would seem ideally suited to it. We have seen that the British in Europe would deploy some 150,000 troops to defend a 60 kilometre sector, obviously stretching back to great depth, and that the density of forces in Europe is likely to produce stasis. If we take India's 1,100,000 strong regular army and 200,000 reserves, and assume that perhaps half would have to be deployed to guard against the risk of Chinese intervention, for internal security duties and to protect rear areas, we get perhaps 600,000 troops available for deployment along the 1,500 kilometre front against Pakistan. Disregarding specific questions of deployment, we get a general density of 400 troops per kilometre, as against 2,500 for the British in Europe. It is immediately obvious that envelopment, outflanking and manoeuvre are far more likely in the India/Pakistan conflict than in Europe, indeed, almost inevitable. Certain areas might be defended and mined, like the Shakergarh bulge in 1971 (see Chapter 4), but it would be almost impossible to do this everywhere, and deep penetration by armour in concert with helicopters would take place. Indian objectives might be to capture Pakistan-occupied Kashmir, destroy Pakisan's armoured strike forces, and to prevent Pakistan making any gains on Indian territory. Pakistan's objectives would be to prevent any big Indian success on the ground, to capture as much of Indian Kashmir as possible and to inflict an obvious and humiliating defeat on India to avenge 1971. Ravi Rikhye has predicted armoured battles of an intensity similar to Yom Kippur: in the centre battle, 100 Indians tanks being destroyed in two hours. The great rivers of the Indus valley would influence operations. In Rikhye's future history prediction the Pakistanis consider a counterattack across the Sutlej (see the map, Figure 4.11) with three reserve divisions, but decide against it because it will probably just add to India's eventual bag.[26] As seen in chapter 3, the use of tactical nuclear weapons cannot be ruled out.

Conflict in South-East Asia will continue to straddle the spectrum of low, middle and full-scale mechanised high intensity war. As the recent veiled conflicts in South-East Asia have shown, a continuous guerrilla struggle can sometimes erupt into full-scale assaults on mountain strongholds with artillery and a certain amount of armour, and subside again. It is almost a reflection of the oriental mind, seeing not clear-cut, defined phases, but a continuum, a wheel rather than a linear scale, returning to the point from which it started, and turning again.[27] That is something which western analysts should study. Swift and decisive results are best achieved by more conventional operations, and the Vietnamese and Chinese have both fought such operations recently. The Chinese Army (PLA) is configured for operations across the full spectrum, and is acquiring sophisticated equipment most effectively employed in large-scale mechanised war. In terms of the historical continuum she is at a point on the wheel not dissimilar to that reached by the Germans in 1918 or the Russians in the Great Patriotic War. The Germans in 1918 had relatively few high-quality trained troops, and found that the best way of using them was to concentrate them in stormtrooper units to lead and accelerate the advance of the more stolid main body.[28] The Soviet mobile groups and forward detachments in the Great Patriotic War fulfilled the same function, making the most of the best equipment. China's army may well find it expedient to concentrate her most modern forces so as to form a spearhead which simultaneously accelerates the flight of the bigger but less dense haft (see Chapter 4).

CONCLUSION

The inevitable uncertainties of the future are compounded by the fact that war is a series of complex interactions. 'The very nature of interaction is bound to make it unpredictable', as Clausewitz said.[29] Can tanks remain dominant, given that the technology for their precise destruction is becoming so advanced? Or is that technology not advanced enough? Anti-tank weapons are threatened by increasingly long ranged and powerful artillery, improved target acquisition and seeking. Every improvement in offence stimulates one in defence, and the reciprocal process between electronics, ECM and ECCM, between electro-optics, EOCM and EOCCM (see Chapter 6) adds another couple of dimensions of interaction. War is not a matter of striking at an inanimate object, of operating on a patient who is tied down.[30] The opponent thinks, reacts and spits venom. All the contradicting tendencies slow down the operation and may well lead to stalemate. As we have seen, massive expenditure of sophisticated ammunition could quickly impose an old-fashioned form on the conflict. Some, like Mikschc, have suggested that this could arise in a battlefield nuclear conflict. It might equally result from a stultifying, oppressive chemical environment. Over and over again, the recurring parallel for European war is that of the World War I. The position of the opposed pacts, the long period of peace and the disbelief in the possibility of a barbaric war, or the belief that if it does occur it will be swift and mobile, the strength of the defence as demonstrated by previous wars (see Chapter 1) which so many have chosen to ignore, the chemical dimension, increased firepower and the corresponding increased dispersion of troops filling the available battlefield and making manoeuvre impossible: all these recall the Great War. A military historian in 1922 might prove to be more prophetic than he has already:

There is, in fact, no real assurance that future war will not partake substantially, of the character of past war, such as that of 1914-18. And such campaigns, we are asked to believe, should be won by quick, imaginative methods. That is a temptation for the ambitious statesman, whether demagogue or despot, to enter into the great adventure lightly.

The other danger is that this extravagant school, if uppermost when a war has once started, may proceed promptly to lose it by some super-Napoleonic stroke such as that on the Aisne in April, 1917, which enthralled the British Prime Minister until it was put to the test.

It is a pity one or two soldiers of note have uttered paradoxes suggesting wars are to be won inexpensively ...

That kind of paradox, or persiflage encourages the super-ficially clever mind.[31]

There is a great deal of persiflage about in the mid-1980s. There are proponents of swift, brilliant strokes (see Chapter 4), or those who believe that the 'attrition' form of war is some kind of devious plot, as opposed to the only way of continuing the conflict if manoeuvre is impossible. Elegant theoretical structures do not necessarily clarify the brutal, horrible, sometimes (perhaps always) irrational phenomenon of war. Drawing distinctions between 'attrition theory' and 'manoeuvre theory' simply obfuscates the real nature of war. Manoeuvre is of value, maybe decisive value, because it increases the rate of attrition (see also Chapter 4). Thus the outflanking move round Boca house by 2 Para at the Battle of Goose Green meant that 'at last the British were able to bring a massive concentation of fire down on the enemy'.[32] How can one say that manoeuvre and attrition are anything other than indistinguishable? At the operational level, it may appear that they are divisible, but to outflank and isolate an enemy formation is to have the potential to destroy it, even if that potential does not have to be used. Clausewitz likened combat in war to the cash transaction in banking: it rarely occurs, but it dominates the entire business. Cash transactions occur more often and more obviously in minor purchases than in those involving millions of pounds or dollars, and similarly the phenomenon of pure destruction is less obvious at the operational level than at the tactical. But it is just as pervasive.

Clausewitz had it right. 'War is an act of violence', he said, and, what is more, 'the maximum use of force is in no way incompatible with the maximum use of the intellect ... it would be futile, even wrong, to try and shut one's eyes at what war really is from sheer distress at its brutality.'[33] Again, the Great War experience is so relevant for today and for the foreseeable future: 'Shells, gas clouds and flotillas of tanks — shattering, starvation, death. Dysentery, influenza, typhus — murder, burning, death. Trenches, hospitals, the common grave — there are no other possibilities.'[34] 'Hard pounding, this, gentlemen. Let's see who will pound longest.'[35]

* * *

The battlefield is expanding. Formations of a given size can dominate a vastly greater area than in either world war. In Europe, deployed forces would fill a battle area some 300 kilometres deep at least. The development of terminally-guided indirect-fire systems and the parallel and indispensable development of air and space surveillance will make forces, including armour deployed tens, even hundreds of kilometres deep, vulnerable. In World War I, indirect fire dominated the battlefield as, for the first time, it could kill troops behind cover and beyond visual range. In a future European war, it would for the first time kill tanks behind cover and far into the enemy depth. The implications of this are uncertain, and this provides yet another parallel with the Great War. There will be manoeuvre of armoured units and helicopters within the fire zone, but the helicopters' bases will have to be far back, because they are so vulnerable. Within this gigantic battle zone, the manoeuvre of armoured brigade and battalions will be like that of trench raiding parties in the Great War, violent, but a tiny part of the overall struggle. To overcome this vast no-man's land, the power indulging in maximum violence will have to either fly over it, or outflank it strategically. In the case of a Soviet assault on Western Europe, a right hook through Norway would seem the most logical plan, especially given the value of that area for naval and strategic deployments. Soviet writings stressing the importance of warfare in special conditions suggest that this must be a favourite option (see Chapter 2). Just as the operational level reflected the expansion of the battlefield before, during and after the Great War, so the modern Soviet concept of the Theatre Strategic Operation (see Chapter 4) reflects the further expansion of the scope of military operations beyond the bounds of continental Europe. Therefore, the immane operations 'of great spatial scope' have grown too big to be a rational option in the Western Theatre of War. The Middle East, Asia and Africa are different. Nations there still do not have the means to conduct such grandiose operations, and Asia is vastly bigger than Europe. As demonstrated in this chapter, strategic operations which would engulf Europe could still be conducted within the confines of Asia without engulfing the protagonists' homelands. Nor are the strategic means available to Asian powers yet sufficiently potent to make major air-land warfare appear a totally unacceptable instrument of policy, as it must surely be for Europe and the superpowers. Therefore, we may, almost certainly will, see major air-land warfare in Asian and North African theatres in the next quarter century. Often this will be connected with, perhaps indistinguishable from, low- and mid-intensity conflict. Guerrilla wars, internal wars or internal wars with external intervention have become the most prevalent forms of war. Sometimes, however, conflict will erupt in the form of classic mechanised air-land war on a large scale. In Europe we have seen the stretch of air-land operations, their greater intensity and cost, thus making war even more total, the intermingling of these operations with those at sea, in the upper air and in cosmic space and their absolute dependence on the latter, not least because of the need for over the horizon target acquisition. All this may well mean that in the Western theatre, major 'air-land warfare' as a discrete phenomenon has, in at least two senses, spaced itself out of existence.

NOTES

1. Opening quote from Sun Tzu *Art of War*, (ed.) (Griffith, ch. 6, 'Weaknesses and Strengths', p. 101: van Creveld, *Military Lessons of the Yom Kippur War* (Washington Papers, Vol. III, No. 2, Sage, Beverly Hills and London, 1975), p. 36.

2. John Terraine, *White Heat: the New Warfare 1914-18* (Sidgwick and Jackson, London, 1982), p. 208.

3. 1914 deployments: Brigadier-General James E. Edmonds and Major A.F. Becke, *Military Operations, France and Belgium 1914: History of the Great War based on official documents* (Macmillan, London, 1917), initial deployment, map facing p. 15; strengths in Appendices 1 (British), 3 (French), 6 (Germans), pp. 447-8, 488-9, 493-5. Space occupied by a division is arguable: Triandafillov, writing after the Great War, considered 12-20 kilometres an extended front; 4 to 8 kilometres was 'normal' in defence, based on positional warfare intensity. If we consider that deployments in 1914 were sparser, 10 kilometres seems sensible. Arguing that a division can dominate a smaller area makes stasis easier to achieve, so it only serves to reinforce the author's argument. Triandafillov, *Kharakter operatsii*, pp. 101-2. Density on modern central front: *NATO and the Warsaw Pact, Force Comparisons* (NATO Information Office, Brussels, 1984), p. 12.

4. Figures from General Tal's paper, *Some Aspects of Strategy* (edited), and conversation with Israeli generals.

5. Sidorenko, *Offensive*, (USAF translation 1976), p. 11.

6. Tizard report, paras. 68 and 79, pp. 30 and 32. Somme from Martin van Creveld, 'Supplying an Army: An Historical View', *RUSI*, June 1978, pp. 56-63, reference on p. 60.

7. New Soviet gun: see the author's *Red God of War* (Brassey's, 1986); quote from van Creveld, 'Supplying an Army', p. 62.

8. Allan R. Millett (ed.), *A Short History of the Vietnam War* (Indiana University Press, 1978), p. 61.

9. Quagmire: 'Lionheart starts', *Sunday Times*, 15 September 1984, p. 2.

10. Colonel-General N. Khlebnikov, *Pod grokhot soten batary (To the Thunder of Hundreds of Batteries)* (extracts translated in *Soviet Military Review*, No. 12, 1977, p. 57).

11. Brigadier-General Avishai Katz, 'The 1985 War — The Untaught War', *Ma'arachot*, nos. 270-71 (October 1979), US translation L-2689, pp. 130-3.

12. Van Creveld, *Military lessons*, p. viii (quote), 'Space for time',

Bidwell, *World War 3* (Hamlyn Paperbacks, 1979), p. 118.

13. Ivan S. Bloch, *Is War Now Impossible?* (London, 1899), being the translation of the *General Conclusions* of *Budushchaya voyna v tekhnicheskom, ekonomicheskom i politicheskom smysle (Future War in its Technical, Economic and Political Aspects)* (6 Vols., St. Petersburg, 1898), p. xxxvii of the former.

14. See Norman Angell, *The Great Illusion* (London, 1914).

15. Stephen T. Hosmer, Konrad Kellen and Brian M. Jenkins, *The Fall of South Vietnam: Statements by Vietnamese Military and Civilian Leaders* (Crane Russak, New York, 1980 edition), pp. 3-4, 9-15, 19.

16. According to the chief of Israeli military intelligence, the Syrians on the Golan heights attacked 'round the clock ... I think we can learn a lot from this about the general Russian pattern in this type of warfare.' Even in Bloch's day, operations lasting from four days to two weeks without a halt were forecast. John J. Emanski and John C. Scharfen, 'Continuous Land Combat Operations: are we only Half Effective?', *RUSI* (June 1978), pp. 26-7; Bloch, *Is War now Impossible?*, p. 52.

17. Van Creveld, *Military Lessons*, pp. 39(quote), 47 and 55 (note 63).

18. Bloch, *Is War now Impossible?*, pp. 57-8.

19. Quotation from Major D.B.A. Bailey, 'The Case for preplaced Field Defences', *IDR*, 7/1984, pp. 887-92. See also Bailey's article, 'Preplaced Hardened Field Defences', *Journal of the Royal Artillery*, March 1983, pp. 28-33, and Major T. Cross, 'Forward Defence — Time for a Change', *RUSI*, June 1985, pp. 19-24.

20. Rodney Cowton, 'The Army changes some entrenched ideas', *Times*, 18 September 1984.

21. Cross, 'Forward Defence'.

22. The chessboard analogy has been suggested by a number of other writers, for example Steven Canby, *The Alliance and Europe; Part IV: Military Doctrine and Technology* (Adelphi Paper, IISS, London, 1974-5), p. 27. The Dragon Variation is the author's own metaphor, a variant of the Sicilian Defence.

23. Max Hastings and Simon Jenkins, *The Battle for the Falklands* (Book Club Associates, London, 1983), pp. 238-53, esp. pp. 251-2 (casualties).

24. Bloch, *Is War now Impossible?*, p. xlix.

25. Yvan Goll, 'Requiem for the Dead of Europe', translated from the German by Patrick Bridgewater, in John Silkin (ed.), *The Penguin Book of First World War Poetry* (Penguin, Harmondsworth, 1979), p. 232.

26. Rikhye, *Indo-Pak War* (ABC Press, New Delhi, 1982), pp. 56-60, 137-9.

27. Palmer, *Summons of the Trumpet* (Ballantine, 1984), p. 83.

28. Terraine, *White Heat* (Sidgwick & Jackson, London, 1982), pp. 279-80.

29. Clausewitz, *On War*, Book 2, chapter 2, p. 139.

30. B.H. Liddell Hart, *Thoughts on War*, 1944, p. xii, cited in Heinl, Col. R.B., *Dictionary of Military and Naval Quotations* (US Naval Institute Press, Annapolis, 1966), p. 132.

31. G.A.B. Dewar and Lt.-Col. J.H. Boraston, *Sir Douglas Haig's Command* (Constable, London, 1922), Vol. 1, p. 167.

32. Hastings and Jenkins, *Battle for the Falklands*, p. 246.

33. Clausewitz, *On War*, Book 1, chapter 1, pp. 75-6 (maximum use of force); Book 1, chapter 2, p. 97 (Cash payment: 'The decision by arms is for all major and minor operations in war what cash is in commerce. Regardless how complex the relationship between the two parties, regardless how rarely settlements actually occur, they can never be entirely absent').

34. Remarque, *All Quiet on the Western Front*, (Putnam, London, 1921), pp. 306-7. Wellington, at Waterloo, Sir Walter Scott, *Paul's Letters* (1815).

Glossary of Acronyms and Initials

AA	Anti-aircraft
ABM	Anti-Ballistic Missile
ACE	Allied Command Europe (North Cape to Turkey)
ACh	Acetyl choline
ADM	Atomic Demolition Mine
ADP	Automatic Data Processing
AFAP	Artillery Fired Atomic Projectile
AFCENT	Allied Forces Central Region
AFNORTH	Allied Forces Northern Region
AFSOUTH	Allied Forces Southern Region
AFV	Armoured Fighting Vehicle
AIFS	Advanced Indirect Fire System
AK	*Avtomat Kalashnikova* (kalashnikov sub-machine gun, Russ.)
ALCM	Air Launched Cruise Missile
AMF(L)	ACE Mobile Force (Land)
APC	Armoured Personnel Carrier
APDS	Armour Piercing Discarding Sabot
APFSDS	Armour Piercing Fin Stabilised Discarding Sabot
ATACMS	Army Tactical Missile System
ATGM	Anti-Tank Guided Missile
ATGW	Anti-Tank Guided Weapon
ATP	Allied Tactical Publication
AVF	All Volunteer Force (US)
AWACS	Airborne Warning And Control System
BAOR	British Army of the Rhine
BM	*Boyevaya mashina* (War Machine), means Rocket Launcher, (Russ.)
BMD	*Bronevaya mashina desantnaya* (Armoured vehicle, airborne) (Russ.)

303

BMEWS	Ballistic Missile Early Warning System
BMP	*Bronevaya mashina pekhota* (Armoured vehicle, infantry) (Russ.)
C^2	Command and Control
C^3(I)	Command, Control, Communications (and Intelligence)
CASTOR	Corps Airborne Stand Off Radar
CCIS	Command Control Information System
CENTAG	Central Army Group within AFCENT
CEP	Circular Error Probable (radius from target within which 50 percent of projectiles fired at it will fall)
CEWI	Combat Electronic Warfare and Intelligence
cGy	CentiGray (equivalent to old rad, measure of radiation)
ChE	Choline Esterase
CLGP	Cannon Launched Guided Projectile
CM	Cruise Missile or, more rarely, Chemical Munitions
CNRI	Combat Net Radio Interface
Comcen	Communications Centre
CPB	Charged Particle Beam
CW	Chemical Warfare or Chemical Weapons
DEW	Distant Early Warning
DF	Direction Finding *or* Dong Feng (East Wind) (Chinese ballistic missile)
DMR	Digital Microwave Radio
DSWS	Divisional Support Weapons System
ECCM	Electronic Counter Counter Measures
ECM	Electronic Counter Measures
EHF	Extremely High Frequency
ELF	Extremely Low Frequency
ELINT	Electronic Intelligence
EMCON	Emission Control
EML	Electro-Magnetic Launcher ('rail gun', in which two rails are connected by a sliding conductor. When a strong current is passed through the conductor it is forced along the rails vapouring into a plasma and driving the projectile with it)
EMP	Electro Magnetic Pulse
EOCCM	Electro-Optical Counter Counter Measures
EOCM	Electro-Optical Counter Measures
ERFB	Extended Range Full Bore

ER/RB	Enhanced Radiation/Reduced Blast
ERSC	Extended Range Sub Calibre
ERW	Enhanced Radiation Weapon (more common but less accurate for ER/RB)
ESM	Electronic Support Measures
EW	Electronic Warfare
FAC	Forward Air Controller
FAE	Fuel Air Explosive
FAESHED	FAE Helicopter Delivered
FEBA	(obsolete) Forward Edge of the Battle Area
FH	Frequency Hopping *or* Field Howitzer
FLOT	Forward Line of Own Troops (has replaced FEBA)
FM	Frequency Modulation or Field
FOFA	Follow On Forces' Attack
FRG	Federal Republic of Germany
GA	tabun
GB	sarin
GD	soman
GDR	German Democratic Republic (East Germany, in German, DDR)
GHz	Gigaherz (1000 million Herz, wavelength 0.3 metres)
GPMG	General Purpose Machine Gun (UK)
GSFG	Group of Soviet Forces Germany (Russian GSVG)
HEAT	High Explosive Anti Tank
HEP	High Explosive Plastic, the same as
HESH	High Explosive Squash Head
HF	High Frequency
HOJ	Home on Jam
HOT	*Haut supersonique Optiquement téléguidé tiré d'un Tube* (French) (High Supersonic Optically guided Tube launched)
HPM	High Powered Microwaves
HTB	Howitzer Test Bed
Hz	Herz (a 300 million metre long wave, which will occur once in a second as electromagnetic waves travel at the speed of light, which is 300 million metres per second)
ICM	Improved Conventional Munition
IDF	Israel Defence Forces (includes Ground Forces)

305

IFV	Infantry Fighting Vehicle
IOSS	Intelligence, Organization and Stationing Study
IR	Infra Red
JIC	Joint Intelligence Committee (UK)
JSTARS	Joint Surveillance Target Attack Radar System
JTACMS	Joint Tactical Missile System (formerly referred to system like ATACMS: now refers to different system)
KGB	*Komitet Gosudarstvennoy Bezopasnosti* (State Security Committee) (Russ.)
KHz	Kiloherz (1000 Herz, wavelength 300,000 metres)
Kilopond	Kilogram force
kN	Kilonewton
Kt	Kiloton (equivalent to 1000 tonnes TNT)
kW	Kilowatt
LANTIRN	Low Altitude Targeting Infrared for Night
LARS	*Leichten Artillerieraketen System* (German)
LAV	Light Armoured Vehicle
LAW	Light Anti-tank Weapon
LGB	Laser Guided Bomb
LHX	Light helicopter Experimental
LLTV	Low Light Television
LPI	Low Probability of Intercept
LRATGW	Long Range Anti Tank Guided Weapon
LSW	Light Support Weapon
MARS	*Mittleren Artillerieraketen System* (German, name for MLRS)
MBAV	Main Battle Air Vehicle
MBT	Main battle Tank
MCV	Mechanized Combat vehicle
MEROD	Message Entry and Read Out Device
MHz	Megaherz (1 million Herz, wavelength 300 metres)
MLRS	Multiple Launch Rocket System (NATO system, *not* general term)
MRL	Multiple Rocket Launcher (general term)
MSE	Mobile Subscriber Equipment
Mt	Megaton (equivalent to 1 million tonnes TNT)
NATO	North Atlantic Treaty Organization
NBC	Nuclear, Biological, Chemical
NIA	Neutron Induced Activity
NORTHAG	Northern Army Group within AFCENT

NSWP	Non-Soviet Warsaw Pact
O Group	Orders Group (traditionally, with subordinate commanders gathered round, now may not exist)
OMG	Operational Manoeuvre Group (Polish *Operacyjna Grupa Manewrowa*, Russian *Operativnaya Manevrennaya Gruppa*)
OOB	Order of Battle
OPSEC	Operational security
ORBAT	Order of Battle
OTC	Officers' Training Corps
OTH	Over The Horizon
PHFP	Preplaced Hardened Fire Position
PLA	People's Liberation Army (Chinese Armed Forces, not just ground forces)
PLO	Palestine Liberation Organization
PLSS	Precision Locating Strike System
POL	Petrol, Oil, Lubricants
PRC	People's Republic of China
psi	pounds per square inch
psig	pounds force per square inch
PTURS	*Protivotankovy upravlyayemy reaktivny snaryad,* Anti-Tank Guided Missile (Russ.)
RDF	Rapid Deployment Force
REB	*Radioelektronnaya bor'ba,* Radioelectronic Combat (Electronic Warfare) (Russ.)
RECS	Radioelectronic Combat Support
REM	*Radioelektronnaya maskirovku,* electronic deception (Russ.)
REP	*Radioelektronnaya podavleniye,* electronic suppression (Russ.)
REZ	*Radioelektronnaya zashchita,* electronic defence (Russ.)
ROK	*Razvedyvatel'no-Ognevoy Kompleks,* reconnaissance fire complex tactical target acquisition and fire control system (Russ.)
ROTC	Reserve Officer Training Corps (US)
RPG	*Reaktivny protivotankovy Granatomët,* anti-tank grenade launcher (Russ.)
RPV	Remotely Piloted Vehicle (Pilotless aircraft)
RSZO	*Reaktivny Sistem Zalpovogo Ognya,* Rocket volley fire system (NATO MLRS) (Russ.)
RUK	*Razvedyvatel'no Udarny Kompleks,*

	Reconnaissance Strike Complex, operational level target acquisition and fire control system (Russ.)
RWR	Radar Warning Receiver (tells you when you have been picked up on somebody else's radar)
SA	Surface to Air missile (western designation for Soviet equipment)
SACEUR	Supreme Allied Commander Europe
SACLOS	Semi Automatic Command Line of Sight Guidance
SADARM	Sense And Destroy Armour
SAM	Surface to Air Missile
Satcom	Satellite communications
SCRA	Single Channel Radio Access
SGL	*Schlüssel Gelände*, key terrain (German)
SHF	Super High Frequency
SIGINT	Signals Intelligence
SL	*Sicherungslinie*, defensive line (German)
SLR	Self Loading Rifle (UK)
SOP	Standard Operating Procedures ('drills')
SOTAS	Stand Off Target Acquisition System
Spetsnaz	*Spetsial'nogo naznacheniya*, 'Of special designation', Special Purpose Forces (Russ.)
SPF	Special Purpose Forces
SS	Surface to Surface missile (western designation used to describe Soviet equipment)
SSM	Surface to Surface Missile
TA	Territorial Army (UK) or Target Acquisition
TEL	Transporter-Erector-Launcher
TERCOM	Terrain Comparison
TGD	Thickened soman
TGW	Terminally Guided Warhead
TMO	Theatre of Military Operations, equals TSMA or TVD
TNT	Trinitrotoluene Troponin T
TOW	Tube launched, Optical tracking, Wire Guided
TRADOC	Training and Doctrine Unit (US)
TREE	Transient Radiation Effect on Electronics
TSMA	Theatre of Strategic Military Action (TVD)
TSO	Theatre Strategic Operation
TV	*Teatr voyny*, theatre of war (Russ.)
TVD	*Teatr voyennykh deystviy*, TSMA (Russ.)
UGS	Unattended Ground Sensor

UHF	Ultra High Frequency
ULF	Ultra Low Frequency
USAREUR	US Army, Europe
USSR	Union of Soviet Socialist Republics
VHF	Very High Frequency
VLF	Very Low Frequency
VRV	*Vorderer Rand der Verteidigund,* Forward Edge of Defence (German)
VR-55	nerve agent
VS	*Vorgeschobene Stellungen,* forward patrols (German)
VX	nerve agent
WARPAC	Warsaw Pact
WIG	Wing In Ground effect craft (Russ. *ekranoplan*)
WP	Warsaw Pact
ZSU	*Zenitnaya samokhodnaya ustanovka,* Anti-aircraft self propelled mounting (Russ.)

Index

Individual formations mentioned are given under the type of formation, for example, Corps ... 1st British ... To find acronyms, except for designations of individual equipments and occasional commonly understood ones such as NATO, consult the glossary and then look up the full description in the index, for example, ABMs, *Anti-Ballistic* Missiles. Figures, tables and footnotes are only indexed if they contain information not directly referred to in the text. Figures and tables are prefixed by the letters f and t, respectively.